THE TOMB OF TUT·ANKH·AMEN

A PORTRAIT OF TUT·ANKH·AMEN

The beaten and burnished gold mask of the young king
representing him at the age of death—about 18 years old.

(See Plate LXXIII)

THE TOMB OF TUT·ANKH·AMEN

DISCOVERED BY THE LATE EARL OF CARNARVON AND HOWARD CARTER

By

HOWARD CARTER

*Hon. Sc.D. (Yale University); Correspondent
Real Academia de la Historia, Madrid*

With Appendices by

DOUGLAS E. DERRY, M.B., Ch.B.: A. LUCAS,
O.B.E., F.I.C.: P. E. NEWBERRY, M.A.: ALEX-
ANDER SCOTT, F.R.S., Sc.D.Camb., D.Sc.Edin.,
and H. J. PLENDERLEITH, M.C., Ph.D.

Volume II

With 153 *Illustrations from Photographs by*
HARRY BURTON
(Of the Metropolitan Museum of Art, New York)

Duckworth

First published in 1927 by Cassell & Company Ltd
Reprinted in 2001 by permission of
The Griffith Institute, Oxford

Gerald Duckworth & Co. Ltd.
61 Frith Street, London W1D 3JL
Tel: 020 7434 4242
Fax: 020 7434 4420
Email: enquiries@duckworth-publishers.co.uk
www.ducknet.co.uk

A catalogue record for this book is available
from the British Library

ISBN 0 7156 3075 X

Printed in Great Britain by Bath Press, Bath

FOREWORD

On 4 November 1922, Howard Carter and his sponsor, the fifth Earl of Carnarvon, made a discovery in Egypt's Valley of the Kings which would change the face of archaeology for good. For the first time in recorded history, diggers had stumbled upon the virtually intact burial of an Egyptian pharaoh – the boy-king Tutankhamun, son and successor of the heretic Akhenaten; and it was a tomb piled high with funerary treasures and gold. The popular perception of Egyptology changed overnight: no longer the worthy pursuit of dusty academics, it was now seen as high-stakes adventure. Without the excitement engendered by Tutankhamun, it is doubtful that Indiana Jones would ever have been born.

The story of the find reads like a fairy-tale fiction: how Carter dug for years with little success in pursuit of the impossible dream; how, in his final season, the tomb he sought was found; how the tomb impacted upon the world, and turned its discoverers into celebrities overnight; and how, with the unexpected death of Lord Carnarvon (supposed victim of 'pharaoh's curse'), the triumph turned sour.

The careful documentation and clearance of Tutankhamun's tomb, and the transportation to Cairo of the objects interred there, took Howard Carter the best part of a decade, with the excavator's personal narrative of the work appearing in three wonderfully written, self-contained volumes published between 1923 and 1933. This, the second in the trilogy, appeared in 1927, and describes the investigation of pharaoh's burial chamber: the opening of the four protective shrines, the extraction of the king's three anthropoid coffins (the innermost of solid gold), and the final examination of the king's splendidly bejewelled mummy. The stuff of fantasy, it is difficult to take in, even today.

For all his riches, Tutankhamun had in life been a relatively insignificant king, too young to impose his personality on the state he ruled and intentionally forgotten by those who came after. With the finding of his tomb by Howard Carter and Lord Carnarvon, Tutankhamun's name was at long last 'made to live': today, more than three thousand years after his death, Egypt's boy-king stands as a veritable icon not only of Egyptology itself, but of archaeological endeavour as a whole.

London, January 2001   Nicholas Reeves

CONTENTS

PREFACE

AS this volume deals with our work of the second, third and fourth seasons upon the tomb of Tut·ankh·Amen, I shall not trouble the reader with any repetition of the dramatic incidents that rendered the first part of the discovery memorable, further than is needed for a general idea.

It will, no doubt, be remembered from the first volume and the accounts published all over the world, describing how, after many years of toil, we at last reached our goal in the discovery of a step cut in the bed-rock beneath the entrance of the tomb of Rameses VI, which proved to be the beginning of a stairway that led down to the tomb of Tut·ankh·Amen.

Great was our feeling of awe when we made the discovery, cleared the stairway and steep descending passage, and entered the Antechamber, when we beheld in that hypogeum for the first time the splendour of the Imperial Age in Egypt, fourteen centuries before Christ. The gorgeousness of the sight, its sumptuous splendour, made it appear more like the confused magnificence of those counterfeit splendours which are heaped together in the property-room of some modern theatre, than any possible reality surviving from antiquity.

The effect was bewildering, almost overwhelming. Moreover, the extent of the discovery had taken us by surprise.

It is true that we had expected to find the tomb of

Preface

Tut-ankh-Amen in the Theban Valley, for reasons already pointed out in the first volume, but our supreme surprise was to find it, for all intents and purposes, intact. Unlike the other royal tombs in the Valley which had all been completely plundered, only a few fragments of their furniture being left, this tomb was for practical purposes intact, save for the early depredations of a few metal robbers. To this fact our great surprise and good fortune were due. Had the tombs of the great Pharaohs of the Theban Empire been found in a similar condition, the tomb of Tut-ankh-Amen would have seemed of comparative insignificance, except that the art of his period would still have remained an outstanding feature.

We soon realized, however, that our first duty was to record, clear and preserve the contents of the Antechamber before attempting any other task. The objects in this chamber were in such dangerous contact that their removal, without causing damage, must be, we saw, a task of some difficulty. It took the greater part of the first season to transport them to the laboratory, where the work of recording, preservation and packing was eventually carried out. It was only after this chamber had been cleared that we were able to penetrate and solve the mystery of the inner sealed door.

Though a shrewd guess anticipated what might be beyond that mysterious sealed door—guarded by two imposing sentinel figures of the king, black and gold, armed with mace and staff—little did we expect the impressive sight revealed as, stone by stone, the masonry blocking the doorway was removed. First, to all appearance, a wall of gold met our gaze, affording no clue to its meaning, until, as the aperture became larger, we realized that what was barring our view was an immense golden shrine, and that we were now at the entrance of the actual burial chamber of the king.

An almost incongruous miscellany of objects and furniture, caskets and beds, chairs, footstools, chariots and statues, filled the Antechamber. These were heterogeneous enough, yet exhibiting, in not a few instances, a kindly art full of domestic affection, such as made us wonder whether, in seeking a tomb of a Pharaoh, we had not found the tomb of a boy. From strange ceremonial couches fashioned in the form of uncanny beasts—demon deities comparable to Greek satyrs—Thoueris, " The Great One," the favourite of the people, in shape partly hippopotamus, partly crocodile and partly feline, personifying " Protection " ; Hathor, " The Abode of Horus," in the form of a cow, the goddess of pleasure and love, the mortal and immortal nurse ; and " The Terrible Goddess of War," or it may be of " The Chase," fashioned like a lion or, perhaps, to be more accurate, a cheetah—from these we passed into the severely simple Burial Chamber occupied almost entirely by its great sepulchral blue and gold shrine.

It would be difficult to describe our emotions when for the first time the light of our powerful electric lamps flooded the Burial Chamber—" That silent seat of a Lord of the West "—illuminating as it did the walls on which were painted representatives of Amentît, the catafalque drawn on a sled by the chief nobles of the land, King Ay before the Osiride Tut·ankh· Amen, and lighting up the immense shrine overlaid with gold, and inlaid with brilliant blue faience tiles, nearly filling up the entire area of the chamber—a space of only one or two feet separating it from the walls on all four sides, while its great roof reached almost to the ceiling.

When we found the first step, when we opened and obtained our first glance at the crowded wonders in the Antechamber; when this sealed door leading to the Burial Chamber was broken through, and when we saw, for the first time in the history of archæology, one of the great sepulchral shrines under which the Pharaohs of Egypt were laid—these, unless my memory misleads me, were the thrilling moments of the first part of the discovery.

There are moments, usually rare and always brief, when life may be vividly stirred by some series of impressive incidents that successively confront us. To these we look back with pleasure, whilst memory loves to contrast their comparative effect on the mind. Such experiences occasionally come to the archæologist to lighten his labours and reward his toil ; and, glancing back now at the second season's work, it seems that our interests were never more deeply stirred than when concentrated on the contents of that simple sepulchre. The task, however arduous, then became enthralling. Our first duty was the removal of the various objects around the shrine, to be followed by the dismantling of the latter with its nest of shrines, shielding in their centre the great yellow quartzite sarcophagus.

Around the emblems, symbols, furniture and monuments associated with Egyptian sepulture, especially when seen for the first time, there always hovers the spirit of mystery and awe, and it was when the lid of the noble sarcophagus was gradually raised, revealing the magnificent outer coffin of the king within, that one of these supremely moving moments was again ours. But life is full of painful disappointments, and it was here that our labours of that winter were destined to be brought to an untimely end.

We had resumed our operations as early in the autumn of 1923 as the heat rendered practicable, in order to have the longest possible period for work in the cooler weather of the winter and spring, but we reckoned in vain, for our object was frustrated by the unfortunate misunderstanding, or rather series of misunderstandings, to which it is now necessary briefly to refer.

As is well known, the late Earl of Carnarvon was deeply interested in Egyptian archæology, his work will never be forgotten, and it had been his practice for many years to entrust to me the superintendence of his excavations in Egypt. And whilst I wish to repeat my feelings expressed in my first volume in the dedication to my beloved friend and late colleague, I must here add my gratitude to Almina, Countess of Carnarvon, for her generous co-operation in the continuance of this work which is devoted to his memory.

It was in the year 1914 that we obtained a concession from the Egyptian Government to excavate in the Valley of the Tombs of the Kings. This concession, as is usual in such cases, was for one year only, renewable annually, and it was still in force in November, 1922, when the tomb was discovered.

It may here be said that, although the concession gave rights to the concessionaire, they were not clearly defined, and to this absence of complete clarity may be attributed a part at least of the trouble that occurred.

Preface

In accordance with the concession (especially the Clause 12 B therein) Lord Carnarvon was justifiably under the impression that all rights of publication with regard to the results of the undertaking were secured to him. Because of that, and with the object of simplifying the distribution of news for which there was an enormous Press demand, he entered into an agreement with *The Times;* for so great and far-reaching was the excitement caused by the first news of the discovery, that almost at once it became evident that, to avoid constant interruption, and consequent danger to the work, some means must be found of issuing news to the world's Press through a single organization.

The contract was not a money-making proposition on either side, since the transaction represented a financial loss so far as *The Times* was concerned, and the money received by the expedition was devoted to the very heavy expenses of the work.

But unfortunately the agreement made with *The Times* gave rise to considerable friction both with the Press and the Egyptian Government.

After the regrettable death of Lord Carnarvon in April, 1923, it was desired that the *déblaiement* of the tomb should be continued in his memory, and by the desire of the family it was arranged that I should continue the operations. As the result of negotiations with the Department of Antiquities, Almina, Countess of Carnarvon, was authorized to continue Lord Carnarvon's enterprise up to November 1, 1924.

When, therefore, I arrived in Cairo on October 8, 1923, the problem before me was how to carry on, with the least possible friction, the absorbing work I had undertaken. Unhappily, however, neither the Press nor the public realized the time and concentrated labour that the *déblaiement* of the tomb entailed. Gradually troubles began to arise. Newspapers were competing for " copy," tourists were leaving no efforts untried to obtain permits to visit the tomb ; endless jealousies were let loose ; days, which should have been devoted to scientific work, were wasted in negotiations too often futile, whilst the claims of archæology were thrust into the background. But this is no place for weighing the merits of a controversy now ended, and it would serve no good purpose to relate in detail the long series of unpleasant incidents which harassed our work. We are all of us human. No man is wise at all times—perhaps least of all the archæologist who finds his efforts to carry out an all-absorbing task frustrated by a thousand pin-pricks and irritations without end. It is not for me to affix the blame for what occurred, nor yet to bear responsibility for a dispute in which at one moment the interests of archæology in Egypt seemed menaced.

How such storms arise is never quite clear. In such conflicts there always enter causes which are intangible, while the spirit of mischief is active in most human affairs. To expect at such times complete fairness and impartiality is to ask too much. Moreover, a man may inherit obligations which it is his obvious duty to carry out, although he personally has not incurred them, and he is certainly not responsible for the acrimony that may be imported by varying sentiments, political and otherwise.

From what has been said it will be readily inferred that much valuable time was wasted over a controversy singularly remote from the calm spirit which should guide research.

By what follows it will be seen that it became easier to work under the new conditions, especially when the rights of both parties were meticulously defined, and original claims of very old standing were forfeited for the good cause.

At the crisis of the irritating situation which developed between the Egyptian Government and myself, Professor Breasted and Sir John Maxwell, and at a still later period Mr. H. E. Winlock, kindly intervened on my behalf. But matters remained so difficult that their friendly efforts were almost fruitless. However, after a long series of lectures beginning in America and ending in Madrid, I returned to Egypt in December, 1924, where I was most cordially received by the new Prime Minister, Ziwar Pasha, and his Cabinet. H.E. Ziwar Pasha expressed the wish that I should continue my work and reopen the tomb. Naturally gratified, I replied I was most anxious to do so, and that Almina, Countess of Carnarvon, was equally desirous that our work should be resumed, but, I added, as her representative, loyalty to her and the work must be my first obligation. A suggestion was made that an equitable solution might be found in the offer to resume the concession on the basis of that which had been previously framed through the kind offices of Mr. Winlock and Maître Georges Merzbach Bey (acting on my behalf), in negotiations with H.E. Abdel Hamid Pasha Bedawi, Conseiller Royal, and the Director-General of the Department of Antiquities.

After a few conferences between these representatives of the Egyptian Government, and Maître

Merzbach and myself, a solution was found, and a final concession drafted to which Their Excellencies the Minister of Public Works and the Prime Minister agreed.

But it was obvious that such problems required the most delicate and careful handling, inasmuch as several important and, to some extent, conflicting claims had to be considered. The question of the division of certain material found could not be disregarded, either from a world or a national point of view, and this became of extreme urgency when we had to deal with material so vast, so important and so diverse as the contents of Tut·ankh·Amen's tomb. With regard to the question of national importance we were of one mind; but another point now arose—that of the heavy work and expenses borne by the Carnarvon estate, and the benefits resulting to Egypt generally. Were these claims to receive acknowledgment and recognition? I am thankful to say that on this particular point an understanding was reached. Apart from the actual new concession in which we relinquished all such claims, the two following letters covering that point were exchanged between H.E. the Minister and myself :—

Le Caire, le 13 *Janvier* 1925.

EXCELLENCE,

J'ai l'honneur de vous informer que le 29 *Décembre* 1924, *j'ai adressé une lettre à S. Ex. le Président du Conseil des Ministres dans laquelle j'ai proposé de reprendre le travail dans la tombe de Tout·Ankh·Amoun, sur la base des conditions générales établies par le projet d'autorisation qui a été communiqué à Almina, Countess Carnarvon, en Juin dernier, tout en demandant que la* question de propriété des objets visés par l'art. 12. de la dite autorisation soit réservée jusqu'au jour où le travail sera terminé et où tous les objets contenus dans la tombe seront consignés au Musée du Caire.   Mercredi dernier une réunion a eu lieu entre M. Lacau et Badaoui Pacha d'une part et Merzbach Bey et moi-même d'autre part, au cours de laquelle j'ai eu l'occasion de préciser ma pensée au sujet de cette autorisation.

Profitant du désir que tant S. Ex. le Président du Conseil que Votre Excellence ont bien voulu exprimer de voir reprendre les travaux en question, je me permets donc de vous soumettre que Almina, Countess Carnarvon, serait reconnaissante à Votre Excellence de vouloir bien lui accorder l'autorisation de les reprendre aux conditions qui lui avaient déjà été communiquées avec les précisions que le Contentieux du Ministère des Travaux Publics et le Service des Antiquités ont accepté d'incorporer dans la dite autorisation.

En recevant les assurances de Votre Excellence qu'elle n'a pas d'objection à accorder l'autorisation dans ces conditions, Almina, Countess Carnarvon, se fera un devoir de renoncer et de faire renoncer aux exécuteurs testamentaires, à toute action, réclamation ou prétention quelconque, tant en ce qui concerne le tombeau de Tout·Ankh·Amoun et les objets en provenant que du chef de l'annulation de l'autorisation et des mesures prises par le Gouvernement à la suite de cette annulation.

Confiant que dans un esprit de bienveillance Votre Excellence voudra bien accorder la dite autorisation, je la prie d'agréer, l'assurance de ma haute considération.

(*Signé*) *HOWARD CARTER.*

S. Ex. le Ministre des Travaux Publics,
  Le Caire.

Preface

LE CAIRE, le 13 Janvier 1925.
Ministère des Travaux Publics,
Cabinet du Ministre,
No. 133–2/4.

MONSIEUR,

J'ai l'honneur de vous accuser réception de votre lettre en date de ce jour, par laquelle vous me faites savoir que Almina, Countess Carnarvon, demande à obtenir l'autorisation de reprendre les travaux dans la tombe de Tout·Ankh·Amoun aux conditions qui lui avaient été communiquées en Juin dernier, avec les précisions que Mon Contentieux et le Service des Antiquités ont accepté d'incorporer dans la dite autorisation.

Pénétré du désir sincère de voir reprendre ces travaux, je n'ai pas d'objection à accorder l'autorisation aux conditions précitées pourvu que Almina, Countess Carnarvon, renonce et fasse renoncer les executeurs testamentaires à toute action, réclamation ou prétention quelconque, tant en ce qui concerne le tombeau de Tout·ankh·Amoun et les objets en provenant que du chef de l'annulation de l'autorisation et des mesures prises par le Gouvernement à la suite de son annulation.

Soucieux de marquer sa reconnaissance pour cette admirable découverte, le Gouvernement tout en ne s'estimant sous aucune obligation en ce qui concerne les objets trouvés dans la tombe se propose comme suite à la suggestion faite par M. Lacau au lendemain de la découverte, de donner dans sa discrétion à Almina, Countess Carnarvon, un choix de doubles aussi représentatif que possible de la découverte, pourvu que ces doubles puissent être distraits de l'ensemble sans dommage scientifique.

De plus, enfin d'éviter au fouilleur tout commentaire

Preface

désagréable, s'il y a lieu de transporter la momie du Roi au Caire, c'est le Service des Antiquités seul qui se chargera de ce transfert et en prendra la responsabilité.

Vouillez agréer, Monsieur, l'assurance de ma consideration distinguée.

Le Ministre des Travaux Publics,
(Signé) M. SIDKY.

Monsieur Howard Carter,
Continental-Savoy, Caire.

It was on this basis, and with good feeling on both sides, that the tomb was reopened and the work resumed on January 25, 1925.

Thus, as will be seen, the third season's work was necessarily brief. It began at the height of the tourist season, in consequence of which no serious work in the tomb could be contemplated. The public interest was great. Luxor was crowded with visitors, and of these not a few were intelligently interested in our researches, and anxious to see the tomb. But whilst the utmost was done to gratify their wish, one part of our work at least was continued, for between February 1 and March 31 of that winter, we were able to prepare the various objects already found, during the preceding season, in the Burial Chamber, for transportation to the Cairo Museum where they were immediately exhibited.

I have no desire to avoid criticism, nevertheless, I feel bound to refer to a small matter. I have been somewhat severely taken to task for slowness in my work. To such criticism I think one is justified in replying that, when one is dealing with fragile objects of different degrees of preservation and of universal importance, one may easily destroy in a minute that which a few days, or may be weeks, of careful and patient treatment can save. Moreover, antiquities that have to be transported to a museum must be adequately strengthened to bear the risks of the journey. There is often great danger in haste.

As a matter of fact we were singularly fortunate in most of our preservation work. Dr. Alexander Scott, who came out to Egypt (winter 1923–24) at our request, as consulting chemist, gave valuable aid in solving many of the complex problems that confronted us, and especially that of the very fragile linen pall. It had to be removed from its ancient wooden struts (*vide* p. 43) and transported to the entrance of the laboratory for relining by the expert hands of Professor and Mrs. Newberry. At the crisis, when my control ceased, the officials who took charge left this most interesting relic in the open inadequately protected, with the result that it almost entirely perished, and that consequently our efforts to save it were of no avail.

When the discovery was first made, Lord Carnarvon and myself found ourselves confronted by a piece of work of overwhelming magnitude, and it was at this critical moment that the Trustees and Director of the Metropolitan Museum of Art, New York, most generously came to the rescue, and at their own sacrifice, lent us the services of Mr. Arthur Mace and Mr. Harry Burton. Up to the last two seasons much of our success in recording and dealing with the antiquities was due to the skill, wide experience and ungrudging help of Mr. Mace. Unfortunately his health, long strained by severe work, failed him in the summer of 1924, and we have, in consequence, been denied his invaluable assistance and encouragement, both in our labours in Egypt and in the compilation of this volume.

With regard to the fourth season, past experience had taught us that it would be well to resume our work on the tomb of Tut·ankh·Amen as soon as the decline of the great summer heat rendered it practicable. Our aim was to carry out the work with due scientific procedure, with the least possible interruption and, to meet the Egyptian Government's wishes, to open the tomb to the public as early as possible during the tourist season. For these reasons I left London in September, and began work early in October. The programme was, in scientific sequence, first to raise the nest of coffins within the sarcophagus, to open and examine them, and then to investigate the king's mummy—a task which took us nearly eight months; that is, until the end of May, 1926.

Throughout the examination of the royal mummy I was fortunate enough to have the invaluable aid of Dr. Douglas Derry, Professor of Anatomy at the Faculty of Medicine, Egyptian University, and of Dr. Saleh Bey Hamdi, Director of the Sanitary Services, Alexandria. It is to them that our thanks are due for the note upon the king's mummy included in this volume. For the chemical and preservation section of the work I had the continued advice and valuable assistance of Mr. A. Lucas, Government Chemist to the Cairo Museum; the Metropolitan Museum of Art, New York, still generously allowing me to retain the services of Mr. Burton for the purpose of carrying out his wonderful photographic records. The very skilful photographs he has made are of extraordinary beauty as well as of great archæological value.

With regard to the tourist side of the question,

between January and March there were over 12,300 visitors to the tomb and some 270 parties to the laboratory.

Now with archæological work the reverse to that which is anticipated almost always occurs. The opening of those elaborate coffins, without causing them harm, proved an intricate undertaking. The procedure which we were obliged to adopt in the examination of the king's mummy was, to say the least, disheartening.

Judging from the external appearance of Tut-ankh-Amen's outer coffin, from the preservation of the royal mummies formerly discovered, and now in the Cairo Museum, after all the depredations they had suffered, one was led to expect that this untouched king would be in almost perfect condition. Unfortunately, that was not the case. We found him in a terrible state. There was every proof that care had been taken in his mummification; he was swathed in masses of the finest cambric-like wrappings; he was literally smothered with every kind of ornament and amulet; he was enclosed in a solid gold coffin; but, the very custom of those last burial rites proved his destruction.

The mummy as well as the gold coffin had been subjected to consecration unguents that had been poured over them in great quantity. Those unguents were of the nature of fatty matter, resin, and possibly wood-pitch, originally in a liquid or semi-liquid condition. In the course of time the decomposition of those unguents acted destructively upon the contents. The consolidated residue of the unguents also formed a hard black pitch-like mass, which firmly stuck both the mummy and its mask to the bottom of the coffin;

and no amount of legitimate force could move them. The mummy had to be examined as it lay *in situ* in the coffin. Thus any systematic unwrapping for which we had hoped, was rendered impossible. The charred linen bandages, which fell to powder at the touch, had to be removed bit by bit. Moreover, the conditions rendered the use of X-rays impossible.

Nevertheless, though the undertaking was not such a clean piece of work as one would have wished, I am glad to say little, if any, data was lost, and all the objects were eventually preserved. The preservation of the latter, the ornaments and amulets, meant many months of work. It necessitated the experience not only of a chemist but of a jeweller. But for the anointing unguents, Tut·ankh·Amen, his wrappings and accessories, in that gold coffin, would have been practically as perfect as when first placed there.

Another of our difficulties was to extricate the gold coffin from the shell of the second coffin. The unguents poured over them had completely filled and consolidated the space between the two coffins, thus sticking them fast together. This problem was eventually solved, and we now have the two perfect and most wonderful coffins yet found.

It is of archæological import to note that all three coffins were not only Osiride in form, but their decoration was of the feathered type. The king's mummy we found neatly made and fashioned to symbolize Osiris. Covering the head and shoulders was a magnificent mask of beaten gold. The outer wrappings were embellished with heavy gold trappings which had somewhat suffered from the action of the unguents. Enclosed within the wrappings were 143 objects, comprising a diadem, daggers, girdles, personal jewellery and amulets. Three of these objects introduced an astonishing feature. They were of iron, which I believe is the first authentic purposed introduction of that metal into Egyptian civilization. It coincides approximately with the period when iron began to overtake bronze in Syria. Another most important historical fact was revealed by the king's mummy— his age at death, and his remarkable structural resemblance to his father-in-law, Akh·en·Aten, which throws light on his probable parentage. It is also of interest to note that there was neither a true heart-scarab upon the body, nor as yet have we found any trace of documents in the way of papyri, either of religious or of literary kind.

The material discovered in this last season has been transported to the Cairo Museum, where most of it is already on exhibition. The king's mummy, re-wrapped, will remain in his tomb enclosed in his sarcophagus.

The thrilling experiences of the last season's work were many, but it seems now, as I look back, that it was when the last of the decayed bandages had been removed, and the young king's features were first revealed, that the summit of these moving impressions was reached. The youthful Pharaoh was before us at last : an obscure and ephemeral ruler, ceasing to be the mere shadow of a name, had re-entered, after more than three thousand years, the world of reality and history ! Here was the climax of our long researches ! The tomb had yielded its secret ; the message of the past had reached the present in spite of the weight of time and the erosion of so many years.

The Store-room of the Burial Chamber and the Annexe to the Antechamber have still to be examined.

Preface

Although in a selfish world it may be easier to remember what we owe to others, than to convey to them the sense of our obligation, I feel that I must at this point express, however inadequately, my thanks to the many friends who have encouraged me with help and sympathy. They are far too many to enumerate. There is one old friend, of many years' standing—Mr. Percy White, who insists that any assistance that it may have been in his power to give me, has had its own reward, as a labour of love. I must nevertheless embarrass him with my warmest thanks for helping me in the compilation of this volume, although for his sake I will say no more.

I must, however, mention that both Dr. Alan Gardiner and Professor Newberry gave me every assistance in translating the various texts that we found, and that the identification of the botanical specimens is entirely due to my old friend and colleague, Professor Newberry.

Last of all come my Egyptian staff and the *Reises* who have served me throughout the heat and burden of many a long day, whose loyal services will always be remembered by me with respect and gratitude, and whose names are herewith recorded: Ahmed Gerigar, Hussein Ahmed Saide, Gad Hassan and Hussein Abou Owad.

Before ending this preface there is one subject to which I consider it my duty to refer. Where knowledge based on evidence ends, it may be said, as a general rule, that mystery begins. Of this the investigator is conscious in whatever direction his studies may lead him. Much must remain dark and obscure in the life of the ancient Egyptians, partly because the main idea behind the cults by which they are revealed to us, was to make clear to the living that which followed after death. The sentiment of the Egyptologist, however, is not one of fear, but of respect and awe. It is entirely opposed to the foolish superstitions which are far too prevalent among emotional people in search of " psychic " excitement.

It is not my intention to repeat the ridiculous stories which have been invented about the dangers lurking in ambush, as it were, in this tomb, to destroy the intruder. Similar tales have been a common feature of fiction for many years, they are mostly variants of the ordinary ghost story, and may be accepted as a legitimate form of literary amusement. But there is another and a serious side to this question which calls for protest. It has been stated in various quarters that there are actual physical dangers hidden in Tut·ankh·Amen's tomb—mysterious forces, called into being by some malefic power, to take vengeance on whomsoever should dare to pass its portals. There was perhaps no place in the world freer from risks than the tomb. When it was opened, scientific research proved it to be sterile. Whatever foreign germs there may be within it to-day have been introduced from without, yet mischievous people have attributed many deaths, illnesses, and disasters to alleged mysterious and noxious influences. Unpardonable and mendacious statements of this nature have been published and repeated in various quarters with a sort of malicious satisfaction. It is indeed difficult to speak of this form of " ghostly " calumny with calm. If it be not actually libellous it points in that spiteful direction, and all sane people should dismiss such inventions with contempt. So far as the living are concerned curses of this nature have no place in the Egyptian ritual.   On the contrary we are piously desired to express our benevolent wishes for the dead. That a similar spirit of wise charity should be absent in the loose-tongued gossips referred to, strongly suggests that, in some respects, our moral progress is less obvious than kindly people generally believe.

HOWARD CARTER.

November, 1926.

LIST OF PLATES

xxix

List of Plates

List of Plates

List of Plates

xxxii

List of Plates

c   xxxiii

List of Plates

INTRODUCTION

REMARKS UPON EGYPTIAN ART

THE controversy that has stirred around the art of the ancient Egyptians, has made it clearer than ever it was before that the aim of all worthy criticism should be to attain a truthful judgment, uninfluenced by the claims of passing fashion, and untrammelled by the habit of crude comparison.

An art which has a standard of its own cannot be justly measured by the values of another brought into being by different national conditions and religious influences. Some of the criticism called forth by the æsthetic activities of this ancient people has been derogatory and unfair in character, and this must be my excuse for the following preliminary and, as it might seem, digressive remarks.

When we are considering this question in all its forms, I trust that if I speak of it with reverence, I may not be understood to infer that this art admitted of no further refinement in its developments, for that is not my meaning. What I do mean is this. Although it may need certain superadditions, it can, in the real sense, be little improved. With all its failings —and to us its apparent incongruities—the real message is there for all who can take it, and perhaps the stronger because it has been kept within its own limits, and has never been purely imitative in character.

Introduction

It has been asserted by those who have never adequately considered the subject, or who have perhaps wearied of it, probably because their judgment has been warped by the absence of perspective, or the obvious remoteness from our conventions, which, to the unaccustomed eye, may give it an aspect of monotony, that on that account Egyptian art is repellent. Such an argument—or may I be pardoned if I use the word subterfuge?—should be regarded as beneath the uses of sound criticism. Every art has its own language. On similar ground the French word *h o m m e* might be objected to because it is not the English word *m a n*. Unfamiliarity with a subject is a blind and most dangerous guide. Such critics have been known to exclaim " What a splendid woman ! " when looking at a finely made young male Bisharee—a justifiable mistake on the part of anyone unacquainted with the physique of that race.

Now when alleged absence of action has been deplored—is it that action is really lacking ? No; action of every kind will be found in the Egyptian reliefs and paintings, as a whole not exaggerated action, but action sober and restrained. Can it be said that there is no grace of line ? Simple grace of line is one of its features. What, perhaps, certain critics really mean is that, owing to the lack of perspective, qualities such as the foreshortening of line which they expect, are unexpressed. If absolute action is sought, any modern instantaneous photograph will produce the undesirable and painful result. From our point of view the fault, if it be a fault, is simply the absence of foreshortening of line due to visual perspective, but as this does not exist in the Egyptian convention—an art complete in every other

2

way—why seek for it ? Add perspective to it and
we have no longer Egyptian art.

There is no doubt that an enormous amount of
Egyptian material labelled " art," was manufactured
to meet the demands of religious superstition. This
demand naturally created a mass of work of small
æsthetic merit which not only ceases to attract, but
may even, in many ways, become actually repellent.
But when one learns to differentiate and to select the
nobler examples, we discover how full they are of
dignity and serenity. In fact, we find in the master-
pieces, a certain feeling and a *finesse* within simplicity
—simplicity rising to an astounding degree—which
have never been surpassed.

We must never forget that, with the Egyptian
artist, each object depicted in his subject is from a
separate point-of-sight, and that the objects are treated
individually, and not relatively to one another.
Therefore the true function of the lines of sight in
linear perspective is eliminated, and its introduction
into such a convention as that of the ancient Egyptian
would give even a falser impression.

To apply to an art so well-balanced and complete
in itself, though it have peculiarities and may even
exhibit incongruities, as well as lack certain qualities
of its more fully developed European offspring, the
same critical methods by which modern art is judged,
is to deviate from the principle by which all useful
criticism should be guided.

There are, however, excuses for some at least of
the loose criticism of which I am now venturing to
complain. Egyptian paintings or bas-reliefs are being
copied for archæological and Egyptological purposes
more and more every day. A great many of these

copies might be supposed to embody their principles, but by being archæological records only, they unfortunately serve merely as accurate records for Egyptological study. From the æsthetic point of view, art is dishonoured when its soul is left out. It is therefore clearly unfair to judge Egyptian ornament from such examples. These works must be studied from the originals if the criticism is to have value.

Speaking of Egyptian ornament, Ruskin, with his eye evidently on the art student, eloquently and justly exclaims :—" the whole mass of it is made up of multitudinous human figures in every kind of action— and magnificent action ; their kings drawing their bows in their chariots, their sheaves of arrows rattling at their shoulders ; the slain falling under them as before a pestilence ; their captives driven before them in astonished troops ; and do you expect to imitate Egyptian ornament without knowing how to draw the figure ? "

It is often asked why Egyptian art never developed as did European art which imbibed its essentials —a question answered collaterally when we inquire why the inhabitants of the Nile Valley never become westernized. There is here a dominant fact that stands out. A culture can be imported into the Nile Valley, but it will never permeate the Nile Valley which colours, as history shows, all it touches. Your importation will be impregnated by that Valley. It is curious to note how, during the Greek domination in Egypt, the Ptolemies accepted, rather than influenced, the Egyptian tradition, not only in art but in religion.

But another reason for absence of progress can

be given. It may be because this art was chiefly concerned with the after-life that the chance of development of the germ was therefore brought within a minimum degree of limitable growth. It was not so much intended to live with as to lie hidden in the subterranean soul-chambers, and thus it came under greater superstitious bondage. Had Egyptian art been relieved of its priestly influence, and been dominated by a pure and more natural study of greater nature, it would probably have broken out into broader fields.

A third and possibly truer reason for its traditional conservatism was that those ancients copied and repeated themselves, a practice which must necessarily lead to a descending rather than to an ascending scale. And it will be noticed that only when new schools or centres arose offering their art fresh life by leading it back to nature, that it escaped from the priest-ridden convention. Leonardo da Vinci says : " The painter will produce pictures of little merit if he takes the works of others as his standard ; but if he will only apply himself to learn from objects of nature he will produce good results. This we see was the case with the painters who came after the time of the Romans, for they continually imitated each other, and from age to age their art steadily declined." Or again to quote Ruskin on the same subject :—" . . . having thus reached a singular perfection, she begins to contemplate that perfection, and to imitate it, and deduce rules from it, and thus forget her duty and ministry as the interpreter and discoverer of truth. And in the very instant when this diversion of her purpose and forgetfulness of her function take place—in that instant, I say begins her actual catastrophe ; and by her fall, so far as she has influence she accelerates the ruin of the nation by which she is produced."

A fourth reason may also be seen when we compare Egyptian and Greek art : Greek art and religion are one artistic ideal. With Egyptian religion and Egyptian art, the one is the motive of the other. " Take a Greek work—the Venus of Melos. That is in no sense a symbol, a suggestion, of anything beyond its own victorious fairness." But take such an Egyptian example of which the Karnak figure of Khensu is a beautiful specimen, this, in a sense, is a symbol of a certain conception or even superstition. One is the love of the fairness of the being ; the other the expression of certain attributed powers, which, by being abstract, have not pure nature as the model.

The ancient Egyptians were undoubtedly great observers of nature, both of its phenomena and in its organic form. Upon it their religion, art and architecture, were assuredly based. But, it should be noted that, although they evidently studied nature, when depicting her they nevertheless produced memorized accepted types, rather than made direct copies. This, I think, would account for the accepted characteristic forms to which they adhered by set rules. This practice, which seems to have been the custom of the race, is more likely to lead to greater conventionalism, than to the absolute or direct interpretation of nature, and such a practice must also influence the art concerned. But here it is as well to recall Walter Pater's words : " The artist is the child of his time," and " every intellectual product must be judged from the point of view of the age and the people in which it was produced."

A very important question is—what are the great

qualities of Egyptian art ? They are the sense of pure feeling that creates an element of serene dignity —and herein lies its supreme essence—and the extraordinary degree of truth, form and character portrayed within such absolute simple and minimum line, by which it stands alone.

Having found in Egyptian art on the one side degrees of excellence, and on the other certain deficiencies, to estimate their value we must now endeavour to discover its purpose. It must firstly be remembered that this decorative ideographic art is a limited art. It was created to form part of the chapel, tomb or temple, wherein it is found—it is fitted for a definite purpose and place, and in both purpose and place it forms part of a great harmonious whole. Its convention therefore is subordinate to a purpose. A great error is to consider this art as pictorially imitative, when in reality it is purely decorative, with religious ideographic meaning ; and had not this idea been kept in view with its statues, no matter how well they might have been executed, incongruity would have been the result.

This art was for the god and the dead to look upon —to show that they were not forgotten, and to perpetuate their memory eternally.

Many of its representations were symbols of an idea, the subject of their faith accepted and adhered to. And to have changed them would have been as, with us now, if we changed the accepted types of our Lord and the Divine Mother. Such designs were regarded by consent as naturally typifying the Being in fact or thought ; and should repetition seem irksome or repellent, such as the frequent representations of the king before numerous divinities, or the deceased before many gods of the dead, directing to them his prayers and justification for his earthly life, it must be remembered that, to a people who believed in this complex theological art, these pictures were of interest and that they were, at least, thoughtful representations that had their uses. To understand this perfectly requires the power of forgetting our own train of thought, and some knowledge of the inner mind of those ancients.

Herodotus tells us that " the Egyptians are religious, far beyond any other race of men,"—a characteristic manifestly displayed in all their records. They believed in an after-life, and on that after-life their thoughts were chiefly bent. " Such, then," says Leighton, " being the mental attitude and such the custom of a race with strong plastic and building instincts, what sort of art should we look for in it ? Should we not look for an art in which the temples of the gods and the abodes of the dead were the most salient features ? And should we not further expect of such a people that whatever connected itself with the glorification of those gods, or with the exhortation of earthly rulers scarcely less divine, or with the service of the departed, would be the inspiring motive of their graphic and plastic art, as well as of their architectural production ? And this art being entirely spontaneous and the sincere expression of the national temper, should it not convey to us a sense of strength, of dignity, of stability, and of repose ? " That was the " intention." The " accident," far from " intention," was the necessity of almost unlimited production, and thus the artist or sculptor often suffered by becoming more the manufacturer and purveyor, than a servant of the close and thoughtful study of nature.

Introduction

When Egypt was the reigning power of the age of copper and bronze, her great periods are generally known as the Old Kingdom, the Middle Kingdom, and the New Empire ; and those periods were just as distinguishable in her art as in her history. In her art they were the Classical Age, the Transitional Age, and the Modern Age. During the Egyptian New Empire her sculpture and painting were never more modern. But, throughout those ages, there was one united convention, a noble convention, not a false convention. Take for example, the beautiful beaten and burnished gold mask of Tut·ankh·Amen found in this tomb covering his head (Frontispiece and Plate LXXIII). Though it retains all the ancient conventions, the moment we become familiar with them, —the strangeness of the head-dress, the conventional beard which in the illustration has been removed— we have a perfect portrait of the young king at the age of his death. Such evidence as this immediately shows that were these conventions not less alien to us we should be better able to recognize individuality, not merely in this one outstanding example, but in all.

That the prevailing Egyptian conventions were noble, cannot be better expressed than in Ruskin's own words, written half a century ago : " The two noblest and *truest* carved lions I have ever seen are the two granite ones in the Egyptian room of the British Museum, and yet in them the lions' manes and beards are represented by rings of solid rock, as smooth as a mirror ! "

THE TOMB OF TUT·ANKH·AMEN

CHAPTER I

TUT·ANKH·AMEN

WHENEVER an archæological discovery lays bare traces of a remote age, and the vanished human lives it fostered, we turn at once instinctively to the facts revealed to us with which we are most in sympathy. And these are invariably human in their interests. A withered lotus flower, some emblem of tender affection, some simple domestic trait, will bring back the past for us, on its human side, far more vividly than the sentiment can be conveyed by austere records or pompous official inscriptions boasting how some dim " King of Kings " overwhelmed his enemies and trampled on their pride.

This is, to a certain extent, true of the discovery of the tomb of Tut·ankh·Amen. Of the young boy king we know very little, but as to his tastes and temperament we can now make some shrewd guesses. As the priestly vehicle through whom divine influence was transmitted to the Theban world, as the earthly representative of Re—the great Sun-god—the young king scarcely takes for us clear or realizable shape, but as a creature of ordinary human dispositions, a lover of the chase, as an eager sportsman, he becomes easily and amiably intelligible. We have here

11

that " touch of nature which makes the whole world kin."

The religious aspects of most races become modified by time, circumstance and education. In some cases their feeling towards death and its mysteries is refined and spiritualized. With the growth of culture, love, pity, sorrow, affection, find tenderer modes of utterance and expression. Of this we have evidence in Greek epitaphs and Latin tomb-inscriptions. But if the more delicate shades of sorrow be less obviously manifested by the ancient Egyptians, it is rather because the gentler human moods seem overwhelmed under the weight of their elaborate burial practices, than that these emotions are absent. Belief in the continuity of the human soul is the idea whence these practices were evolved. To strengthen this conviction and impress it on the world, no sacrifice was deemed too great. The after-life seems in their eyes to have been more important than their worldly existence, and the most careless student of their customs may wonder at the lavish generosity with which this ancient people launched their dead on their last mysterious journey.

If, however, tradition and priestly practice governed ancient Egyptian burial ceremonial, as the contents of Tut·ankh·Amen's tomb suggest, their ritual left room for a personal side which confronted the grief of the mourners, whilst it aimed at encouraging the dead on their journey through the dangers of the Underworld. This human sentiment has not been concealed by the mysterious symbolism of a complex creed. It dawns on the observer gradually as he pursues his investigations. The impression of a personal sorrow is perhaps more distinctly conveyed

to us from what we learn from the tomb of Tut·ankh·
Amen than by most other discoveries. It meets us
as an emotion which we are accustomed to deem
comparatively modern in origin. The tiny wreath
on the stately coffin, the beautiful alabaster wishing
cup (Vol. I, Plate XLVI) with its touching inscription,
the treasured reed with its suggestive memories—
cut by the young king himself by the lake-side—
these, and other objects, help to convey the message
—the message of the living mourning the dead.

The sense of premature loss faintly haunts the
tomb. The royal youth, obviously full of life and
capable of enjoying it, had started, in very early
manhood—who knows under what tragic circumstances?—on his last journey from the radiant
Egyptian skies into the gloom of that tremendous
Underworld. How could grief be best expressed?
In his tomb we are conscious of this effort, and the
emotion thus gently and gracefully exhibited is the
expression of that human regret which knits our
sympathies with a sorrow more than three thousand
years old.

As has been already mentioned in Volume I,
politically we gather that the king's brief reign and
life must have been a singularly uneasy one. It may
be that he was the tool of obscure political forces
working behind the throne. This, at least from the
sparce data that we have, is a reasonable conjecture.
But however much Tut·ankh·Amen may have been
the tool of political religious movements, whatever
political influence the youthful king may have possessed, or whatever his own religious feelings, if any,
may have been—and this must remain uncertain—
we do gather not a little information as to his tastes

and inclinations from the innumerable scenes on the furniture of his tomb. It is in these that we find the most vivid suggestions of Tut·ankh·Amen's affectionate domestic relations with the young queen, and that evidence of his love of sport, of the royal and youthful passion for the chase, which makes him so human to our sympathies after the lapse of so many dark centuries.

What, for instance, could be more charming than the tableau upon the throne (Vol. I, Plate II), so touchingly represented? Such impressions, for the moment, seem to lift us across the gulf of years and destroy the sense of time. Ankh·es·en·Amen, the charming girlish wife, is seen adding a touch of perfume to the young king's collar, or putting the last touches to his toilet before he enters into some great function in the palace. Nor must we forget that little wreath of flowers, still retaining their tinge of colour, that farewell offering placed upon the brow of the young king's effigy as he lay within his quartzite sarcophagus.

Other incidents represented suggest even a touch of humour. Among episodes of the daily private life of the king and queen on a small golden *naos* (Vol. I, Plate LXVIII), we find Tut·ankh·Amen accompanied by his lion-cub, shooting wild-duck with bow and arrow, whilst, at his feet, squats the girlish queen (Plate I, B.). With one hand she is handing him an arrow, while with the other she points out a fat duck. On the same *naos* the young spouse is represented offering to him sacred libations, flowers and collarettes, or tying a pendant around his neck. Here we have the young couple in various simple and engaging attitudes. The queen accompanies the king on

14

another fowling expedition in a reed canoe. She is seen affectionately supporting his arm as though he were wearied by State affairs, and then again—and there is a suggestion of playfulness in these little glimpses of their private life—we find him pouring sweet perfume on her hand as they are resting in their cabinet (Plate I, A). These are charming scenes and full of the kindliness which it pleases us to consider modern.

Upon a golden fan (Plate LXII), found between the sepulchral shrines that covered and protected his sarcophagus, a fan, such as we see pictured in Roman times, and actually used to-day in the Vatican, is a beautifully embossed and chased picture of Tut·ankh·Amen, hunting ostriches for the plumes for that very flabellum. On its reverse side he is seen returning home triumphant, his attendants carrying his quarry—two dead ostriches, and the coveted feathers under his arm.

Scenes of the young sportsman's activities constantly confront us. Upon trappings of the chariot-harness he is shown practising archery. We gather, too, that, like some of our earlier kings, he was a lover of the bow. And, as proof of his proficiency in archery, there was treasured in his tomb, among boomerangs and similar missiles of the chase, a magnificent bow-of-honour (Vol. I, Plate LXXVI), covered with sheet-gold, decorated with fine filigree gold-work, and richly adorned with semi-precious stones and coloured glass. In a long box in the Antechamber (Vol. I, Plate XVII) of his tomb were a number of different kinds of bows of the neatest workmanship—composite bows decorated with ornamental barks and finely fashioned arrows, while lying nearest to him, under the golden shrines that shielded his sarcophagus, were other bows and arrows. The sheath of a handsome gold dagger, found girded to his waist within the wrappings of his mummy, has also wild animals embossed upon it (Plate LXXXVIII). Even his cosmetic jar bears evidence of his pastime. On it are portrayed bulls, lions, hounds, gazelle and hare— the huntsman's favourite game (Plates L, LI). His slughi hounds are especially included in scenes suggesting fondness of field sport and of an open-air life.

There can be little doubt that in the Theban neighbourhood, in those days, the greater area of morass attracted and harboured large quantities of game. Game also abounded on its desert borders, and in the scrub of the desert wady. In the marshes the boy king shot all kinds of wild-fowl. In extensive preserves the desert afforded a varied field for the skill of the royal sportsman, who hunted in his chariot, while his courtiers followed in cars and his attendants coursed on foot. Within these preserves it would seem to have been the custom to collect every variety of game. When hunting, the young Tut·ankh·Amen shot with bow and arrow, his slughi hounds being loosed in turn on the game when sighted.

Of his interest in sport, as thus exhibited, we have striking evidence in a delightful and vigorous sketch found while nearing the entrance of his tomb, and possibly drawn by one of the artisans employed in making the sepulchre : it is on a flake of limestone and represents the young king, aided by his slughi hound, slaying a lion with a spear (Plate II, A). When an ordinary artisan is capable of such vigorous work, we naturally expect art of extreme beauty from the highly-trained craftsmen employed by the rulers of

Egypt, who seem to have been generally men of artistic discernment. The treasures in Tut·ankh· Amen's tomb showed how fully this expectation was justified.

One of the great artistic treasures is a painted wooden casket found in the Antechamber (Vol. I, Plate XXI). Its outer face, completely covered with gesso, has, upon this prepared surface, a series of brilliantly coloured and exquisitely painted designs : hunting scenes upon its curved lid, battle scenes upon its sides, wherein Tut·ankh·Amen and his suite are most energetically engaged, whilst upon the ends of the box are representations of the king, in lion form, trampling upon his alien foes (Vol. I, Plates L–LIV). The vigour, imagination, and dramatic force displayed in these scenes is extraordinary, and incomparable in Egyptian art. In the war scenes we see the youthful but all-conquering monarch trampling under foot, with great gusto, his African and Asiatic enemies. Fine as they are we must admit the braggart spirit is not absent. The mighty monarch, for the sake of effect no longer a slender youth, is shooting down his enemies from his chariot, panic is before him, the dead at his feet. Such pictures of Egyptian kings are, of course, traditional. They are probably, in this case, merely the customary homage of the Court painter. That he took the field of war in person, especially at his age, is improbable, but of such polite fiction, kings and conquerors in the Oriental world have always been singularly tolerant. The paintings on the casket's lid are wonderfully spirited. Here we have hunting scenes full of the sense of speed and movement. Incident and action are manifold, and in them all Tut·ankh·Amen is accompanied by his slughi hounds.

Even in the battle scenes his dogs are seen pulling and tearing at the defeated foe. The king in his chariot, drawn by prancing steeds, gorgeous in their trappings, is pursuing desert fauna. Before him flee antelope and ostrich, wild ass and hyena—all the denizens of the desert, including lions and lionesses. Seen between the flying figures of the animals and the feet of his followers, tufts of gay desert flora, forming the scrub of the wady, are charmingly suggested. Tut·ankh·Amen, with his slughi hounds around him —his followers at respectful distance—is thundering down the wady-bed, the panic-stricken quarry fleeing on all sides. The agonized beasts are rendered with the utmost realism. There are moments—in the group of hunted lions (Plate III) for example—when the artist reaches almost tragic force. The agonized, shaft-pierced beasts are portrayed with splendid power. One of them—the King Beast—stricken to the heart—having sprung into the air in the final spasm of death, is falling headlong to the ground. Another clutches with his paw at a shaft which has entered his open mouth, and hangs broken in his jaws, meanwhile the half-grown cub is slinking away with tail between its legs, whilst wounded comrades lie in tortured postures of pathetic suffering. But if the historical accuracy of this beautiful work be doubted, there can be no two opinions as to its merits in interpreting the king's true passion and inclinations. These exquisite pictures in delicate miniature painting are, in fact, idealized hunting scenes wherein the young man's tastes and temperament, as well as the spirit of the chase, have been captured and interpreted.

Evidences of the kindlier affections are traits we scarcely expect to find among a Pharaoh's relics.

His predecessors have left too few memories of the gentler feelings, still the messages of archæology are not always those we most expect, and we are surprised, as well as touched, by the expression of the simpler human feelings charmingly portrayed on Tut·ankh·Amen's funerary furniture. From them we gather that he was a gallant and amiable youth, loving horse and hound, sport and military display. But there is another side to the picture. The traditional ornament, worked in gold on the chariots, the beautiful carving of African and Asiatic prisoners bound to the king's walking-sticks (Vol. I, Plates LXIX, LXX), and on his furniture all suggest the formidable Pharaoh, bent, metaphorically at least, on " making his enemy his footstool " (Vol. I, p. 119), and typify the braggart spirit associated with the character of Egypt's ancient rulers, although we have it here, is less overwhelmingly expressed than in other tombs.

The silver trumpets (Plate II, B) dedicated to the legions or units of the Egyptian army, found in the Antechamber and Burial Chamber, appeal to the imagination. The military experience of Tut·ankh· Amen must have been small indeed, but we may nevertheless imagine him surrounded by his generals, State officials and courtiers, taking the salute whilst the massed legions in military pageant passed by.

His mummy, like his statues, shows him to have been a slim youth with large head, presenting structural resemblance to the dreamer Ankh·en·Aten, who in all probability was not only his father-in-law but also his father.

Thus step by step, the excavator's spade, in various departments of archæology, is revealing to us the world of the past, and the more our knowledge extends, the greater grows our wonder—possibly our regret—that human nature should have so little changed during the few thousand years of which we have some historical knowledge. Especially our gaze is fixed on ancient Egypt which has given us such vivid glimpses of a wonderful past. On painted casket, decorated chair, on shrine, tomb chapel or temple wall, her ancient life passes in strange and moving pageant. In many points our sympathies meet, but it is chiefly by her art that we are brought nearest to her feeling, and that we recognize in the royal sportsman, the dog-lover, the young husband and the slender wife, creatures in human taste, emotion and affection, very like ourselves.

Thus we learn not to overvalue the present, and our modern perspective becomes less complacent and more philosophical. There are, we are tempted to believe, certain characteristics which became innate in man in those dim ages as yet but slightly touched by archæological research. There are glimmering atavisms of which we are barely conscious, and it may be these that awaken in us sympathy for the youthful Tut·ankh·Amen, for his queen, and all the life suggested by his funerary furniture. It may be these instincts which make us yearn to unravel the mystery of those dim political intrigues by which we suspect he was beset, even whilst following his slughi hounds across marsh and desert, or shooting duck among the reeds with his smiling queen. The mystery of his life still eludes us—the shadows move but the dark is never quite uplifted.

CHAPTER II

THE TOMB AND BURIAL CHAMBER

THE fear and awe associated with death were at least as deeply implanted in the minds of the ancient as in those of the modern world. These emotions have reached us through dim ancestral channels, colouring successive mythologies, moulding human conduct, nor have they left Christian theology untouched. At all times and on all races, death has loomed as the most tremendous mystery and the last inevitable necessity that man's obscure destiny must face—and pathetic have been his efforts to throw light on the darkness shrouding his future. His life and art were once mainly concerned with this insoluble problem. Human reason has always attempted to calm human fears ; man's mind, yearning and active, has instinctively endeavoured to find in his beliefs solace for them—to call up some protection against the dangers that fill the dark gulf of the Unknown. But one touching glimmer of hope has always shone through the gloom. On the threshold of death he has sought comfort in the love and affection which he hoped would knit him to the living—a natural yearning revealed in ancient burial rituals. It is apparent in the expressed desire—as in Jacob's request to his son—that his bones should be laid amid his kin, and the beloved surroundings of his native land, and the evidence of scientific investigation suggests that the instinct was atavistic in its origin. But from the very earliest times the means of obtaining comfort in this great problem have been modified, whilst fundamental tradition has remained. In the Valley of the Nile a simple shallow grave developed into a great pyramid-tomb and mortuary chapel. From the most grandiose and impressive of all sepulchral efforts to guard the memory of the dead, change after change has moulded custom, until such simplicity has been attained that those vast ancient preparations have shrunk to a brief epitaph and a wreath of flowers. However, of those varied epoch-making transitions, we deal here with but one, that of the Egyptian New Empire.

Many of the funeral customs of the older Egyptian periods were widely practised in the Theban New Empire; where some of them disappear it was only to make room for more elaborate conceptions which were intended to be equally beneficial for the dead. One of the innovations was the increased amount of household furniture and personal effects that were placed in the tomb. Another, instead of the king's mortuary chapel and sepulchre being contiguous, in the New Empire the royal mummies were buried in elaborate hypogea excavated in the cliffs far away from their mortuary buildings. These were as sumptuous in decoration as their chapels. But in the Eighteenth Dynasty they began by decorating only the sepulchral chamber with texts deemed most necessary for the dead. Later, in the Nineteenth and Twentieth Dynasties, the preceding corridors, passages and antechambers, which led to the burial chamber— called "The-Golden-Hall"—were covered from end to end with elaborate texts and scenes taken principally from the sacred books concerning the realms of the

The Tomb and Burial Chamber

dead, such as the books of " Amduat," " The Gates,"
" The Caverns," and " The Hymns to the Sun-god."

Most of these rock-cut hypogea were excavated in
the desolate Valley of the Kings, actually some
twenty-eight in number, while their mortuary chapels,
many of them of the dimensions of great temples,
were constructed on the desert plain bordering the
arable land. It was in these buildings where ceremonies and offerings to the dead monarchs were
celebrated, while " Osiris " (that is the deceased)
rested in solitude, far away in the Valley, sealed within
his " Silent Seat "—the tomb.

In the mortuary chapels upon the plain we find,
as well as religious scenes, records of the individual
reign to which they belong ; but in the Valley tombs,
or hypogea, texts concerning the realms of the dead
and welcoming wishes of the gods of the West are
alone found.

Commencing from the beginning of the Empire
these rock-cut hypogea show stages of evolution, they
gradually expand in importance, reaching their climax
at the time of Thothmes iv, from which reign onwards, though we find certain additions, these
additions disappear, and the tomb-plan gradually
falls into decadence. It is only in the case of the
tombs of the so-called heretic kings belonging to the
" Aten " or monotheistic religion, that the orthodox
pattern of the New Empire has not been adhered to.
Hence, it is no surprise to find Tut·ankh·Amen's
tomb unorthodox in type, though he reverted to the
older religion—the worship of Amen. Contrary to
Tut·ankh·Amen and King Ay, Hor·em·heb, who
usurped the throne and founded the Nineteenth
Dynasty, in making his tomb in the Valley, reintro-

duced the orthodox plan in all its component parts.
And in Hor·em·heb's tomb one directly sees the
transition from the Eighteenth Dynasty bent tomb
to the straightened tomb form of his dynasty and of
those which followed.

In the place of an elaborate series of corridors,
sunken staircases, protective well and vestibule, further descending passages, antechamber, sepulchral
hall, crypt and a series of four store-rooms, of the
orthodox Theban plan, Tut·ankh·Amen's tomb merely
comprises a sunken entrance-staircase, a descending passage, an antechamber with annexe, a burial
chamber and one store-room, all small and of the
simplest kind (*see* plan, Vol. I, p. 223). In fact, it
only conforms with the Theban pattern of the New
Empire royal tomb in orientation, by having its
burial chamber alone painted of a golden hue corresponding with " The-Golden-Hall," and by having in
its walls niches for the magical figures of the four
cardinal points.

The subjects painted upon the walls of this chamber, though resembling in many ways those of the
tomb of his successor, King Ay, differ from those
found in any of the other sepulchral chambers in the
Valley. The style of painting is also not of Theban
type, it shows distinct traits of El Amarna art. In
contradistinction to this the decoration of Hor·em·
heb's tomb has distinct affinity with the art displayed
in all the other royal tombs in the Valley, so much so
that it led the late Sir Gaston Maspero into the sup-
position that it was the work of the same artists
employed in Seti's tomb, constructed some twenty-
five years later.

In orientation the Burial Chamber, as well as its

nest of four shrines, sarcophagus, coffins and mummy, is east and west, accurate to within four degrees of magnetic north (Nov., 1925). The doors of the shrines, in accordance with the guide-marks upon them, were intended to face west, but for reasons not altogether clear they were actually erected facing east : it may be that had the shrines been placed in their correct and intended orientation, access to their folding doors would have been most difficult, and their purpose constricted in that very small chamber, as it would have been wellnigh impossible to have introduced objects such as were found between the outermost and second shrines. In the following chapter (p. 47) other reasons for this incorrect orientation are suggested.

In shape the Burial Chamber is rectangular, having its long axis (east and west) at right angles to that of the Antechamber. With the exception of a difference in floor levels of about 3 feet, the Antechamber and Burial Chamber were originally continuous, but were afterwards separated by a dry-masonry partition wall, in which was left a doorway guarded by the two sentinel statues of the king elsewhere described (Vol. I, p. 99).

The walls of the Burial Chamber were coated with a gypsum plaster, and were painted yellow with the exception of a dado which was coloured white. The rock ceiling was left plain in its rough and unfinished state. It is here interesting to note that traces of smoke, as from an oil lamp or torch, are visible upon the ceiling in the north-east corner.

The construction of the partition wall (Plate x) dividing the Antechamber from the Burial Chamber, and the plastering and decoration of the chamber itself, must have taken place after the burial of the king, the closing of the sarcophagus and the erection of the four shrines. This is proved by the following facts : the introduction of the sarcophagus, the burial, and the placing of the shrines, could not have been effected after the partition wall had been built, the doorway through it being insufficiently large. Again, the plastering and painting that covered the inner face of the partition wall was uniform with the rest of the decoration of the chamber. Thus the plastering and painting of the chamber must necessarily have been done after the erection of the shrines, under exceptionally difficult conditions and in a very confined space, which may account for the crudeness of the workmanship. The surfaces of the walls are covered with small brown fungus growths, the original germs of which were possibly introduced either with the plaster or the sizing of the paint, and were nourished by the enclosed humidity that exuded from the plaster after the chamber had been sealed up.

The subjects treated in the paintings upon the walls are of funerary and religious import. One scene is unprecedented, and that is the figure of the reigning King Ay presiding over the obsequies of his dead predecessor or co-regent.

Depicted on the east wall is a scene of the funeral procession wherein the deceased Tut·ankh·Amen upon a sledge is being drawn by courtiers to the tomb. The mummy is shown supported upon a lion-shaped bier, within a shrine on a boat, which rests upon the sledge. The bier painted here resembles that actually found in the sarcophagus under the coffins, while the shrine is of similar design to that which encloses the canopic chest and jars in the store-room of this tomb.

The Tomb and Burial Chamber

Over the dead king are festoons of garlands ; on the boat in front of the shrine is a sphinx rampant ; before and behind the shrine are the mourning goddesses Nephthys and Isis respectively ; and attached to the prow and stern of the boat, as well as on both sides of the shrine, are red and white pennants. The courtiers and high officials forming the cortège are divided up in the following order : A group of five nobles, then two groups of two nobles each, two officials wearing garments such as distinguish the viziers, and lastly a courtier. Each personage wears upon his wig or bare shaven head, as the case may be, a white linen fillet such as is usually found in funeral processions illustrated in private tomb chapels, and like those still used by the modern Egyptian on such occasions to distinguish relatives and retainers of the deceased's household. A legend above this procession tells us : " The Courtiers of the Royal Household going in procession with the Osiris King Tut·ankh·Amen to the West. They ' voice ' : O King ! Come in peace ! O God ! Protector of the Land."

The wish calls to mind the not uncommon custom still in vogue in the Nile Valley, the deceased being often carried around the grave by the bearers to ensure approval, and the scene vividly calls to mind (Genesis, ch. 50, vv. 4–7) Joseph's burial of his father Jacob : " And when the days of his mourning were past, Joseph spake unto the house of Pharaoh, saying, If now I have found grace in your eyes, speak, I pray you, in the ears of Pharaoh saying, My father made me swear, saying, Lo, I die : in my grave which I have digged for me in the land of Canaan, there shalt thou bury me. Now therefore let me go up, I pray thee, and bury my father, and I will come again.

And Pharaoh said, Go up, and bury thy father, according as he made thee swear. And Joseph went up to bury his father : and with him went up all the servants of Pharaoh, the elders of his house, and all the elders of the land of Egypt."

On the north wall, east corner, we find the scene of historical importance of Ay as king with royal insignia, clad in a leopard's skin of the *Sem* priest (Plate LIV). Here King Ay officiates at the funeral ceremony of " The Opening of the Mouth " of the dead Tut·ankh· Amen represented as Osiris (Plate IV, A). Between the living and the dead monarchs are the objects connected with the ceremonial laid out upon a table, which are the adze, a human finger, the hind limb of an ox, the fan of a single ostrich feather, and a double plume-like object : these are surmounted by a row of five gold and silver cups containing what may be balls of incense such as we found in the Antechamber.

In the centre of the north wall Tut·ankh·Amen, wearing a wig, fillet and white kilt, stands before the goddess Nût, " Lady of Heaven, Mistress of the Gods," who gives " health and life to his nostril " (Plate IV, B).

The third scene, at the west end of the wall, refers to the king's spiritual rather than his bodily form : it shows Tut·ankh·Amen followed by his " Ka " (spirit) embracing Osiris (Plate IV, C).

On the west wall are vignettes selected from certain chapters of the Book concerning Amduat (that which is within the Underworld), which are repeated among the mural decorations in the tomb of King Ay in the Wâdyein : the outstanding features here being the assembly of the sacred cynocephalus apes, the " Kheper-boat-of-Re " and a procession of deities named : Maa, Nebt·uba, Heru, Ka·shu and Nehes (Plate IV, D).

The south wall, wherein was the sealed doorway to the chamber, was composed partly of the built partition wall and the bed-rock itself. Depicted upon it are scenes of the king before certain divinities. At the west end, King Tut·ankh·Amen is figured between Anubis and Isis. He wears the *Khat* head-dress. The goddess Isis repeats here the same wishes as those of Nût upon the north wall, the words of which I have already given. Behind Anubis, the goddess Isis is again figured and she holds in both her hands symbols of water. She is accompanied by three " Great Gods, Lords of Duat " (i.e. of the Underworld).

These paintings, rough, conventional and severely simple as they are, have not the same austere character of the more elaborate texts and vignettes in the other Theban royal tombs ; neither in their rendering do they show that affinity common to the art of those tombs. In fact, they might be described as almost transitional—between El Amarna and Theban style—the subjects themselves being curtailed in the greatest possible degree. These artistic traits are equally noticeable in the art displayed by the funerary furniture found in the tomb.

The rest of the tomb, i.e. the Antechamber, Annexe and Store-room, is quite simple and, like the descending passage, their well-cut rock surfaces are left unsmoothed.

We now turn to the contents of the Burial Chamber. When we entered it we found, lying beside a small hole made by the robbers through the masonry of the door which had been subsequently reclosed by the ancient Egyptian officials, portions of two necklaces dropped by a thief. Around the four sides of the great shrine which occupied almost the entire area of the chamber, were divers objects and emblems. A brief examination of the shrine and the objects surrounding it, showed that little damage had been done in this chamber by the predatory intruders, except that the folding doors of the great shrine had been opened for the purpose of peering in, and that the sealings of the wine-jars, placed between the shrine and the walls of the chamber, had been broken. But although the Burial Chamber had suffered little from the activities of the thieves, many objects had been stolen from the small Store-room beyond. Standing in the south-east corner was a lamp resting upon a trellis-work pedestal, carved out of pure translucent calcite (Plate XLV). This lamp of chalice form, flanked with fretwork-ornament symbolizing " Unity " and " Eternity," ranks among the most interesting objects we had so far discovered. Its chalice-like cup, which held the oil and a floating wick, was neither decorated on its exterior nor interior surfaces, yet when the lamp was lit the king and queen were seen in brilliant colours within the thickness of its translucent stone (Plate XLVI). We, at first, were puzzled to know how this ingenious effect was accomplished. The explanation would seem to be that there were two cups turned and fitted, one within the other, and that on the outer wall of the inner cup a picture had been painted in semi-transparent colours, visible only through the translucent calcite when the lamp was lit.

Beneath this unique lamp, wrapped in reeds, was a silver trumpet (Plate II, B), which, though tarnished with age, were it blown would still fill the Valley with a resounding blast. Neatly engraved upon it is a whorl of calices and sepals, the prenomen and nomen of Tut·ankh·Amen, and representations of the gods Re, Amen and Ptah. It is not unlikely that these gods may have had some connexion with the division of the field army into three corps or units, each legion under the special patronage of one of these deities—army divisions such as we well know existed in the reign of Rameses the Great. At the Dog River in Phœnicia are three military stelæ of that reign, one to each of these gods, which were probably erected by the respective corps of the army. On a stele recently discovered in Beisan in Palestine the same divisions or corps occur. We may assume, therefore, that this silver trumpet with its gold mountings is of military significance, and that the creation of those three legions patronized by Re, Amen and Ptah, of the Imperial army organization, existed in the Eighteenth Dynasty and probably before Tut· ankh·Amen's reign.

At the eastern end of the shrine were two massive folding doors, closed with ebony bolts shot into copper staples, their panels decorated with strange figures —headless demon guardians of the caverns of the Underworld. Before these doors stood an exquisite triple-lamp (Plate XLVII) of floral-form, carved out of a single block of translucent calcite, in shape three lotiform cups, with stems and leaves springing from a single circular base, strangely suggestive as symbolizing the Theban Triad and resembling the *Tricerion* or three-branched candlestick that typifies the Holy Trinity of the Christian era. In front, standing along the east wall, was Amen's sacred goose (*Chenalopex Ægyptiacus*, Linn.) of wood, varnished black, and swathed in linen (Plate LII,A); beside it were two rush-work baskets collapsed with age, and a wine-jar bearing the legend: "Year 5, wine of the house of (?) Tut·ankh·Amen, from the Western river Chief of the Vintners, Kha."

Resting upon the ground, between the shrine and the north wall, were magic oars (Plate V) to ferry the king's barque across the waters of the Nether World, and with them, one at each end, curious devices in varnished black wood: one representing a *hes* vase between *propylæ* (Plate LIII,A), the other having "Feathers of Truth" between two kiosks (Plates V, LIII,B), which contained faience cups filled respectively with natron and resin. At the western end of the chamber, in the northern and southern corners, were austere golden emblems of Anubis hung on lotiform poles (Plates V, VI), erect, standing some five or six feet in height, in alabaster pots, placed upon reed mats. They may belong to the dark world under the earth, where the sun sinks, and where also the dead sleep: emblems it may be to guide the dead through this domain, for was not Anubis—the Jackal—a prowler of the dusk, and did not Re send him forth to bury Osiris? But, in truth, their meaning is obscure and probably nearly as remote from Tut·ankh·Amen as his day from ours. With these emblems were four gilt wooden objects (Plate LII,B) which may signify the swathing linen of the dead; on the other hand, these curious symbols of gilt wood, according to Dr. Alan Gardiner, have given rise to the phonetic hieroglyph "to awake," thus one might infer that they may have some connexion with the awakening of the dead. On the floor, beside these curious symbols, were four small rough clay troughs, in which they may have stood. Resting against the south-west corner was an immense [funerary bouquet (*Vide* Vol. I, Plate XXVII) composed of twigs and branches of the persea (*Mimasops Schimperi*) and olive (*Olea Europa*).

When we drew back those ebony bolts of the great shrine, the doors swung back as if only closed yesterday, and revealed within yet another shrine, in type like the first, save for the blue inlay. It has similar bolted doors, but upon them was a seal intact, bearing the name of Tut·ankh·Amen and a recumbent jackal over Egypt's nine foes. Above the shrine drooped a linen pall. This bespangled linen pall brown with age, still hanging on its curious wooden supports, was rent by the weight of the gilt bronze marguerites sewn to its fabric (Plate IV). The shrine, dazzling from the brilliance of its gold, was decorated with scenes wrought, in beautiful incised-relief, from the book " Of that which is in the Underworld "—that guide to the Hereafter, which points out to the deceased the road he should take, and explains to him the various malefic powers he must meet during his subterranean journey. According to this book two routes led him to the land of the blessed, one by water, the other by land, and it further shows that there were by-ways leading to seething rivers of fire by which he must not travel.

The pall made us realize that we were in the presence of a dead king of past ages. The unbroken seal upon the closed doors of the second shrine gave us the data we were seeking. Had the tomb-robbers, who had entered the Antechamber, its Annexe, the Burial Chamber and its Store-room by any chance reached the king ? The shrine was intact, its doors bore their original seal uninjured, indicating that the

33

robbers had not reached him. Henceforth, we knew that, within the shrine, we should be treading where no one had entered, and that we should be dealing with material untouched and unharmed since the boy king was laid to rest nearly three thousand three hundred years ago. We had at last found what we never dreamed of attaining—an absolute insight into the funerary customs followed in the burial of an ancient Pharaoh. Ten years of toil had not been wasted and our hopes were to be realized with a result far exceeding our expectations.

In front of the shrine's doors stood the king and queen's perfume vase carved of pure semi-translucent alabaster (calcite), a rare masterpiece of intricate stone-carving embellished with gold and ivory (Plates XLVIII, XLIX). It would seem that the royal lapidary delighted in intricate design typifying the " Union of the Two Countries," Upper and Lower Egypt, symbolized by a knot of stems of conventional papyrus and lotus flowers, but here he has even surpassed himself by adding to his favourite theme two charming epicene figures of Hapi. They represent the Upper and Lower Nile, and they embrace not only the flanking floral ornament, but also slender sceptres encircled by uræi bearing the red and white crowns of the " Two Kingdoms." The lip of the vase itself the artist has surmounted with a vulture with wide spreading wings. Unhappily, so delicate was the workmanship, the intumescence of the sacred material it held had burst the vase asunder. In front of this beautiful object, partially covered by fallen portions of the pall, stood another powerful piece of conventional art embodying, in this case, certain characteristics of the Eastern Mediterranean. This was a

cosmetic jar of various kinds of carved calcite (Plates
L, LI) which still contained its cosmetic (*see* p. 206),
plastic and fragrant. This jar is remarkable for its
unique design ; it is cylindrical in shape, rests on four
prisoners of African and Mediterranean type, it has a
Bes column on either side, a delightful recumbent lion
with long protruding red tongue on the lid, and upon
its sides are scenes among desert flora, incised and
filled in with pigment, of lions attacking bulls, hounds
chasing antelope, gazelle and hare.

On either side, between the two shrines, stacked
in the right and left corners, were numerous ceremonial maces, sticks, staves and bows, some carefully
wrapped in linen. Perhaps the choicest of them all
are the gold and silver sticks, made of two thin
tubular shafts supporting tiny statuettes of the youthful monarch, cast and chased in their respective
metals (Plate VII). It would be almost impossible to
describe the refinement of these graceful figures of
sedate but youthful bearing. Chubby little figures
are here represented very subtly modelled. Their
crowns and skirts are chased. The gesture of their
hands is of youthful simplicity. Both are exactly
alike save for their metals. They are clearly the
production of a master hand. These gold and silver
sticks were in all probability intended for ceremonial
and processional purposes. They call to mind the
gold and silver stick borne on State occasions by the
Gentlemen-at-Arms to-day.

A series of curved batons, most elaborately decorated with minute marquetry of variegated barks,
iridescent elytra of beetles, and broad bands of burnished gold with scroll-pattern borders, next claimed
our admiration (Plate VIII,A). One of these was

completely veneered with intricate ivory and ebony patterns, divided by bands of floral decoration, and had carved hunting devices on its ivory tips (Plate VIII, B). Among other sticks of perhaps more personal nature, was a simple plain gold stick with lapis lazuli glass top, inscribed " Take for thyself the wand of gold in order that thou mayest follow thy beloved father Amen, most beloved of gods ; " another was encrusted with exquisite glass inlay intermingled with gold filigree work on the handle, called " The beautiful stick of His Majesty ; " the third was a plain reed mounted with broad gold and electrum ferrules and plaited gold wire. We wondered why such an ordinary and plain reed should have been so richly mounted, but the legend written upon it gave the touching solution : " A reed which His Majesty cut with his own hand." The remainder of this remarkable collection of royal appurtenances was of a more ceremonial and religious kind, such as maces, *Uas* sceptres, crooked and forked sticks, made of wood covered with gesso and gilt.

Such were the appointments of the Burial Chamber, mostly of a religious character, some of them almost austere, but all of them in some way conveying an insight into the past, and expressing a fine art in the service of superstition. One could not but be deeply impressed by this superb example of solicitude for the well-being of the dead, animated as it was by extreme felicity. In fact, the whole chamber and its appointments beautifully represented the mentality of those ancients. Mingled with a fear of the very gods and demons of their own creation, one is conscious of sincere feeling and affection for the dead. From its very severity it might be the actual burial of the god himself, instead of his representative on earth who, in passing from this earthly life, became one of the " Lords of the West." Its appointments, like those of the Antechamber, may almost be divided into two categories : the personal and the religious—the personal objects reflecting the tastes of the young king, the religious objects reflecting the superstitions of the past. The former were placed there in tender thought for the deceased, the latter for his protection in the grim Underworld—for even when the great Sun-god himself entered on his nocturnal journey, his path through those dark regions was beset by all kinds of snares.

But the problems here suggested are difficult. The meaning of some of the emblems placed in the tomb, giving rise, as they do, to much conjecture to-day, may have been almost as obscure to the ancient Thebans as to ourselves. It is doubtful whether they could have given us a reason for placing many of them in the tomb. The true significance of the symbols might well have been lost years before the age of Tut·ankh·Amen and tradition may have held them to be necessary for the welfare of the dead long after the reason for their use had been forgotten.

Beside this traditional paraphernalia necessary to meet and vanquish the dark powers of the Nether World, there were magical figures placed in small recesses in the walls, facing north, south, east and west, covered with plaster, conforming with the ritual laid down in the Book of the Dead, for the defence of the tomb and its owner. Associated with these magical figures are incantations " to repel the enemy of Osiris [the deceased], in whatsoever form he may come." Magic for once seems to have prevailed.

37

The Tomb of Tut·ankh·Amen

For of twenty-seven monarchs of the Imperial Age of Egypt buried in this valley, who have suffered every kind of depredation, Tut·ankh·Amen, throughout those thirty-three centuries, alone has lain unscathed, even though predatory hands violated the chambers of his tomb—or may we believe, as those ancient Thebans might readily claim, that Tut·ankh·Amen's long security is due to Amen·Re's protection of his convert who, in acknowledging that Theban god's triumph over the religious revolution of Akh·en·Aten, reconstructed his sanctuaries and re-endowed his temples?

CHAPTER III

CLEARING THE BURIAL CHAMBER AND OPENING THE SARCOPHAGUS

THE second season's work actually began in the laboratory, under Mr. Mace, who dealt with the magnificent chariots and the ceremonial couches that were left over from the first season. While he was carrying out this work of preservation and packing, with the aid of Mr. Callender, I began by removing the two guardian statues (Plate IX) that stood before the doorway of the Burial Chamber, and then, as it was necessary, demolished the partition wall dividing it from the Antechamber (Plate X).

Without first demolishing that partition wall, it would have been impossible to have dealt with the great shrines within the Burial Chamber, or to remove many of the funereal paraphernalia therein. Even then our great difficulty was due to the confined space in which we had to carry out the most difficult task of dismantling those shrines, which proved to be four in number, nested one within the other.

Beyond the very limited space and high temperature which prevailed, our difficulties were further increased by the great weight of the various sections and panels of which those complex shrines were constructed. These were made of $2\frac{1}{4}$-inch oak[1] planking,

[1] For the identification of the wood as oak, I am indebted to Mr. L. A. Boodle of the Jodrell Laboratory, Royal Gardens, Kew.

and overlaid with superbly delicate gold-work upon gesso. The wood-planking, though perfectly sound, had shrunk in the course of three thousand three hundred years in that very dry atmosphere, the gold-work upon the gesso had, if at all, slightly expanded; the result in any case was a space between the basic wood-planking and the ornamented gold surface which, when touched, tended to crush and fall away. Thus our problem was how to deal in that very limited space with those sections of the shrines, weighing from a quarter to three-quarters of a ton, when taking them apart and removing them, without causing them undue damage.

Other complications arose during this undertaking, and one of them was due to the fact that those sections were held together by means of secret wooden tongues let into the thickness of the wood-planking of the panels, roof sections, cornice pieces and " styles." It was only by slightly forcing open the cracks between those different sections, and by that means discovering the positions of the tongues that held them together, inserting a fine saw and severing them, that we were able to free them and take them apart. No sooner had we discovered the method of overcoming this complication, had dealt with the various sections of the great outermost shrine, and become proud of ourselves, anticipating that we had learnt how to treat the next shrine or shrines, than we found that, in the very next shrine, although held together in a similar manner, many of the hidden tongues were of solid bronze, inscribed with the names of Tut·ankh·Amen. These could not of course be sawn through as in the first case. We had therefore to find other methods. In fact, contrary to our expectations, the farther we proceeded, although the space in which we could work had been increased, new and unforeseen obstacles continually occurred.

For instance, after our scaffolding and hoisting tackle had been introduced it occupied practically all the available space, leaving little for ourselves in which to work. When some of the parts were freed, there was insufficient room to remove them from the chamber. We bumped our heads, nipped our fingers, we had to squeeze in and out like weasels, and work in all kinds of embarrassing positions. I think I remember that one of the eminent chemists assisting us in the preservation work, when taking records of various phenomena in the tomb, found that he had also recorded a certain percentage of profanity! Nevertheless, I am glad to say that in the conflict we did more harm to ourselves than to the shrines.

Such was our task during the second season's work in the Burial Chamber. First we had to remove those strange guardian figures in the Antechamber bearing the impressive legend : " The Good God of whom one be proud, the Sovereign of whom one boasts, the Royal KA of Harakhte, Osiris, the King Lord of the Lands, Neb·kheperu·Re ; " next to demolish the partition wall that divides the Antechamber from the Burial Chamber, built as it was of dry masonry, bonded with heavy logs of wood, and covered on both sides with a coat of hard plaster ; finally to dismantle the great shrines within the chamber ; and, in so doing, to unmask the magnificent yellow quartzite sarcophagus containing the mortal remains of the king shielded in their centre. The undertaking took us eighty-four days of real manual labour. It will give some idea of the magnitude of that operation when it is mentioned that the outermost of those golden shrines, occupying nearly the whole of the Burial Chamber, measured some 17 feet in length, 11 feet in width, and over 9 feet in height, and that the four shrines comprised in all some eighty sections, each section or part having to be dealt with by a method different from the last, and every section needing first to be temporarily treated so as to allow it to be handled with the least risk of damage.

The demolition of the partition wall gave a clear view of the great outermost shrine (Plate LIV), and we were able, for the first time, to realize its grandeur, especially its admirable gold-work and blue faience inlay, overlaid with gilt protective emblems—*Ded* and *Thet* alternately.

Having got thus far, the next procedure was to remove and transport to the laboratory all the portable funerary equipment that had been placed around the chamber, between the walls and the sides of the outermost shrine, and then to construct, and introduce the necessary scaffolding and hoisting tackle preparatory to dismantling the outermost shrine. Our gear, necessarily of primitive kind, being placed in position, we began by first unhanging the very heavy folding doors of the outermost shrine, which were hinged on copper pivots inserted in corresponding sockets in the lintel and in the threshold. This was a very tedious and hazardous task, as the front part of the entablature of the shrine, had to be slightly raised to free the upper and lower pivot-hinges fixed on the back rails of the doors. We then hoisted and removed the three roof sections (Plate XI) that were tongued to the entablature. After that, we took apart the entablature which comprised four sections of cornice moulding and frieze, tongued to their corresponding panels, and held together, at the four corners, by means of heavy copper **S**-shaped dowels, each bearing inscriptions such as north-east, south-west, etc., to show their correct orientation.

Having removed the entablature, the panels of the shrine had to be dealt with. They now stood unsupported save for our temporary struts and the four corner uprights to which they were tongued. The panels were comparatively easy to free, but there being insufficient room to permit of their egress, we had to lean them against the corresponding walls of the chamber and leave them there, pending some future time when they could be passed out—in other words until after the dismantling and removal of the inner shrines, which, at that time, prevented their exit. The removal of the corner pieces completed our primary task—the dismantling of the first (outermost) shrine.

The next and very delicate problem was the linen pall that completely covered the second shrine. Its tissue was much decayed and in very fragile state; its drooping edges were badly torn from the weight of its own material, and by the metal marguerites that were sewn to it. Happily, as a result of Dr. Alexander Scott's experiments, duroprene (a chlorinated rubber compound dissolved in an organic solvent such as zylene) proved most efficacious in reinforcing the deteriorated fabric. It strengthened the tissues sufficiently to enable us to roll it (Plate LV,A) on to a wooden roller, expressly made for the purpose, and transport it to the laboratory where eventually the fabric could be finally treated and relined.

The linen pall and the wooden framework forming

43

its curious supports (Plates LV,B, and LVI) being disposed of, we were able to study the question of the second shrine—a beautiful gilt construction almost exactly similar to the first, save for the absence of the blue faience inlay (Plate LVII). The doors of this second shrine were bolted top and bottom, and carefully fastened with cord tied to metal staples and sealed (Plate LX). The clay seal upon this cord was intact. It bore impressions of two distinct seals, one bearing Tut·ankh·Amen's prenomen, Kheperu·neb·Re, surmounting "A Jackal over nine Foes," the second bore the device of the Royal Necropolis Seal, "The Jackal over nine Foes," without other distinguishing mark or royal insignia (Plate LX). Here was a great piece of luck, as manifestly behind those two seals we should be dealing with material unharmed since the burial of the king. It was with great care that the cords were severed, those folding doors opened (Plate XII), which, when swung back, revealed yet a third shrine, also sealed and intact—the seal impressions upon this third shrine being identical to those on the second.

At this point of our undertaking we realized that it would now be possible, by opening those further doors, to solve the secret the shrines had so jealously guarded throughout the centuries. I therefore decided before any other procedure to make the experiment. It was an exciting moment in our arduous task that cannot easily be forgotten. We were to witness a spectacle such as no other man in our times has been privileged to see. With suppressed excitement I carefully cut the cord, removed that precious seal, drew back the bolts, and opened the doors, when a fourth shrine was revealed, similar in design and even more brilliant in workmanship than the last. The decisive moment was at hand ! An indescribable moment for an archæologist ! What was beneath and what did that fourth shrine contain ? With intense excitement I drew back the bolts of the last and unsealed doors; they slowly swung open (Plate xiii), and there, filling the entire area within, effectually barring any further progress, stood an immense yellow quartzite sarcophagus (Plate xiv), intact, with the lid still firmly fixed in its place, just as the pious hands had left it. It was certainly a thrilling moment, as we gazed upon the spectacle enhanced by the striking contrast—the glitter of metal —of the golden shrines shielding it. Especially striking were the outstretched hand and wing of a goddess sculptured on the end of the sarcophagus, as if to ward off an intruder. It symbolized an idea beautiful in conception, and, indeed, seemed an eloquent illustration of the perfect faith and tender solicitude for the well-being of their loved one, that animated the people who dwelt in that land over thirty centuries ago.

We were now able to profit by the experience we had acquired and had a much clearer conception of the operation immediately before us : the three remaining shrines would have to be taken to pieces and removed before the problem of the sarcophagus could be contemplated. And thus it was that we laboured for another month, first dismantling the second shrine, then the third, until the fourth (innermost) shrine, the last and smallest, was completely freed. When this was achieved we saw that this last shrine had all the appearance of a golden tabernacle (Plate lviii). Upon its folding doors and west end, were winged figures of the tutelary goddesses of the dead, in fine bas-relief, majestic in their protective significance (Plate LIX), whilst the walls of the shrine were covered with religious texts.

We found between the third and fourth (innermost) shrines ceremonial bows and arrows, and with them, a pair of the gorgeous flabella (Plate LXI)—the insignia of princes, fans so prominent in scenes where kings are depicted, carried by inferior officers behind their chief. Beautiful specimens they were—one lying at the head, the other along the south side of the innermost shrine. The one at the head, wrought in sheet-gold (Plate LXII), bears a charming and historical scene of the young King Tut·ankh·Amen in his chariot, followed by his favourite hound, hunting ostrich for feathers for the fan, as the inscription upon the handle says in " the Eastern desert of Heliopolis ; " on the reverse side of the fan, also finely embossed and chased, the young " Lord of Valour " is depicted returning triumphant, his quarry, two ostriches, borne on the shoulders of two attendants who precede him, the plumes under his arm. The second fan, larger and perhaps more resplendent, was of ebony (Plate LXIII), overlaid with sheet-gold and encrusted with turquoise, lapis lazuli, and carnelian-coloured glass, as well as translucent calcite : the palm of the fan being emblazoned with the titulary of Tut·ankh· Amen. Unfortunately, only the debris remained of the actual feathers of these two flabella. Although these had suffered from the havoc of insects, enough still remained to show us that they once had been alternate white and brown plumes—forty-two on each fan.

The roof and cornice of the fourth (innermost)

shrine, contrary to our expectations, was of different form, and was made in one piece (Plate xv), instead of in several sections as in the case of the roofs of the preceding shrines. It was thus very heavy, and the question was how to raise it and turn it in that very narrow space. It was one of our most difficult problems, and it took several laborious days before it could be lifted, gradually turned, and hauled into the Antechamber where it now rests. Taking apart the sides, ends and doors of this innermost shrine was a much easier undertaking. It enclosed and, as it proved, exactly fitted the sarcophagus. It was the last of those complex problems involved in the dismantling of the four shrines, hallowed as they were by ancient memories. Our task of over eighty days was thus ended.

During the process of our work it became clear that the ancient Egyptian staff of undertakers must have had extreme difficulty in erecting the shrines within that limited space. Their task, however, was perhaps easier than ours, as in their case, the wood was new and pliable, the gold ornamentation firm and strong. In that narrow area it must have been necessary for them first to have placed the parts of the four shrines in correct order around the four walls of the chamber : the various parts and panels of the outermost shrine being introduced first, and those of the innermost shrine last. The next logical step in that operation must have been first to erect the innermost shrine and lastly the outermost. And that was what apparently occurred. The carpentry and joinery of those constructions exhibited great skill, and each section was carefully numbered and oriented to show not only how they fitted, but also their correct orientation. Hence the constructors of those shrines were manifestly past-masters in their work, but on the other hand there was evidence that the obsequies had been hurriedly performed, and that the workmen in charge of those last rites were anything but careful men. They had, with little doubt, placed those parts around the sarcophagus, but in their carelessness had reversed their order in regard to the four cardinal points. They had leant them against the four walls around the sarcophagus they were to shield, contrary to the instructions written upon the different parts, with a result that, when they were erected, the doors of the shrines faced east instead of west, the foot ends west instead of east, and the side panels were likewise transposed. This may have been a pardonable fault, the chamber being too small for correct orientation, although there were other signs of slovenliness. Sections had obviously been banged together, regardless of the risk of damage to their gilt ornamentation. Deep dents from blows from a heavy hammer-like implement are visible to the present day on the gold-work, parts of the surfaces in some cases had been actually knocked off, and the workmen's refuse, such as chips of wood, had never been cleared away.

The raising of the roof of the last shrine bared the lid of the sarcophagus, the removal of the three sides and doors of that shrine freed that great stone monument. We were more than repaid. For there, free standing from all surrounding structure, stood, as if in state, a magnificent sarcophagus of wonderful workmanship, carved out of a solid block of finest yellow quartzite, measuring 9 feet in length, 4 feet 10 inches in width, and 4 feet 10 inches high (Plate LXIV).

It was on February 3 that we first had a clear view

of this sepulchral masterpiece, ranking as it does among the finest specimens of its kind the world possesses. It has a rich entablature consisting of a cavetto-cornice, taurus moulding and frieze of inscription. But the outstanding features of the sarcophagus are the guardian goddesses Isis, Nephthys, Neith and Selkit, carved in high relief on each of the four corners, so placed that their full spread wings and outstretched arms encircle it with their protective embrace (Plate LXV). Round the base is a dado of protective symbols *Ded* and *Thet*. The corners of the casket rested upon alabaster slabs. Between the last shrine and the sarcophagus there were no objects, save for a *Ded*-symbol placed on the south side for " Strength " and possibly " Protection " of the owner (Plate LXV).

As our light fell on the noble quartzite monument, it illumined, in repeated detail, that last solemn appeal to gods and men, and made us feel that, in the young king's case, a dignity had been added even to death. With the profound silence that reigned the emotion deepened, the past and present seemed to meet—time to stand and wait, and one asked oneself, was it not yesterday that, with pomp and ceremony, they had laid the young king in that casket ?—so fresh, so seemingly recent, were those touching claims on our pity that, the more we gazed on them, the more the illusion gathered strength. It made one wish that his journey through those grim tunnels of the Underworld might be unperturbed until he attained complete felicity !—as those four goddesses, sculptured in high relief at the corners, seemed to plead as they shielded their charge. For in them had we not a perfect Egyptian elegy in stone ?

The lid (Plate LXIV) made of rose granite tinted to

match the quartzite sarcophagus, was cracked in the middle and firmly embedded in the rebated top edges. The cracks had been carefully cemented and painted over to match the rest, in such a way as to leave no doubt that it had not been tampered with. Undoubtedly the original intention must have been to provide a quartzite lid in keeping with the sarcophagus itself; it would therefore appear that some accident had occurred. It may be that the intended lid was not ready in time for the burial of the king, and that this crudely made granite slab was substituted in its place.

The crack greatly complicated our final effort, the raising of this lid, for had it been intact the operation would have been far easier. The difficulty, however, was overcome by passing angle irons along and closely fitting the sides of the slab, which permitted it to be raised by differential pulleys as one piece. At this last ceremony many were present : The Governor of the Keneh Province and Mohamed Zaglûl Pasha (Under-Secretary of State for Public Works), Mr. E. S. Harkness (Chairman of the Board of Trustees of the Metropolitan Museum of Art, New York), Dr. Breasted (Professor of Egyptology and Oriental History in the University of Chicago), the Chief Inspector of Antiquities, Upper Egypt ; Mr. A. M. Lythgoe (Curator of the Egyptian Department of the Metropolitan Museum of Art, New York), Professor Newberry (Honorary Reader of Egyptian Art at the Liverpool University), Dr. Alan Gardiner, the well-known philologist ; Mr. H. E. Winlock (Director of the Egyptian Expedition of the Metropolitan Museum of Art, New York), Mr. Norman de Garies Davies (of the same museum), Dr. Douglas Derry (Professor of Anatomy at the Kasr-el-

Aini School of Medicine, Cairo), Mr. Robert Mond,
M. Foucart (Directeur de l'Institut Français d'Arché-
ologie), M. Bruyère (Directeur de l'Expedition Fran-
çaise), Major the Hon. J. J. Astor, Messrs. Mace,
Callender, Lucas, Burton and Bethell and the Assistant
Curator of the Cairo Museum.

Many strange scenes must have happened in the
Valley of the Tombs of the Kings since it became the
royal burial ground of the Theban New Empire, but
one may be pardoned for thinking that the present
scene was not the least interesting or dramatic. For
ourselves it was the one supreme and culminating
moment—a moment looked forward to ever since it
became evident that the chambers discovered, in
November, 1922, must be the tomb of Tut·ankh·
Amen, and not a cache of his furniture as had been
claimed. None of us but felt the solemnity of the
occasion, none of us but was affected by the prospect
of what we were about to see—the burial custom of a
king of ancient Egypt of thirty-three centuries ago.
How would the king be found ? Such were the
anticipatory speculations running in our minds during
the silence maintained.

The tackle for raising the lid was in position. I
gave the word. Amid intense silence the huge slab,
broken in two, weighing over a ton and a quarter, rose
from its bed. The light shone into the sarcophagus.
A sight met our eyes that at first puzzled us. It was
a little disappointing. The contents were completely
covered by fine linen shrouds (Plate xvi). The lid
being suspended in mid-air, we rolled back those
covering shrouds, one by one, and as the last was
removed a gasp of wonderment escaped our lips, so
gorgeous was the sight that met our eyes : a golden

effigy of the young boy king, of most magnificent workmanship, filled the whole of the interior of the sarcophagus. This was the lid of a wonderful anthropoid coffin (Plates LXVI, LXVII), some 7 feet in length, resting upon a low bier in the form of a lion, and no doubt the outermost coffin of a series of coffins, nested one within the other, enclosing the mortal remains of the king. Enclasping the body of this magnificent monument are two winged goddesses, Isis and Neith, wrought in rich gold-work upon gesso, as brilliant as the day the coffin was made. To it an additional charm was added, by the fact that, while this decoration was rendered in fine low bas-relief, the head and hands of the king were in the round, in massive gold of the finest sculpture, surpassing anything we could have imagined. The hands, crossed over the breast, held the royal emblems—the Crook and the Flail—encrusted with deep blue faience. The face and features were wonderfully wrought in sheet-gold. The eyes were of aragonite and obsidian, the eyebrows and eyelids inlaid with lapis lazuli glass. There was a touch of realism, for while the rest of this anthropoid coffin, covered with feathered ornament, was of brilliant gold, that of the bare face and hands seemed different, the gold of the flesh being of different alloy, thus conveying an impression of the greyness of death. Upon the forehead of this recumbent figure of the young boy king were two emblems delicately worked in brilliant inlay—the Cobra and the Vulture—symbols of Upper and Lower Egypt, but perhaps the most touching by its human simplicity was the tiny wreath of flowers (Plate LXVII) around these symbols, as it pleased us to think, the last farewell offering of the widowed girl queen to her husband, the youthful representative of the " Two Kingdoms."

Among all that regal splendour, that royal magnificence—everywhere the glint of gold—there was nothing so beautiful as those few withered flowers, still retaining their tinge of colour. They told us what a short period three thousand three hundred years really was—but Yesterday and the Morrow. In fact, that little touch of nature made that ancient and our modern civilization kin.

Thus from stairway, steep descending passage, Antechamber and Burial Chamber, from those golden shrines and from that noble sarcophagus, our eyes were now turned to its contents—a gold encased coffin, in form a recumbent figure of the young king, symbolizing Osiris or, it would seem, by its fearless gaze, man's ancient trust in immortality. Many and disturbing were our emotions awakened by that Osiride form. Most of them voiceless. But, in that silence, to listen—you could almost hear the ghostly footsteps of the departing mourners.

Our lights were lowered, once more we mounted those sixteen steps, once more we beheld the blue vault of the heavens, where the Sun is Lord, but our inner thoughts still lingered over the splendour of that vanished Pharaoh, with his last appeal upon his coffin written upon our minds : " Oh Mother Nût! spread thy wings over me as the Imperishable Stars."

CHAPTER IV

The State Chariots

EVERY addition to our knowledge of the subject tends to increase our admiration for the technical skill displayed by the ancient Egyptian craftsmen when they were dealing with the relatively limited means at their disposal.

That they were adepts in vehicular structure has already been established by the paintings upon the walls of their tomb chapels, and also by the beautiful specimens of their chariots discovered in Egypt during the nineteenth and twentieth centuries.

A specimen exhibited in the Egyptian collection at Florence, another in the Cairo Museum discovered by Mr. Theo. M. Davis in the Tomb of Yuaa and Tuaa, are striking examples of their proficiency. They are well constructed, strong and at the same time exceedingly light. They consist of a bent-wood framework, strengthened, and in one case ornamented, with leather, but though well made and having beautiful lines, these are of a type such as were used by the Theban notables, and might be described as curricles since they have none of the magnificence of the State chariots, of which the " body " discovered in the tomb of Thothmes IV was our first example. This last, also discovered by Mr. Davis and in the Cairo Museum, had unfortunately been broken up by the early plunderers of that tomb. Its wheels, axle and pole had been destroyed, but the " body," the only portion that was left of the chariot, was not only a wonderful example of vehicular construction, but must have been a masterpiece of artistic workmanship. It was covered on both outside and inside with battle scenes and traditional ornament modelled in low relief upon an extraordinary light panelled bent-wood framework, the surfaces of which were prepared with canvas and gesso, no doubt, once overlaid with gold, but the full extent of its splendour was never realized until the more complete specimens were discovered in the Antechamber of this tomb.

We found them here heaped together in confusion, and they, too, had unfortunately suffered, the thieves having very roughly handled them in their endeavours to tear off the more valuable portions of the gold decoration. But the confusion in which we found these State chariots was not merely due to those plunderers. The entrance passage of the tomb was too narrow to admit of their ingress in their complete form, so they had been taken to pieces, and even their axles sawn in two to get them in the chamber, where their dismembered parts had been heaped one upon the other (Vol. I, Plate xix). However, with the exception of some minor details of the ornamentation that had been wrenched away, and of the leather-work melted from humid heat to a viscid mass, they are otherwise complete, even to the remains of their rugs, and can, when time allows, be put together again. Their admirable design and gorgeousness will justify any amount of time and work bestowed upon them. Covered from top to bottom with gold, every inch of which is decorated with embossed patterns and traditional scenes, they have upon their borders and framework elaborate ornament of semi-precious stones and polychrome glass encrusted upon the gold casing.

Like all the other examples, the bodies of these chariots are not provided with a seat. The royal charioteer always stood, and rarely if ever sat while driving. They are entirely open at the back, so that the driver might readily leap to the ground and up again as might be necessary. The floor consisted of a mesh of interlaced leathern thongs which were covered either with an animal skin or a linen rug of very long pile, in order, by its elasticity, to render the motion of the carriage more easy. This elastic bottom to the body was the early form of spring—the true, or more efficacious spring, such as we use to-day, was not applied to wheel carriages in Europe until the seventeenth century. Before that period the bodies of carriages were suspended by long leather straps from pillars erected upon the under-carriage. With the Egyptian chariots additional ease was provided by placing the wheels and axle-tree as far back as possible, and thus utilizing as much of the springiness of the pole as was practical.

The carriage proper of these chariots comprises an axle-tree and (two) wheels. This, for reasons already stated, was set under the extreme back of the body, but as the body rested partly on the pole, and the pole was permanently fixed to the axle-tree, the pole also formed part of the under-carriage or carriage proper. Thus as the body of the chariot rested on the axle-tree and pole, the pole was especially bent at that extremity so that the floor of the body would, when harnessed to the horses, be approximately horizontal. The weight of the body and charioteer was therefore taken partly by the wheels and partly by the horses, but as the charioteer stood well back in the body, the carriage proper received the greater part of this weight. The body was bound by leathern thongs both to the axle-tree and the pole, and it was also stayed by means of thick leathern straps attached to its upper front rim and the shaft of the pole. Hence, it will be seen that the pole acted not only as the means of yoking the horses, but also partly as the under-carriage or carriage proper.

The wheels, of six spokes or radial bars, show in their construction a special mechanical knowledge on which we have made little advance. They, in the lightest manner possible, are constructed so as to be the strongest and most durable form for a nave and radial bars for a wooden wheel.

As some of these specimens are encased with sheet-gold, and their uniqueness forbids their being taken to pieces for proper examination (Plate xl), I shall use as an example the fragments of a wheel discovered during Lord Carnarvon's researches in the tomb of Amen·hetep iii, in Wâdyein—a branch valley of the Valley of the Tombs of the Kings. They are, no doubt, from the same royal workshops and are not more than (at most) twenty-five years earlier. With these frag-ments of a wheel were found a few parts of the frame-work of the body of the chariot, and also a few frag-ments of the harness saddles, all of which have every appearance of being of similar construction to that of the more perfect specimens found in Tut·ankh·Amen's tomb. The fragments of the wheel are from the nave, the lower parts of the radial bars, and por-tions of the inner and outer flanges of the nave, to which a good deal of their leather bindings still adhere. The structure consists of :—six **V**-shaped parts made of bent-wood, each so devised as to comprise a segment of the nave and half-section of two radial bars or spokes of the wheel. These V-shaped parts when put together, form a nave or hub and six complete radial bars. In the hub portion of each of these six V-shaped sections are two mortice halvings so devised that, when united, they form six mortice slots in the nave, designed to receive corresponding dovetail tenons upon the rims of the two cylindrical flanges, which were fitted to the inner and outer sides of the nave of the wheel. Thus these long cylindrical flanges, contrived to keep the wheel upright during any lateral movement, served also a very important constructive purpose—their tenons, when fitted into the mortice slots of the nave, interlocked all the parts and formed a perfect hub. The flanges, hub, and radial bar sections, when assembled, were bound with raw hide which, when it dried, shrunk and held them tight.

If I have made myself clear, it will be seen that this ingenious form of chariot wheel possesses not only all elements of lightness, but it tends to neutralize risk of splitting, and to combine even greater solidity when under any reasonable weight. So excellent is the joinery that in portions of the specimen under discussion, even though it has suffered very rough handling, the joints are hardly visible to the naked eye. The radial bars appear to have been morticed to the felloe or outer rim of the wheel, and the splitting element eliminated by having shoulders to the tenons. The tyres were of leather.

The industry of carriage-making depends, to a great extent, upon the selection of the materials. The ancient Egyptians selected, as we now do, suitable woods for the different parts. The woods were artificially (mechanically) bent. Carriage-making necessitates a combination of crafts rarely united in one trade, embracing as it does such divers materials. In the ancient Egyptian mural paintings and sculptures, the Egyptian artists have not failed to point out what parts were the peculiar province of the carpenter, wheelwright, currier and other craftsmen.

The draught gear, such as the yoke (Plate XLI), fixed to the end of the pole and attached to the harness saddles upon the withers of the horses, sufficed for all purposes of draught, as well as for backing the chariot; it also kept the horses at the same distance and in the same relative position. Spur-like goads (Plate XLIII,B) were fixed to the breast harness and the bridle in such a manner as to prevent the horses from breaking from the line of draught—as there were two of these spur-like goads to each chariot found in this tomb, it would appear that only one was attached to each horse, and that on the outside.

From various paintings of the king in his chariot (Vol. I, Plates L–LIII), we know that the horses were decked with sumptuous housings, neck coverings, and that a crest of ostrich feathers was fastened to the head-stall and bridle. Of these trappings there were no traces whatever in the tomb. The actual harness of leather, evidently of breast type, had unfortunately perished, but as the greater part of its decoration—embossed sheet-gold—was there, with careful study and time the bulk of it can be reconstructed. As yet we do not know what kind of bit was employed for command over the horses—the robbers took all the heavy metal they could carry away and, no doubt, also the metal bits. From the gait and general demeanour of the horses portrayed upon the painted casket in this tomb, one would expect to find that the bits were of a heavy " curb " type. The r. ins were evidently passed through rings attached to the breast harness, and were long enough to be tied round the royal waist, so that the king's arms would be free to defend himself—for the king always drove alone in his chariot. Blinkers were used—several pairs were preserved in the tomb—and the chariots were richly mounted with quivers full of arrows, the bow being the principal arm of attack. One of the predominant features peculiar to the royal chariots was a golden-solar-hawk (Plate XLIV), fixed upon the end of the pole. It was the cockade, so to speak, of the Royal House, which like the crests of ostrich feathers upon the heads of the horses, were only used by the king and princes of the household.

The four chariots discovered in the Antechamber (there are others in the Store-room of the Burial Chamber not yet touched) can be divided into two categories : State chariots and curricles. Of these, the latter were more open, of lighter construction probably for hunting or exercising purposes.

The gold encased State chariots, with their sumptuous housings and harness trappings (cf. Plate III), must have produced a magnificent effect in the royal pageants, especially when it is remembered how the burnished metal must have reflected the brilliant Eastern sun—a fact emphasized by the following quotation from a tablet of Akh·en·Aten, demarcating the limits of his city : " His Majesty ascended a great chariot of electrum, like Aten when he rises from his horizon and filling the land with his love . . ."

From the following somewhat brief description, but more especially from the accompanying illustrations of the chariots and their parts, it is hoped that some idea may be gathered of their gorgeousness. Their effect when in motion under Egyptian skies must have been one of dazzling splendour, with the jewelled trappings flashing back the light, the horses' plumes waving, in a pageant of brightness, colour, gleam and richness, probably rarely surpassed at any other period, or by any other splendour-loving race. Some such impression as this we gather, not only from the monuments, but from what time and circumstance have left us in this tomb.

As will at once be seen in the illustrations (Plates xxxvii and xxxviii), the " bodies " of the State chariots are not only quite open at the back, but they have lozenge-shaped openings at the sides. Attached to the bent-wood upper rim of the body is a secondary rim which forms a shelf-like projection, the space between these two rims being filled in with an open-work design consisting, in the centre, of the traditional device of " Unity of the Two Kingdoms," and on either side the captive foes of Egypt (Plate xxi,A). The gold casing on the front of the bodies is embossed and encrusted with traditional ornament : in one case with elaborate coil-pattern (Plate xvii,A), in the other with feather, scroll, and ox-eye ornament (Plate xvii,B), and in each case with a panel bearing the titulary of the king. Similarly on the inside of the body of the chariots is the king's titulary supported by the symbolical " Union " of the " Two Countries," to which, on one example, are tied Northern and Southern prisoners, and below that a wonderful frieze of conquered foes, with their arms lashed behind them (Plate xviii), kneeling before Tut·ankh·Amen triumphant as a human-headed lion crushing Egypt's alien

61

enemies (Plates XIX, XX). Traditional ornament of this kind, wherein the conquered races are typified by separate figures conventional in attitude, but individual in character and detail, was regarded by general consent as naturally symbolizing the power of the monarch. This desire to humiliate the foe, the absence of magnanimity in conquerors, are but the spirit of unbridled imagination rendered pictorially in those Pharaonic battle scenes, wherein the vigour and variety of the mêlées are of incomparable intensity. On the other example, the interior, like the outside, is decorated with a simple feather, scroll and ox-eye pattern. Added to this decoration are encrusted medallions of silver and gold, fixed on the lower part of the panels (Plate XVII,B).

On both of the chariots, the lozenge-shaped openings in the sides of the bodies have margins of floral design, encrusted with semi-precious stones, glass and faience (Plates XIX, XX). At the juncture where the body rests on the axle, are highly ornamented bosses of stone (Plate XXI,C), in one instance surmounted by a grotesque gold head of the god Bes (Plate XXI,B). Their wooden axles have at intervals, collars of gold richly encrusted with glass and semi-precious stones, worked in floral devices, and the names of enemy countries (Plate XXXIX). Each pair of wheels has its spokes, hub and rims covered with thin sheet-gold; the tyres being of leather (Plate XL). The wooden poles are left plain save for a gold cap at the end, whereon the royal golden-solar-hawk (Plate XLIV) was fixed. Embossed, and completely filling the field of the disk upon the head of the solar-hawk, is a device incorporating the king's prenomen. As the Pharaohs were looked upon as the Sun-god's earthly representatives, would it be a too daring hypothesis to suggest that this device symbolized his supposed solar origin ?   The bent-wood yokes, which were joined to the pole, were overlaid with gold and, in one case, have alien captives forming the curved ends (Plate XLI).

The ends of the harness saddles (Plate XLII) to which the yokes were fixed, are decorated with heads of the household god Bes.   Through the god's widely-opened mouth passed the girth straps.   This combined scheme of ornament and strap fastening, may possibly have been inspired by the fact that this god is represented throughout the tomb furniture with long protruding tongue—the straps here issuing from the mouth convey that idea.   Surmounting the back of the harness saddles are centre-pieces with reels of aragonite decorated with fine red-gold filigree-work.   With each chariot a pair of spur-like goads (Plate XLIII,B), already mentioned, were found ; and also the ever necessary horsehair fly-whisks (Plate XLIII,C).   In Fig. A, Plate XLIII, are examples of the quaintly ornamented blinkers from the bridles of the horses.

These highly ornate chariots may well be said to have taken in Egyptian ceremonial the place of the State coach in modern pageant.

CHAPTER V

THE OPENING OF THE THREE COFFINS
(SEASON 1925–26)

PAST experience had taught us that it would be well to resume our work on the tomb of Tut·ankh·Amen as soon as the decline of the great heat rendered it practicable, our aim being to carry it out with due scientific procedure, with the least possible interruption and to be able to open the tomb to the public as early as possible during the tourist season. Our anticipations were fully justified, for, between January 1 and March 15, 1926, there were over 12,000 visitors to the tomb, and during the same period I received 278 applications for permission to inspect the objects and the work in the laboratory.

After having purchased necessary materials for the campaign, I left London on September 23 and arrived in Cairo on the 28th. There was as usual not a little to be done in Cairo before I could leave for Luxor. In work of this sort in Egypt, delays may be anticipated and must be patiently accepted. Monsieur Lacau, the Director-General of the Department of Antiquities, was absent in Europe. On October 1 I saw Mr. Edgar, acting for Monsieur Lacau at the Museum, when I arranged with him that the electric light in the Valley of the Tombs of the Kings should be in readiness to start from October 11, and at the same time I took the opportunity to discuss with him the general programme for the season's work.

Opening the Three Coffins

The first task obviously would be to raise the nest of coffins from the sarcophagus, to open and examine them one by one; secondly to examine the king's mummy, with the aid of Dr. Douglas Derry, Professor of Anatomy in the Medical School at Kasr-el-Aini, and Dr. Saleh Bey Hamdi, formerly Director of the same school; lastly, if time allowed, to investigate, clear and record the contents of the Store-room leading out of the Burial Chamber—undertakings which, as every object would need preserving and packing for transport to Cairo, would more than provide ample occupation for the season. However, the last part of the programme—that of the Store-room—proved impossible of realization on account of the state of the mass of material found on the king's mummy. Even raising and opening the nest of three coffins, as it proved to be, took far longer than was anticipated.

It was also arranged that Mr. A. Lucas should go with me to Luxor on October 6 and resume his duties as chemist in the work of preservation.

The question arose as to whether M. Lacau, who was on leave in Europe, would wish to be present during the actual unwrapping of the mummy. Upon finding that he would not be back in Egypt before November, I suggested, in order to avoid any possible delay, that a cable should be sent to ascertain the date of his return, and in the event of its being deferred, to ask whether he would object to Mr. Edgar representing him during the examination.

On the following day a reply was received from Monsieur Lacau saying that he desired to be present at the examination of the Royal mummy and that he trusted that the delay might not inconvenience me. To meet his wishes upon the matter, I arranged with

Drs. Derry and Saleh Bey to defer their coming to Luxor until November 10.

With archæological work the reverse of what is anticipated almost always occurs. As events turned out the work of dealing with the actual coffins fully occupied the intervening period, and we were only just ready for the examination of the mummy when M. Lacau and the doctors arrived.

On October 3 I inspected the Tut·ankh·Amen exhibits in the Cairo Museum with Mr. Lucas, in order to study them from the point of view of preservation, a problem of extreme interest and importance in dealing with antiquities, especially of a fragile nature. The throne had undoubtedly darkened since it had been exhibited in the museum, and it was decided that this discoloration could be removed by hot wax treatment, a protective measure which we proposed to carry out during the spring. There was little doubt that the objects which allowed of the paraffin wax treatment had been improved by it, and were consequently in better condition; it was therefore agreed that this method was permanently the most effective and generally the best.

The Press is a great and necessary force in modern civilization, but it is occasionally eager for more news than actually exists. It is, too, exceedingly competitive. Research of all kinds owes much to intelligent publicity and it was hoped that the machinery organized by the Egyptian Government for distributing the news would prove adequate, but soon after my arrival, I was a little disappointed to discover that the correspondents, both local and foreign, were imperfectly satisfied.

Before I left Cairo I had an agreeable interview

with H.E. Abdel Hamid Pasha Bedawi, Conseiller Royal to the Public Works Ministry, to whom I explained our plans. They met his complete approval, and on the following evening, accompanied by Mr. Lucas, I started for Luxor, whence, on the following day, after an interview with the Bey, the Marmour of Luxor, and Tewfik Effendi Boulos, the Chief Inspector for the Department of Antiquities of Upper Egypt, we crossed over to the village of Gurna —Western Thebes.

In spite of the heat it was pleasant to be back in those familiar but ever impressive surroundings, still unawakened from the silence of their summer sleep. A brief inspection soon showed us that the tomb, the magazine and the laboratory were all in good order. It was a relief to see how well the men had carried out their various duties, for on resuming work after a lapse of some months, one is always haunted by a faint sense of apprehension lest something should have miscarried.

I at once instructed my *Reises* to enrol the necessary labour—some twenty-five men and seventy-five boys—and to set to work to uncover the entrance of the tomb on the following morning.

To begin a new season's work is a less simple task than is perhaps generally imagined. There is always much to be done. The first few days are usually employed in getting ready—in putting in order and testing the various instruments and gear. To begin work, under conditions so different from those prevailing in Europe, in a country where many simple appliances and facilities are not easily obtainable, needs much prearrangement and forethought. The problem, especially in the desert, consists mainly in the simplification of one's requirements or the adapting of the material available. Even with that especially ordered from England, or elsewhere, it may happen, on examination on the spot, that it proves slightly too large or too small, and needs to be fitted to the requirements, whilst the men in charge have to be taught its uses. Thus several tedious days may be spent in preparation brightened, however, by the broad smiles on the *Reises'* faces when they first realize the advantages of some new gadget as a practical help in their forthcoming labours.

It was on October 10 at 6.30 a.m. that the uncovering of the entrance of the tomb commenced. The men and boys set to work with a will to remove the mass of rubbish heaped over the entrance staircase for protective purposes at the end of the previous season's work. They laboured like ants, and although the temperature in the Valley was ranging from 97° to 105° Fahrenheit, and the air grey with dust, their swing and go suggested an enthusiasm for their task. It was a pleasure to see them as they worked.

With the help of an extra number of boys for carrying the rubbish, the clearance of the entrance to the tomb was finished on the following day, when we were able to connect up our electrical installation with that of the Royal Tombs, and make an inspection of the interior.

First we removed the watertight timber-blocking before the entrance doorway, composed of Turkish oak beams interlaced with soft deal boards, by which the wooden portcullis door of the passage entrance had been screened; then the wooden portcullis of the passage was unlocked; at the farther end of the descending passage, we removed the sheet screening the securely locked steel gate, and once more entered the Antechamber and Burial Chamber.

Familiarity can never entirely dissipate the feeling of mystery—the sense of vanished but haunting forces that cling to the tomb. The conviction of the unity of past and present is constantly impressed upon the archæological adventurer, even when absorbed in the mechanical details of his work. These are varied enough. For instance, it was encouraging to find that, save for a few grains of disintegrated plaster fallen from the ceiling on the black modern pall with which I had covered the sarcophagus, hardly a trace of dust had settled in the tomb since it was closed down the previous year.

It was interesting to note the effect, on the invading forms of minute insect life, of the various insecticides with which I had then sprinkled the tomb. It is true that a few traces of those fish-like insects usually found in dark places, were still left, but the insecticides, on the whole, had acted effectively, for these pests had been almost entirely destroyed.

And now once more our powerful electric lamps lit up the great quartzite sarcophagus. Under the plate-glass screen which I had placed over it, was revealed the gold-encased coffin that seems to gather power of appealing to the emotions the more it is seen. With the shadows of the ancient gods there can be no vulgar intimacy.

The inspection over, and everything having been found in satisfactory condition, the tomb was reclosed. We then made our way to the laboratory, of which the entrance, for the summer months, had been protected by a heavy wooden screen. Here everything was free from dust and insects and, like the magazine, was in good order.

Thus our season had begun. The Valley, awakened from its summer sleep for the last two days by bawling workmen and screaming boys, was at peace again, and quiet will possess it until the winter migrants and their followers invade its golden silence.

The Antechamber freed of its beautiful furniture, the Burial Chamber denuded of its golden shrines, leaves the now open stone sarcophagus in the centre with its coffins within alone retaining their secret.

The task before us now was to raise the lid of the first outermost coffin, as it rested in the sarcophagus.

This great gilded wooden coffin (Plate LXVI), 7 feet 4 inches in length, anthropoid in shape, wearing the *Khat* head-dress, with face and hands in heavier sheet-gold, is of *Rishi* type—a term applied when the main decoration consists of a feather design, a fashion common to coffins of the preceding Intermediate and Seventeenth Dynasty Theban periods. During the New Empire, in the case of burials of high officials and commoners, the style of decoration of coffins completely changes at the beginning of the Eighteenth Dynasty ; but in the case of the royal coffin, as we now see, the older fashion still survived, with only very slight modification, such as the addition of figures of certain tutelary goddesses. This is a complete inversion of the usual order of things—fashion generally changing more rapidly with the upper than with the lower stations in life. May not this connote some religious idea in connexion with a king ? There may be tradition behind it. The goddess Isis once protected the dead body of Osiris by taking him within

her wings, thus she protects this new Osiris as represented by the effigy.

After careful study of the coffin it was decided that
the original silver handles—two on each side—manifestly made for the purpose, were sufficiently well
preserved still to support the weight of the lid, and
could be used without danger in raising it. The lid
was fixed to the shell by means of ten solid silver
tongues, fitted into corresponding sockets in the
thickness of the shell (four on each side, one at the
head-, and one at the foot-end) where they were held
in place by substantial gold-headed silver pins.
Could we remove the silver pins by which the lid was
fixed to the shell of the coffin without disturbing the
coffin in the sarcophagus? As the coffin filled up
nearly the whole of the interior of the sarcophagus,
leaving only the smallest space, especially at the head-
and foot-ends, it was by no means easy to extract
the pins. By careful manipulation, however, it was
found possible to withdraw them, with the exception
of the pin at the head-end where there was only space
enough to pull it half out. It had therefore to be
filed through before the inner half could be with-
drawn.

The next step was to place in position the hoisting
tackle necessary for lifting the lid. This tackle consisted of two sets of three sheaf pulley-blocks provided with automatic brakes, fixed to an overhead
scaffold, the pulleys being slung so as to come immediately above the centre of the lid opposite each pair
of handles. The tackle was attached to the handles
of the lid of the coffin by means of slings, and thus a
correct centralization of its weight was assured, otherwise there would have been a danger of the lid bumping

against the sides of the sarcophagus the moment it became free and pendent.

It was a moment as anxious as exciting. The lid came up fairly readily, revealing a second magnificent anthropoid coffin, covered with a thin gossamer linen sheet, darkened and much decayed. Upon this linen shroud were lying floral garlands, composed of olive and willow leaves, petals of the blue lotus and corn-flowers, whilst a small wreath of similar kind had been placed, also over the shroud, on the emblems of the forehead (Plate XXII). Underneath this covering, in places, glimpses could be obtained of rich multi-coloured glass decoration encrusted upon the fine gold-work of the coffin.

Some time was spent in the previous summer working out the methods to be followed in this under-taking, and in providing the necessary appliances, thus it was completed in one morning when otherwise it would have occupied several days at least. The tomb was closed, everything being left undisturbed to await Mr. Harry Burton's photographic records.

Thus far our progress had been fairly satisfactory, but we now became conscious of a rather ominous feature. The second coffin which, so far as visible through the linen covering, had every appearance of being a wonderful piece of workmanship, showed dis-tinct signs of the effect of some form of dampness and, here and there, tendency for its beautiful inlay to fall away. This was, I must admit, disconcerting, sug-gesting as it did the existence of former humidity of some kind within the nest of coffins. Should this prove the case, the preservation of the royal mummy would be less satisfactory than we had hoped.

On October 15 Mr. Burton arrived, and on the

17th, early in the morning, he successfully completed the photographic records of the shroud and floral garlands that covered the second coffin, as it rested within the shell of the first, in the sarcophagus.

These records complete, we had now to consider how best to deal with the second coffin, as well as the shell of the first. Manifestly, our difficulties were increased on account of the depth of the sarcophagus, and it was evident that the outer shell and the second coffin, neither of which was in a condition to bear much handling, must be raised together. This was eventually accomplished by means of pulleys as before, attachment being attained by means of steel pins passed through the tongue-sockets of the first outermost shell. In this way hoisting was possible with the minimum of handling.

In spite of the great weight of the coffins—far heavier than at first seemed possible—they were successfully raised to just above the level of the top of the sarcophagus, when wooden planks were passed under them. In the confined space, and with the restricted head-room available, the task proved one of no little difficulty. It was much increased by the necessity of avoiding damage to the fragile gesso-gilt surfaces of the outermost coffin.

Further records having been taken, I was then able to remove the chaplet and garlands, and roll back the covering shroud (Plate XXIII,A). It was one more exciting moment. We could now gaze, with admiring eyes, upon the finest example of the ancient coffin-maker's art ever yet seen—Osiride, again in form, but most delicate in conception, and very beautiful in line. As it now lay in the outer shell which rested upon the modern improvised trestles, it presented a wonderful picture of Majesty lying in State (Plate XXIII,B).

The chaplet and garlands placed upon the shroud in memory of " the wreaths given to Osiris on his triumphant exit from the Judgment-hall of Heliopolis," which, as Dr. Gardiner remarks, reminds us of the " crown of righteousness " (2 Tim. iv. 8), were but illustration of Pliny's description of ancient Egyptian wreaths. When the care and precision with which these are fashioned is recognized, there is strong reason for the belief that this particular occupation with the ancient Egyptians, as in later days, must have been a specialized trade.

This second coffin, 6 feet 8 inches in length, sumptuously inlaid on thick gold-foil with cut and engraved opaque glass, simulating red jasper, lapis lazuli and turquoise respectively, is similar in form and design to the first (Plates LXVIII, LXIX). It symbolizes Osiris, it is *Rishi* in ornament, but it differs in certain detail. In this case the king wears the *Nemes* headdress, and in place of the protective figures of Isis and Nephthys, the body is embraced with the wings of the vulture Nekhebet and of the serpent Buto. The arresting feature is the delicacy and superiority of the conception, which confer upon it at once the position of a masterpiece.

We were now faced by a complicated problem, not unlike the one we had to solve two seasons before when the covering shrines were dismantled. It was again a case of the unexpected happening. Conclusions drawn from former evidence or example are not to be trusted. For some unknown reason the reverse too often proves to be the case. On seeing that there were handles on the outer coffin for lowering or raising it, we were led to expect similar metal handles on the second coffin. There was none, and their absence placed us in a dilemma. The second coffin proved exceedingly heavy ; its decorated surface very fragile ; it fitted the outer shell so closely that it was not possible to pass one's little finger between the two. Its lid was fixed, as in the case of the outer coffin, with gold-headed silver pins which, as the coffin lay in the outer shell, could not be extracted. It was evident that it would have to be lifted in its entirety from the outer shell before anything further could be done. Thus the problem which confronted us was to discover a method of doing this with the minimum risk of damage to its delicate inlay, that had already suffered from some kind of humidity, the origin of which was then unknown.

It may be, under the strain of such operations as these, that one is too conscious of the risk of irreparable damage to the rare and beautiful object one desires to preserve intact. Much in the early days of Egyptian archæological research has undoubtedly been lost to us by too eager or careless handling, more still from want of necessary appliances at the right moment ; but against ill luck, even when every possible precaution has been taken, no man is secure. Everything may seem to be going well until suddenly, in the crisis of the process, you hear a crack—little pieces of surface ornament fall. Your nerves are at an almost painful tension. What is happening ? All available room in the narrow space is crowded by your men. What action is needed to avert a catastrophe ? There is, too, another danger. As the lid is being raised, the excitement of seeing some new and beautiful object may attract the workmen's attention; for a moment their duty is forgotten and irreparable damage in consequence may be done.

Such are often the anxious impressions uppermost in the archæologist's memory when his friends inquire what his emotions in these thrilling moments may have been. Only those who have had to handle heavy yet fragile antiquities in circumstances of similar difficulty, can realize how exacting and nerve-racking the strain and responsibility may become. Moreover, in the case before us, we could not be sure that the wood of the coffin was sufficiently well preserved to bear its own weight. However, after long consultations, and having studied the problem for nearly two days, we devised a plan. To remove the second coffin from the shell of the first, some points of attachment were necessary. There were, it will be remembered, no handles, so it was judged best to make use of the metal pins which fastened down the lid.

Inspection showed, however, that although the space between the shell of the outer coffin and the second coffin was insufficient to enable us to withdraw these pins entirely, they could still be pulled out about a quarter of an inch, so as to permit stout copper wire attachments to be fixed to them and to the overhead scaffold. This we did successfully. Strong metal eyelets were then screwed into the thickness of the top edge of the shell of the outer coffin, so as to enable it to be lowered from the second coffin by means of ropes working on the pulleys.

On the following day, after these preparations, we were able to proceed with the next stage. It proved to be one of the most important moments in the dismantling of the tomb. The process adopted was the reverse of that which might at first appear to be the natural order of things. We lowered the outer shell from the second coffin, instead of lifting the second coffin out of the first. The reason for this was that the head-room was insufficient, and the weight being stationary, there would be less risk of undue stress upon those ancient silver pins. The operation proved successful. The shell of the outer coffin was lowered once more into the sarcophagus, leaving for a moment, the second coffin suspended in mid-air by means of the ten stout wire attachments. A wooden tray sufficiently large to span the opening of the sarcophagus was then passed under it, and thus the second coffin strongly supported, stood before us free and accessible (Plate LXVIII). The wire attachments having been severed, the overhead gear removed, Mr. Burton made his records, and we were able to turn our energies to the raising of its lid.

The entire inlaid surface was indeed, as already mentioned, in a very fragile condition, and any handling, so far as possible, had to be avoided. In order therefore to lift the lid without causing injury, metal eyelets, to serve as handles, were screwed into it at four points where there would be no danger of permanent disfigurement. To these eyelets our hoisting tackle was fixed, the gold-headed silver nails were extracted and the lid was slowly raised.

There was at first some slight tendency for the lid to stick, but gradually it rose from its bed and, when high enough to clear the contents of the coffin, it was lowered on to a wooden tray placed at the side to receive it.

This revealed a third coffin which, like its predecessors, was Osiride in form, but the main details of the workmanship were hidden by a close-fitting reddish-coloured linen shroud (Plate xxiv). The burnished gold face was bare; placed over the neck and breast was an elaborate bead and floral collarette, sewn upon a backing of papyrus, and tucked immediately above the *Nemes* head-dress was a linen napkin (Plate xxxvi).

Mr. Burton at once made his photographic records. I then removed the floral collarette and linen coverings. An astounding fact was disclosed. This third coffin, 6 feet 1¾ of an inch in length, was made of solid gold! The mystery of the enormous weight, which hitherto had puzzled us, was now clear. It explained also why the weight had diminished so slightly after the first coffin, and the lid of the second coffin, had been removed. Its weight was still as much as eight strong men could lift.

The face of this gold coffin (Plates lxx, lxxi) was again that of the king, but the features though conventional, by symbolizing Osiris, were even more youthful than those on the other coffins. In actual design it reverted to that of the outermost coffin, inasmuch as it was *Rishi*, and had engraved upon it figures of Isis and Nephthys (Plate lxxii), but auxiliary to this design were winged figures of Nekhebet and Buto (Plate lxxi). These latter protective figures, emblematic of Upper and Lower Egypt, were the prominent feature, for they are superimposed in gorgeous and massive cloisonné work over the richly engraved ornament of the coffin—their inlay being natural semi-precious stones. In addition to this decoration, over the conventional collarette of " the Hawk "—again in auxiliary cloisonné work—was a double detachable necklace of large disk-shaped beads of red and yellow gold and blue faience, which enhanced the richness of the whole effect. But the ultimate details of the ornamentation were hidden by a black lustrous coating due to liquid unguents that had evidently been profusely poured over the coffin. As a result this unparalleled monument was not only disfigured—as it afterwards proved, only temporarily—but was stuck fast to the interior of the second coffin, the consolidated liquid filling up the space between the second and third coffins almost to the level of the lid of the third.

These consecration unguents, which had obviously been used in great quantity, were doubtless the cause of the disintegration observed when dealing with the outer coffins which, as they were in a practically hermetically sealed quartzite sarcophagus, cannot have been affected by outside influences. As a further result it may be mentioned that the covering shroud and floral collarette mingled with blue faience beads had suffered, and although these at first appeared to be in good condition, they proved so brittle that the material broke the very instant it was touched.

We raised the third coffin contained in the shell of the second, which now rested on the top of the sarcophagus, and moved them into the Antechamber where they were more accessible, both for examination and manipulation. It was then that the wonder and magnitude of our last discovery more completely dawned upon us. This unique and wonderful monument—a coffin over 6 feet in length, of the finest art, wrought in solid gold of $2\frac{1}{2}$ to $3\frac{1}{2}$ millimetres in thickness—represented an enormous mass of pure bullion.

How great must have been the wealth buried with those ancient Pharaohs! What riches that valley must have once concealed! Of the twenty-seven

monarchs buried there, Tut·ankh·Amen was probably of the least importance. How great must have
been the temptation to the greed and rapacity of
the audacious contemporary tomb robbers ! What
stronger incentive can be imagined than those vast
treasures of gold ! The plundering of royal tombs,
recorded in the reign of Rameses ix, becomes easily
intelligible when the incentive to these crimes is
measured by this gold coffin of Tut·ankh·Amen. It
must have represented fabulous wealth to the stone-
cutters, artisans, water-carriers and peasants—to contemporary workers generally, such as the men impli-
cated in the tomb robberies. These plunderings
occurred in the reigns of the later Ramessides (1200–
1000 B.C.) and are recorded in legal documents now
known as the Abbott, Amherst, Turin, and Mayer
papyri, discovered in Thebes about the beginning of
last century. Probably the thieves, who made their
practically ineffectual raid on Tut·ankh·Amen's tomb,
were aware of the mass of bullion covering the remains
of the young Pharaoh under its protective shrines,
sarcophagus and nested coffins.

Our first object now was to protect from injury
and, so far as was possible for the moment, to conserve
the delicate inlay on the shell of the second coffin.
The process used we knew to be effective. It was,
therefore, lightly brushed to remove loose dust, sponged
with warm water and ammonia, and when dry, the
whole surface covered with a thick coating of paraffin
wax applied hot with a long brush. This wax as it
cooled and solidified held the inlay securely in position
so that the coffin could be handled with impunity.
The great advantage of this system is that the wax
coating may be removed by heat at any time should

further restoration be considered necessary, and the mere reheating of the wax has also a cleansing quality.

The next problem for consideration, requiring a certain amount of experimental work, was to ascertain the most satisfactory, and at the same time the most expeditious manner, of dealing with those ancient consolidated consecration unguents, that not only covered the body of the coffin but completely filled the space between the two, thus sticking them fast and for the moment preventing further progress in investigation. Mr. Lucas made a preliminary analysis of this substance. In appearance it was black, and resembled pitch; in those places where the layer was thin, as on the lid of the coffin, the material was hard and brittle, but where a thicker layer had accumulated, as was the case under and between the coffins, the interior of the material was soft and plastic. Its smell when warm was penetrating, somewhat fragrant, not unpleasant, and suggestive of wood-pitch. Naturally a complete chemical analysis was not then possible, but, as a result of a preliminary examination, it was found to contain fatty matter and resin. There was no mineral pitch or bitumen present, and even the presence of wood-pitch, which was suggested by the smell, could not then be proved. There can be little doubt from the manner in which this material had run down the sides of the third coffin and collected underneath, that it was in a liquid or semi-liquid condition when employed.

On account of its nature, it follows that this substance could be melted by heat and dissolved by certain solvents, but neither of these methods in the existing circumstances was practicable. So we decided to raise the lid and examine the contents before any further procedure, and before applying any drastic measures. Luckily the line of junction between the lid and the coffin was visible and, with difficulty, accessible, except at the extreme foot-end where the second and third coffins practically touched.

The lid was fastened to the shell by means of eight gold tenons (four on each side), which were held in their corresponding sockets by nails. Thus, if the nails could be extracted the lid could be raised. In the narrow space between the two coffins ordinary implements for extracting metal pins were useless, and others had to be devised. With long screw-drivers converted to meet the conditions, the nails or pins of solid gold, that unfortunately had to be sacrificed, were removed piecemeal. The lid was raised by its golden handles and the mummy of the king disclosed.

At such moments the emotions evade verbal expression, complex and stirring as they are. Three thousand years and more had elapsed since men's eyes had gazed into that golden coffin. Time, measured by the brevity of human life, seemed to lose its common perspectives before a spectacle so vividly recalling the solemn religious rites of a vanished civilization. But it is useless to dwell on such sentiments, based as they are on feelings of awe and human pity. The emotional side is no part of archæological research. Here at last lay all that was left of the youthful Pharaoh, hitherto little more to us than the shadow of a name.

Before us, occupying the whole of the interior of the golden coffin, was an impressive, neat and carefully made mummy (Plate xxv), over which had been poured anointing unguents as in the case of the outside of its coffin—again in great quantity—consolidated and blackened by age. In contradistinction to the general dark and sombre effect, due to these unguents, was a brilliant, one might say magnificent, burnished gold mask (Plate LXXIII and Frontispiece) or similitude of the king, covering his head and shoulders, which, like the feet, had been intentionally avoided when using the unguents. The mummy was fashioned to symbolize Osiris. The beaten gold mask, a beautiful and unique specimen of ancient portraiture, bears a sad but calm expression suggestive of youth over-taken prematurely by death. Upon its forehead, wrought in massive gold, were the royal insignia—the Nekhebet vulture and Buto serpent—emblems of the Two Kingdoms over which he had reigned. To the chin was attached the conventional Osiride beard, wrought in gold and lapis-lazuli-coloured glass; around the throat was a triple necklace of yellow and red gold and blue faience disk-shaped beads; pendent from the neck by flexible gold inlaid straps was a large black resin scarab (Plate xxvi,A) that rested between the hands and bore the *Bennu* ritual. The burnished gold hands, crossed over the breast, separate from the mask, were sewn to the material of the linen wrappings, and grasped the Flagellum and Crozier—the emblems of Osiris. Immediately below these was the simple outermost linen covering, adorned with richly inlaid gold trappings pendent from a large pectoral-like figure of the *Ba* bird or soul (Plate xxvi,B), of gold cloisonné work, its full-spread wings stretched over the body. As these gorgeous trappings had been subjected to the consecration unguents, their detail and brilliance were hardly visible, and to this must be attributed the disastrous deterioration which we discovered to have taken place in the case of many of the objects.

But through this obstruction it could be faintly seen that these trappings, made of heavy gold plaques held together by threads of beads (Plate xxvii,A), bore welcoming speeches of the gods—for example, on the longitudinal bands down the centre, the goddess of the sky, Nût, the Divine Mother, says :—" I reckon thy beauties, O Osiris, King Kheperu·neb·Re ; thy soul livest : thy veins are firm. Thou smellest the air and goest out as a god, going out as Atum, O Osiris, Tut·ankh·Amen. Thou goest out and thou enterest with Ra . . ." The god of the earth, the prince of the gods, Geb, says :—" My beloved son, inheritor of the throne of Osiris, the King Kheperu· neb·Re ; thy nobility is perfect : Thy Royal Palace is powerful ; Thy name is in the mouth of the Rekhyt, thy stability is in the mouth of the living, O Osiris, King Tut·ankh·Amen, Thy heart is in thy body eternally. He is before the spirits of the living, like Re he rests in heaven." While the texts upon the transverse bands open with words, such as " Honoured before Anubis, Hapy, Kebeh·sen·uef, Dua·mutef," and " Justified before Osiris."

Accompanying these bands along the sides of the mummy, from the shoulders to the feet, were festoons of even more ornate straps attached to the transverse bands, and made up of elaborate small inlaid gold plaques also threaded together with beads (Plate xxvii,B). The devices on these side straps were of geometrical patterns, *Ded* and *Thet* symbols, solar uræi, and cartouches of the king. These, when cleaned, seemed to have been made up in part of a residue from Smenkh·ka·Re's burial, for some of the cloisonné plaques bore on the back texts from the " Chapter of the Heart " wherein Smenkh·ka·Re's names were introduced, and had, in most cases, been afterwards purposely defaced.

When these trappings were cleaned it became clear, that the jeweller had made the main part of these trappings (texts and festoons) to measure, that the finished mummy proved larger than was originally expected, and that pieces were cut, others added, to make them fit.

Though the attributes upon this mummy are those of the gods, the likeness (Plate LXXIII, and Frontispiece) is certainly that of Tut·ankh·Amen, comely and placid, with the features recognizable on all his statues and coffins. From certain aspects the face here recalls his father-in-law Akh·en·Aten, in others, especially in profile, perhaps an even stronger likeness to the great Queen Tyi, Akh·an·Aten's mother, or, in other words, as those features gazed at you, there was an incipient gleam of affinity to both of those predecessors.

Those liquid unguents so lavishly used would seem to have been applied as part of the burial ritual for the consecration of the dead king, before his entrance into the presence of the great god Osiris of the Underworld. It was particularly noticeable that, both on the third coffin and the king's mummy itself, the head and feet had been carefully avoided, although some of the same liquid had been poured on the feet (only) of the first outermost coffin (*see* p. 90). One's thoughts turned, as one mused on the nature of that last ceremony and its intention, to that touching scene " in the house of the leper," when " there came a woman having an alabaster box of ointment of spikenard very precious " and to Christ's words : " she is come aforehand to anoint my body to the burying " (Mark xiv. 8).

When the detailed photographic records were made by Mr. Burton, we were better able to make a closer examination of the actual state of things, and the preservation of the mummy. The greater part of the flagellum and crozier was completely decomposed, and had already fallen to dust ; the threads that once held the hands and trappings in place upon the outer linen covering, were decayed, and in consequence the various sections fell apart at the slightest touch ; the black resin scarab was covered by minute fissures, probably the result of contraction ; consequently, these external trappings and ornaments had to be removed, piece by piece, and placed in corresponding order and position upon a tray for future cleaning and remounting. The farther we proceeded the more evident it became that the covering wrappings and the mummy were both in a parlous state. They were completely carbonized by the action that had been set up by the fatty acids of the unguents with which they had been saturated.

But, alas ! both the mask and the mummy were stuck fast to the bottom of the coffin by the consolidated residue of the unguents, and no amount of legitimate force could move them. What was to be done ?

Since it was known that this adhesive material could be softened by heat, it was hoped that an exposure to the midday sun would melt it sufficiently to allow the mummy to be raised. A trial therefore was made for several hours in sun temperature reaching as high as 149° Fahrenheit (65° C.) without any success and, as other means were not practicable, it became evident that we should have to make all further examination of the king's remains as they lay within the two coffins.

As a matter of fact, after the scientific examination of the king's mummy *in situ*, and its final removal from the gold coffin, that very difficult question of removing the gold mask and extricating the gold coffin from the shell of the second coffin, had to be solved.

Originally something like two bucketsful of the liquid unguents had been poured over the golden coffin, and a similar amount over the body inside. As heat was the only practical means of melting this material and rendering it amenable, in order to apply a temperature sufficiently high for the purpose, without causing damage to those wonderful specimens of ancient Egyptian arts and crafts, the interior of the golden coffin had to be completely lined with thick plates of zinc, which would not melt under a temperature of 968° Fahrenheit (520° C.). The coffins were then reversed upon trestles, the outside one being protected against undue heat and fire by several blankets saturated and kept wet with water. Our next procedure was to place under the hollow of the gold coffin several Primus paraffin lamps burning at full blast. The heat from the lamps had to be regulated so as to keep the temperature well within the melting-point of zinc. It should be noted here that the coating of wax upon the surface of the second coffin acted as a pyrometer—while it remained unmelted under the wet blanketing there was manifestly no fear of injury.

Although the temperature arrived at was some 932° Fahrenheit (500° C.), it took several hours before any real effect was noticeable. The moment signs of movement became apparent, the lamps were turned out, and the coffins left suspended upon the trestles, when, after an hour, they began to fall apart. The movement at first was almost imperceptible owing to the tenacity of the material, but we were able to separate them by lifting up the wooden shell of the second coffin, thus leaving the shell of the gold coffin resting upon the trestles. Its very nature was hardly recognizable, and all we could see was a dripping mass of viscous pitch-like material which proved very difficult to remove, even with quantities of various solvents—the principal of which was acetone.

In the same manner that the outside of the golden coffin was covered with a viscid mass, so was the interior, to which still adhered the gold mask. This mask had also been protected by being bound with a folded wet blanket continually fed with water, its face padded with wet wadding. As it had necessarily been subjected to the full power of the heat collected in the interior of the coffin, it was freed and lifted away with comparative ease, though to its back, as in the case of the coffin, there adhered a great mass of viscous unguents, which had eventually to be removed with the aid of a blast lamp and cleaning solvents.

We have now, in the natural sequence of our work, to return to the first coffin that had still to be raised out of the sarcophagus. This was successfully achieved, as in previous operations, by means of our hoisting tackle attached to the overhead scaffolding. After it had been lifted sufficiently high to clear the top of the sarcophagus, a wooden tray was passed beneath it, and it was thus carried up to the laboratory where its lid was already under treatment. It proved to be of great weight, and like the shrines, was probably of an oak wood. It had unfortunately suffered from humidity evaporated from those liquid unguents, which had caused the gesso-gilt surfaces to blister and buckle to such an extent that, in many places, this overlaying decoration had become detached from the basic wood. Fortunately this injury need not be permanent. By patiently filling in the interstices with hot paraffin wax, in time, with patience and care it can be repaired, and the decorated surfaces once more be made good and firm.

The only remaining object in the sarcophagus was the gilt bed-shaped bier with lion's head and feet. It stood on the bottom and served as a support to the first (outermost) coffin. It was made of a stout and heavy wood covered with gesso-gilt ; but the astonishing fact was that, after supporting the weight of those three great coffins—more than a ton and a quarter—for over thirty centuries, it was still intact. Strips of broad webbing were passed under it, and this splendid example of ancient Egyptian construction was raised out of the sarcophagus. It stands about 12 inches in height, 7 feet 6 inches in length, and is curved so as to receive and to fit the base of the outermost coffin. The central panel is designed in low relief to represent a cord-mesh—like the string mesh of the Sudanese *Angarîbes* (bedsteads) of to-day. The joints of the framework are hardly sprung, thus bearing witness to the good quality of the wood and the extreme excellence of the joinery.

Lying on the bottom of the sarcophagus beneath this bier were a number of wooden chips bearing traces of gesso-gilt ornamentation. These were at first puzzling, but their presence was accounted for upon further examination. The design on the gesso-gilt surface was identical with that on the edge of the first (outermost) coffin, from which pieces had been crudely hacked away by some sharp instrument like a carpenter's adze. The obvious explanation is that the foot-end of the coffin, as it rested on the bier, was too high to allow the lid of the sarcophagus to be lowered in place, and it was therefore cut down by those whose duty it was to close the sarcophagus. This is evidence of want of forethought on the part of the workmen. This mutilation of the coffin had not been noticed before, owing to its having been hidden by the anointing unguents, the presence of which, in this case only on the feet, might have been an endeavour to cover the disfiguring scar, and thus may not be of religious significance.

Besides these chips were some rags, a stout wooden lever, portions of floral garlands fallen from the burial, and the transcending example of religious handicraft —the highly ornamented gold and silver receptacle for sacred unguents presented and described on Plate LXXIV.

The Burial Chamber and sarcophagus were now empty and, looking back, we were able, for the first time, to consider more closely the funerary customs followed in the burial of a Pharaoh, as revealed to us by Tut·ankh·Amen's tomb, and something, I venture to think, has been added to our knowledge.

The more one considers it the more deeply one is impressed by the extreme care and enormous costliness lavished by this ancient people on the enshrinement of their dead. Barrier after barrier was raised to guard their remains from the predatory hands against which, in death, these great kings too ineffectually sought protection. The process was as elaborate as it **was** costly.

First we have the golden shrines profusely decorated and of magnificent workmanship. They were sealed and nested one in the other over an immense and superbly sculptured monolithic quartzite sarcophagus. The sarcophagus, in its turn, contained three great anthropoid coffins of wood and gold which bear the likeness of the king with repeated *Rishi* and Osiride symbolism.

Everywhere there was evidence of the accomplished artist and skilful craftsman, intent on the mysteries of a vanished religion, and the problems of death. Finally we reach the monarch himself, profusely anointed with sacred unguents and covered with numberless amulets and emblems for his betterment, as well as personal ornaments for his glory.

The modern observer indeed is astounded at the enormous labour and expense bestowed on these royal burials, even when the titanic excavations of their rock-cut tombs is disregarded. Consider the carving and gilding of the elaborate shrines ; the hewing and transport of that quartzite sarcophagus ; the moulding, carving, inlaying of the magnificent coffins, the costly and intricate goldsmith's work expended upon them, the crowd of craftsmen employed, the precious metal and material so generously devoted to the princely dead. But we do not know all, there are the contents of two more chambers yet to be seen !

CHAPTER VI

Points of Interest in Egyptian Burial Customs

UNDOUBTEDLY the greatest ceremony which awaited every Egyptian, in due proportion to his rank, was his funeral.

With the ancient Egyptian in all stations of life, from the Pharaoh to the peasant, there was a profound yearning for a good burial. To secure this wish he made, in accordance with his rank, elaborate preparations and it was naturally his desire that his survivors would see that they were carried out. The general attitude of mind of the ancient Egyptians towards the benefits of a good burial is expressed, with simple dignity, in the story of a certain Sinuhe which has come down to us from the Middle Kingdom, some forty centuries ago, and is translated by Dr. Alan Gardiner :

Remember then the day of burial, the passing into beatitude ; when the night shall be devoted to thee with oils and with bandages, the handiwork of Tayt [i.e. the goddess of weaving]. There is a procession to be made for thee on the day thou art reunited with the earth : thy mummy-case of gold, with head of lapis lazuli, a heaven [i.e. shrine] above thee—the while that thou art placed upon the hearse, and oxen drag thee. Then shall musicians await thy coming, and the dance of the *Muu* be performed at the door of thy tomb. The words of offering shall be pronounced on thy behalf, and victims slaughtered at the door of thy stele.[1]

[1] "The Tomb of Amenemhet," p. 56.

This may be regarded as a general expression of optimism prevailing among those ancient people, but pessimists have existed in all ages, and we have an Egyptian poet lamenting in the following lines the uselessness of fine sepulchres : " He who built there in granite, who constructed a hall in a pyramid ; who supplied there what was beautiful in fine work . . . his altar shall be as empty as those of the weary, who die on the canal embankment without leaving any survivors." [1]

These quotations convey to us both the sanguine and dissenting views held on this subject, but although the latter is of rare occurrence, we have some idea of what was the practice. Actual cliff-tombs were commenced during the lifetime of the deceased : for example, Queen Hat·shep·sût prepared for herself a cliff-tomb on the western side of the mountain of Thebes, when she was consort to Thothmes ii, and another, and later one, in the Valley of the Tombs of the Kings, when she actually reigned as a monarch. In a similar way Hor·em·heb had two tombs, one as general of the army, the other as king after he had usurped the throne. But perhaps the most striking instance of all is that of King Akh·en·Aten, who as early as the sixth year of his reign, when he was about eighteen years of age, when setting up tablets demarcating the limits of his city Akh·et·Aten (El Amarna), decrees :

There shall be made for me a sepulchre in the Orient Mountain ; my burial shall be (made) therein in the multitude of jubilees which Aten my father hath ordained for me, and the burial of the chief wife of the king, Nefertiti, shall be made therein in that multitude of years . . . (and the burial of) the

[1] Erman, " Egyptian Religion," p. 127.

king's daughter Mert·Aten shall be made in it in that multitude of years. [1]

Further, Akh·en·Aten decrees that, should he, his queen, Nefertiti, or his eldest daughter, Mert·Aten, die " in any town " outside the limits of his city, that they shall be brought to, and buried in, the sepulchre prepared by him " in the Orient Mountain " of his city. There are other examples of this kind which need not be quoted.

Not only was the cliff-tomb commenced during life, but also the stone sarcophagus was prepared, as in the case of Queen Hat·shep·sût ; and, if the Turin papyrus relating to the tomb of Rameses IV be accepted as a project, as I think it really was, so were the covering gilt wooden shrines, and some of the essentially religious funerary objects. But the results of archæological research suggest also that the greater part of the burial equipment was made after death, though no doubt the deceased had made preliminary provisions. This point is strongly indicated by the fact, that, on practically all funerary furniture, the names, titles, and rank, are those of the deceased at the time of death. The objects which obviously belonged to his lifetime are the exception.

In the case of Tut·ankh·Amen's tomb there is sufficient evidence to show that at least most of the funerary appurtenances were made after death, during the period of mummification, and the subsequent period, whatever it may have been, necessary for the carrying out of the customs prior to burial. This point is confirmed by the fact that the funerary statues, statuettes, coffins and mask show a certain hurried workmanship, and depict Tut·ankh·Amen

[1] N. de G. Davies : "The Rock Tombs, El Amarna," Part V, p. 30.

at the age of his death, as is proved by his mummy. While, in contradistinction, an obvious piece of El Amarna palace furniture, such as the throne (Vol. I, Plate LXIII), bears his early and original *Aten* name, and the ceremonial gold and silver sticks (Plate VII) which depict him about the age he became king.

It therefore becomes clear that a great part of the funerary appurtenances which could not be made during the lifetime of the deceased depended largely on the fidelity of his successor.

Herodotus, writing some nine centuries after the death of Tut·ankh·Amen, gives a short account of the way in which the Egyptians conducted their mournings, and also of the method of mummification employed in his day : " On the death in any house of a man of consequence, forthwith the women of the family beplaster their heads, and sometimes even their faces, with mud; and then, leaving the body indoors, sally forth and wander through the city, with their dress fastened by a band, and their bosoms bare, beating themselves as they walk. All the female relations join them and do the same. The men too, similarly begirt, beat their breasts separately. When the ceremonies are over, the body is carried away to be embalmed."

" There are," he wrote, " a set of men in Egypt who practice the art of embalming, and make it their proper business. These persons, when a body is brought to them, show the bearers various models of corpses, made of wood, and painted so as to resemble nature. The most perfect is said to be after the manner of him whom I do not think it religious to name in connexion with such a matter ; [1] the second

---

[1] Meaning undoubtedly, Osiris, the great god of the dead.

sort is inferior to the first, and less costly ; the third is the cheapest of all. All this the embalmers explain, and then ask in which way it is wished that the corpse should be prepared. The bearers tell them, and having concluded their bargain, take their departure, while the embalmers, left to themselves, proceed to their task." Referring to " the most perfect process," as he terms it, Herodotus, after telling us how the brain and softer parts of the body are treated, proceeds : " Then the body is placed in natrum for seventy days, and covered entirely over. After the expiration of that space of time, which must not be exceeded,[1] the body is washed, and wrapped round, from head to foot, with bandages of fine linen cloth, smeared over with gum, which is used generally by the Egyptians in place of glue, and in this state is given back to the relatives, who enclose it in a wooden case which they have had made for the purpose, shaped in the figure of a man. Then fastening the case, they place it in a sepulchral chamber, upright against the wall."

Although the method of embalming described by the great Greek historian refers to a much later date, the process, as archæological research has shown, was very similar to that employed in earlier times.

In ordinary cases the practice was certainly one likely to lead to abuses, and we may be sure that the neighbourhood of the burial grounds was peopled by hungry professional embalmers, and the meaner priests, eager to prey upon the relations. In the case of a royal and sacred personage, no doubt, the operation would be carried out within the palace or its

---

[1] On account of the risk of the natron corroding the flesh and converting it into the condition of pulp.

adjuncts in pomp and ceremony and under special supervision.

The length of time for mummification given by Herodotus is confirmed by a Theban stele of a noble of the reign of Thothmes III, ably translated and published by Dr. Alan Gardiner.[1] The stele also throws valuable light upon the burial rites about a century before Tut·ankh·Amen.

" A goodly burial arrives in peace, thy seventy days having been fulfilled in thy place of embalming. Thou art placed on the bier . . . and art drawn by bulls without blemish, thy road being besprinkled with milk until thou reachest the door of thy tomb. The children of thy children, united of one accord, weep with loving hearts. Opened is thy mouth by the lector, and thy purification is made by the *Sem* priest. Horus adjusts for thee thy mouth, and opens for thee thy eyes and ears, thy flesh and thy bones being perfect in all that appertains to thee. There are recited for thee spells and glorifications. There is made for thee an offering-which-the-King-gives, thy own true heart being with thee. . . . Thou comest in thy former shape, even as on the day wherein thou wast born. There is brought to thee the son thou lovest, the courtiers making obeisance. Thou enterest into the land given of the King, into the sepulchre of the West. There are performed rites for thee as for those of yore. . . ."

But upon the subject of the period for mummification, and for the mourning of the dead, I should also refer the reader to the well-known passage in Genesis (Ch. 50, vv. 2 & 3), wherein " Joseph commanded his servants the physicians to embalm his father : and the physicians embalmed Israel. And forty days were fulfilled for him : for so are fulfilled the days of those which are embalmed : and the Egyptians mourned for him three score and ten days."

Some evidence of the obsequies of Tut·ankh·Amen is afforded by the material found in a cache of large

[1] " The Tomb of Amenemhet," p. 56.

pottery jars, discovered by Mr. Theo. M. Davis (1907–8) in the Valley, a little distance from the king's tomb (Vol. I, p. 77). Their contents proved to be accessories used during the funeral ceremonies of the young king, and afterwards gathered together and packed away within jars—which seems to have been the custom in Egyptian burials. Among the material there were clay seals of Tut·ankh·Amen and of the royal necropolis, and floral collars of a kind represented as worn by mourners in burial scenes. The floral collars, sewn upon sheets of papyrus, are the counterparts of that found on the gold coffin ; the pottery vases are also similar to specimens in the tomb. This discovery indicates that pottery vases were broken as well as that the seals on certain objects were removed, and that linen head-shawls and floral collars were worn during the royal funerary ritual ; but the material throws no light upon the ministrations of the " divine servants " and lectors who must have officiated at the burial. However, that King Ay, Tut. ankh·Amen's successor, was present, and that he acted as the *Sem* priest, is clear from the scene depicted on the north wall of the Burial Chamber of the tomb (p. 28). Also the scene on the east wall of the same chamber shows that the king's mummy, on its sledge, was dragged to the tomb, at least for some distance, by courtiers and high officials (p. 27), instead of by oxen which were used in non-royal funerals.

It is manifest, after the actual burial ceremonies, that the tomb must have remained open and have been in the hands of workmen for a long time, for it is obvious that the nest of shrines, covering the sarcophagus, could only have been erected after the great coffins were placed in position, and the sarcophagus closed. In the same way the partition wall, dividing the Antechamber from the Burial Chamber, must have been built after the erection of the shrines, and the furniture filling both chambers subsequently introduced.

These last facts open up an interesting question : where were all the valuable and delicate objects that eventually filled those rooms, while these lengthy operations—the erection of the shrines and the building of the partition wall—were being carried out ? As we have no evidence that any store-room existed in the Valley, although there might have been temporary constructions serving for that purpose, does it mean that the funerary furniture was brought from the royal workshop only when their place was ready ? If these objects were not brought to the tomb simultaneously, the obsequies would be of a different character from that generally supposed. It has been usually imagined that all the furniture was carried behind the coffin in the funeral procession, thus forming a gorgeous pageant. But, as we have just seen, it would appear that many of the funerary objects must have been transported to the tomb after the actual burial of the king, when the chambers were ready to receive them.

When the tomb was eventually closed and sealed, the seals of the dead king were used (Vol. I, Plate xiv) instead of those of his successor.

To return to Tut·ankh·Amen : his mummy and his coffins were all scrupulously fashioned to represent and symbolize the one great god of the dead, Osiris. For this we seem to have an impressive reason. The close association in funeral custom with that deity, was in all probability due to the belief that Osiris was

in many ways nearer than any other deity to man.
For on this earth he suffered the pangs of death, was
buried, and rose again from mortal death to immortal
life. The mummy itself was carefully orientated east
and west and, as it will be seen in the succeeding chapter, the insignia were so placed on it as to agree in
position with the Two Kingdoms, Upper and Lower
Egypt. The amulets and ornaments of religious
import were conscientiously disposed within its wrappings, in accordance with the ritual of the Book of the
Dead.

As will have been already gathered from the preceding chapter, we found, to our dismay, that the
mummy of Tut·ankh·Amen was in poor condition,
due, as is now clear, to the profuse anointing to which
it had been subjected. It was, however, evident that
this anointing formed an essential part of the king's
burial.

There was the amplest evidence that the body had
been carefully mummified, wrapped and adorned with
all the accessories, before the liquids had been poured
over it. In all probability those once liquid unguents
were merely of pious significance, and had been
applied for a sacred purpose either before or during
the burial rites, to consecrate or purify the dead king,
or to help him towards initiation on his journey
through the mysteries of the shadowy Underworld.
Egyptian ritual was full of symbolism. The anointing by the gods of the body of Osiris would give the
ceremony all the weight of religious tradition.

That there had been method in the pouring of
these liquids was also evident. Apparently they had
not been dispensed without design. Both on the
effigy on the (innermost) coffin of gold, and over the

wrappings of the mummy itself, the liquid had been poured over the body and legs only. The face and feet had been avoided, except in the case of the first (outermost) coffin, whereon a small amount had been definitely poured on the feet only (*see* Plate LXVI), though, as already suggested in the previous chapter, this may possibly have been for quite another purpose.

But whatever the sacred intention, the result, so far as archæology is concerned, has been unfortunate. There can be little doubt that the use of the liquids within the wood and metal coffins was the main cause of the extremely bad condition of their contents. The action of the composite liquid employed has been threefold : first, the decomposition of the fatty matter, by producing fatty acids, has acted destructively upon certain qualities of the glass inlay and cement of the objects ; secondly, the oxidation of the resin has given rise to a kind of slow spontaneous combustion, resulting in the carbonization of the linen fabric and, in a less degree, of the tissues and even of the bones of the mummy ; thirdly, the quantity of liquid poured both over the innermost coffin and mummy itself was sufficient to form a pitch-like cement which consolidated the contents.

The result is disappointing to this extent. Time and mischance, aided by the chemical decomposition suggested, have robbed archæology of part at least of what might have been a great opportunity—the scientific examination, the systematic unwrapping of the mummy, for which we had hoped, were consequently rendered nearly impossible.

Naturally a question here arises as to whether all the other royal mummies of the Egyptian New Empire were subjected to similar treatment in respect to anointing ? I believe, although those remains show but slight traces of similar resinous matter, such a ceremony was common to all.

It must be remembered in the case of the royal mummies discovered both in the cache of Deir el Bahari and in the tomb of Amen·hetep II (*vide* Vol. I, p. 72) that not one of them had either their original wrappings or coffins, rough coffins having been substituted by the priests in the Twentieth and Twenty-first Dynasties. Thus, by having been denuded of their original coverings and coffins, those royal mummies at an early date were freed from the destructive elements from which Tut·ankh·Amen's mummy suffered. In other words, the royal tomb-robberies occurred before there had been sufficient time for the unguents to penetrate far into the voluminous wrappings, or set up much decomposition.

The alabaster jars belonging to Rameses II and Mer·en·ptah containing those very unguents, discovered by Lord Carnarvon and myself in the Valley in 1920, are evidence of the constant use of those materials. The hieratic inscriptions upon the jars mention, " Oil of the first quality from Libya " ; " oil of the first quality of divine things," and " fat of *Tauat*."

But for the anointing oils, I believe that the wrappings, and all accessories of Tut·ankh·Amen's mummy in the solid gold coffin, would have been found practically as perfect as when first placed in the coffin.

We might now with advantage reconsider some impressions gathered from our investigation of the burial rites of the ancient Egyptians, so far as the discovery of this tomb has added to our knowledge. In the first place, former documentary evidence makes it clear that it was a constant belief in the religion of the ancient Egyptians that the solicitude of the living ensured the welfare of the dead : also that the rare dissenting traces of pessimistic philosophy which have come down to us, throwing doubts on the utility of constructing vast mortuary temples, chapels and tombs in their honour, could obviously have had but little influence on the strength and intensity of this cult.

We gather from this tomb that in the case of a royal burial, the succeeding king acts as the *Sem* priest in the ritual of " the opening of the mouth," and that courtiers and high officials replaced oxen in dragging the bier.

Our knowledge gathered from other sources for the period of mummification, shows that it was at least seventy days, or possibly more, but whether the period of mourning was contemporaneous with it is still uncertain, though it seems clear that the funeral took place immediately after the completion of mummification. However this may be, it is now evident that, between a royal burial and the closing of the tomb, some time must have elapsed for the various intricate preparations before the chambers were ready to receive their full equipment, and that consequently it does not seem probable that the whole of the funerary furniture could have been carried in the procession of the mummy. It is difficult to conceive that the great quantity of delicate and extremely valuable articles, not to mention boxes of jewellery and gold vessels, etc., such as filled the Burial Chamber and its adjacent rooms, could have been stacked there, while the workmen and tackle necessary for closing the sarcophagus, erecting the shrines and building the thick masonry partition wall, were present. Further, it would have been wellnigh impossible for the workmen to have carried out their task, had those chambers been encumbered with furniture as we found them. I might here note that upon the outermost shrine there were distinct splashes of plaster, whereas the funerary furniture bore no such evidence.

In the case of royal burials we may also infer that it was the custom to bury the late king behind necropolis seals bearing his own name. If then each Pharaoh was buried behind his own seals, a question arises as to when the seal of the successor came into force and that of the late king became obsolete. To this no clear answer can yet be given. When the tomb of Tut·ankh·Amen was reclosed after the depredations of the tomb-thieves, which probably occurred not long after his burial, the seals then used were those of the royal necropolis which bore no royal names; and this was also the case when King Hor·em·heb ordered the tomb of Thothmes IV to be restored after its violation by robbers.

Whether the whole of the tomb equipment was made before or after the king's death, is a question of interest upon which some evidence has been gathered. In some instances there is little doubt. Some objects bear a distinct clue; in the case of others, deduction evades us. Thus we gather that some objects were made during his lifetime—even at an early age—and that others were made immediately following or soon after his death.

Another important and interesting fact borne on the mind, is the tenacity of the Osiris cult throughout the history of ancient Egypt. The mummy and its coffin were consistently made in the form of the deity, whose mortal experiences brought him nearer than any other god of the Egyptian pantheon to human sympathies, and it is the mysterious influence of this divinity that shines through the cults of more than one later creed.

There remains but one other fact to be noted. The discovery of Tut-ankh-Amen's tomb has brought to light a custom hitherto little known—that of profusely anointing the royal mummy—which, in the case of the young King, has worked such deplorable havoc from an archæological point of view. We had expected to find the mummy in better condition than most of those that have come down to us, torn as they had been from their coffins by profane hands in dynastic times. But alas ! we were disappointed, and here we have a grim example of the irony which may sometimes await research. The tomb-robbers who dragged the remains of the Pharaohs from their coverings for plunder, or the pious priests who hid them to save them from further violations, at least protected those royal remains against the chemical action of the sacred unguents before there was time for corrosion.

CHAPTER VII

THE EXAMINATION OF THE ROYAL MUMMY

TO most investigators, and especially to those absorbed in archæological research, there are moments when their work becomes of transcending interest, and it was now our good fortune to pass through one of these rare and wonderful periods. The time that immediately followed we shall ever recall with the profoundest satisfaction. After years of toil—of excavating, conserving and recording—we were to see, with the eye of reality, that which we had hitherto beheld only in imagination. The investigation for us had been one of the greatest interest, nor will it, I venture to hope, be entirely without importance to archæology. Something at least has been added to confirm or extend our knowledge of the funeral rituals of the Pharaohs in relation to their ancient myths and traditions.

On November 11, at 9.45 a.m., the examination of the royal mummy was commenced. There were present H.E. Saleh Enan Pasha, Under-Secretary of State to the Ministry of Public Works; H.E. Sayed Fuad Bey el Khôli, Governor of the Province of Keneh; Monsieur Pierre Lacau, the Director-General of the Department of Antiquities; Dr. Douglas Derry, Professor of Anatomy in the Faculty of Medicine, Egyptian University; Dr. Saleh Bey Hamdi, Director of the Sanitary Services, Alexandria; Mr. A. Lucas, Government chemist, Department of Antiquities;

Examination of the Royal Mummy

Mr. Harry Burton of the Metropolitan Museum of Art, New York; Tewfik Effendi Boulos, Chief Inspector of the Department of Antiquities, Upper Egypt; and Mohamed Shaaban Effendi, Assistant Curator, Cairo Museum (Plate xxviii).

The external ornaments and inlaid gold trappings described (pp. 83-85, Plates xxvi, xxvii) having been removed, the king's mummy lay bare with its simple outer coverings and gold mask. It occupied the whole of the interior of the gold coffin, measuring in total length 6 feet 1 inch (Plate xxix).

The outer wrappings consisted of one large linen sheet, held in position by three longitudinal (one down the centre and one at each side) and four transverse bands of the same material, corresponding in position to the flexible inlaid gold trappings already mentioned. These linen bands had evidently been fastened to the linen covering by some such adhesive as Herodotus has described. They were doubled, and varied from $2\frac{3}{4}$ to $3\frac{1}{2}$ inches in width. The central longitudinal band, beginning in the middle of the abdomen (in reality thorax), was passed under the lower layer of each of the three transverse bands, over the feet, under the soles, and doubled back below the second layer of transverse bands. At each side of the feet the linen wrappings had been rubbed, the result probably of friction against the sides of the metal coffin during transport to the tomb. The mummy lay at a slight angle, suggesting that it had been subjected to some shock when lowered into the sarcophagus. There was also similar evidence to imply that the unguents had been poured over the mummy and coffin before they were lowered into the sarcophagus—the liquid being at different levels on the two sides, suggesting the tilting of the coffin.

In consequence of the fragile and carbonized condition of the linen swathing, the whole of the exposed
surface was painted over with melted paraffin wax of
such a temperature that when congealed it formed a
thin coating on the surface, with minimum penetration
of the decayed wrappings beneath. When the wax
had cooled, Dr. Derry made a longitudinal incision
down the centre (Plate xxviii) of the outer binding to
the depth penetrated by the wax, thus enabling the
consolidated layer to be removed in large pieces. Nor
did our troubles end here. The very voluminous
under-wrappings were found to be in even worse
condition of carbonization and decay. We had hoped,
by removing a thin outer layer of bandage from the
mummy, to free it at the points of adhesion to the
coffin so that it might be removed, but in this we were
again disappointed. It was found that the linen
beneath the mummy and the body itself had been so
saturated by the unguents which formed a pitch-like
mass at the bottom of the coffin and held it embedded
so firmly, that it was impossible to raise it except
at risk of great damage. Even after the greater
part of the bandages had been carefully removed, the
consolidated material had to be chiselled away from
beneath the limbs and trunk before it was possible to
raise the king's remains.

The bandages that actually enveloped the head
were in a better state of preservation than those on
the rest of the body, inasmuch as they had not been
saturated by the unguents, and consequently had only
suffered from indirect oxidation. This was also the
case to a large extent with the wrappings on the feet.

The general system of bandaging so far as could be
discovered was of normal character : it comprised a

series of bandages, sheets and pads of linen, where the latter were required to complete the anthropoid form, the whole showing evidence of considerable care. The linen was evidently of a very fine cambric-like nature. The numerous objects found upon the mummy were enclosed in alternate layers of the voluminous wrappings, and literally covered the king (Plate xxx) from head to foot; some of the larger objects were caught up in many different layers of bindings which were wound crosswise and transversely.

Although the actual examination had necessarily to be carried out beginning from the feet upwards, for the sake of clarity, in the following description, I will describe it from the head downwards, enumerating each object and point of interest in proper sequence.

Upon the top of the head was a large pad of conic form, composed of wads of linen, wrapped in the manner of a modern surgical head-bandage, and in shape suggestive of the *Atef* crown of Osiris, without such accessories as the horns and feathers. The purpose of this pad is obscure; from its shape it might be thought to be a crown, but, on the other hand, it could well be merely a tall pad to support and fill the empty space within the hollow of the *Nemes* head-dress of the gold mask, especially in view of the fact that the mask is an integral part of the external equipment of the mummy, making it coincide with the effigies upon the coffins.

Beneath this crown-like pad, lying on the back of the mask, was a small amuletic *Urs* pillow, or head-rest (Plate LXXVII,B), made of iron, which, according to the 166th Chapter of the "Book of the Dead," has the following significance : " Rise up from non-existence, O prostrate one . . . overthrowest thou thy enemies,

triumphest thou over what they do against thee."
Such amulets are usually made of hæmatite, but in
this case pure iron has taken the place of that ore, a
fact that gives us a very important milestone in the
development and growth of the history of civilization
—of this more anon.

Next to the pad and encircling the top of the head,
was a double tie (the Arabic *aqal*), not unlike that of
the Bedouin head-dress (Plate LXXVI,C), made of fibre
tightly bound with cord and having loops at the ends
to which were doubtless attached tapes for tying at
the back of the head. Its use is unknown, its like or
parallel never before having been found. It suggests
a relief to the head from the pressure of a crown.

The removal of a few layers of wrappings revealed
a magnificent diadem (Plate LXXV) completely encircling the king's head—an object of extreme beauty
and of simple fillet type. In design it comprises a
richly ornamented gold ribbon of contiguous circles
of carnelian, having minute gold bosses affixed to
their centres, with, at the back, a floral and disk-
shaped bow, from which hang two ribbon-like gold
appendages similarly decorated. On both sides of
the fillet are appendages of a like but broader kind,
and having a massive pendent uræus attached to
their front margins. The insignia of northern and
southern sovereignty of this diadem, I should here
mention, were found lower down, separate, and on
the right and left thighs (Plate XXX,R, s) respectively,
and as the king lay within the sarcophagus, east
and west—his head towards the west—the uræus of
Buto being on the left side, and the vulture of Nekhebet on the right, the insignia took their correct
geographical position, as did also those emblems on

the coffins. Both of these golden emblems of royalty have grooved fastenings on the back, into which fit corresponding T-shaped tongues upon the diadem. They are thus movable and could be fitted on to whatever crown the king might have worn.

The golden Nekhebet with obsidian eyes (Plate LXXVI,A) is a remarkable example of fine metal-work. The shape of the head, occiput covered with wrinkles, and at the back of the neck a partial collar of short stiff feathers, make it quite clear that the bird, representing the Upper Egyptian goddess, was *Vultur auricularis*, Daud.—the sociable vulture. This particular species is to-day plentiful in Nubia, not uncommon in the middle and southern provinces of Egypt, but seldom if ever seen in Lower Egypt.

This diadem must have had a very early origin, inasmuch as it seems to have derived its name *Seshnen* and form from the circlet-ribbon worn on the head by men and women of all classes, as far back as the Old Kingdom, some 1,500 years before the New Empire. Moreover, there is evidence enough to show that we may consider it to be among ancient Egyptian funerary appurtenances, since it is to be found mentioned among the coffin texts of the Middle Kingdom, and diadems of this kind are known to have been found thrice in connexion with royal burials : once analogous, but not identical, at Lahun, among the jewellery discovered by Professor Sir William Flinders Petrie, of a Princess Sat·Hathor·iunut of the Middle Kingdom ; and twice in the royal Theban pyramid-tombs of the Seventeenth Dynasty—one upon a burial of an Antef, the other mentioned in connexion with the ancient Egyptian plunderers of the burial of Sebek·em·Saf. In both the latter cases, curiously enough, they were found by professional tomb-thieves : that of Sebek·em·Saf is mentioned in the records of the famous royal tomb robberies which occurred during the reign of Rameses IX, when the king's diadem and the rest of the treasure found, was divided up among the thieves as metal. The discovery of the third diadem, that of an Antef king, was made less than a century ago by predatory Arabs, when it passed from hand to hand until finally it found its way to the Leyden Museum.

More than often when this type of diadem is depicted upon the monuments, the king is represented wearing it around a wig in conjunction with, and surmounted by, the *Atef* crown of Osiris.

Around the forehead, underneath a few more layers of linen, was a broad temple-band (Plate LXXVII,A) of burnished gold terminating behind and above the ears. At its extremities are slots through which linen tapes were passed and tied in a bow (Plate LXXVI,C) at the back of the head. This band held in place, over the brow and temples, a fine cambric-like linen *Khat* head-dress, unfortunately reduced by decay to such an irreparable condition that it was only recognizable from a portion of the kind of pigtail at the back (Plate LXXVI,C), common to this head-dress. Sewn to this *Khat* head-dress were the royal insignia, being a second set found upon the king (Plate LXXVI,D). The uræus, with body and tail in flexible sections of gold-work threaded together, and bordered with minute beads, was passed over the axis of the crown of the head as far back as the *lambda*, whilst the Nekhebet vulture (in this case with open wings, and with characteristics identical with those already described) covered the top of the head-dress, its body being parallel with the uræus. In order that the soft linen of this head-dress should take its conventional shape, pads of linen had been placed under it and above the temples.

Beneath the *Khat* head-dress were further layers of bandaging that covered a skull-cap of fine linen fabric, fitting tightly over the shaven head of the king, and embroidered with an elaborate device of uræi in minute gold and faience beads (Plate xxxii). The cap was kept in place by a gold temple-band similar to that just described (Plate lxxvii,a). Each uræus of the device bears in its centre the *Aten* cartouche of the Sun. The fabric of the cap was unfortunately much carbonized and decayed, but the bead-work had suffered far less, the device being practically perfect, since it adhered to the head of the king. To have attempted to remove this exquisite piece of work would have been disastrous, so it was treated with a thin coating of wax and left as it was found.

The removal of the final wrappings that protected the face of the king needed the utmost care, as owing to the carbonized state of the head there was always the risk of injury to the very fragile features. We realized the peculiar importance and responsibility attached to our task. At the touch of a sable brush the last few fragments of decayed fabric fell away, revealing a serene and placid countenance, that of a young man (Plate xxxi). The face was refined and cultured, the features well formed, especially the clearly marked lips, and I think I may here record, without wishing to encroach on the province of Drs. Derry and Saleh Bey Hamdi, the first and most striking impression to all present : namely, the remarkable structural resemblance to his father-in-law, Akh·en·

Aten—an affinity that has been visible on the monuments.

This strong likeness—for it is too evident to be set down to mere accident—presents the historian of this period with an entirely new and unexpected fact, and one which may throw some light on the ephemeral Smenkh·ka·Re, as well as on Tut·ankh·Amen, both of whom acquired the throne by marrying Akh·en·Aten's daughters. The obscurity of their parentage becomes intelligible if these two kings were the offspring of an unofficial marriage—an hypothesis by no means improbable since there are precedents for it in the royal family of the Eighteenth Dynasty. Thothmes I, son of Amen·hetep I, by an unofficial wife, Sensenb, became king by his marriage to the Crown Princess Ahmes. Hat·shep·sût was married to her half-brother, Thothmes II. In fact, when the royal wife had no male issue or surviving son, such marriages were generally the rule.

The further the problem suggested by this structural affinity visibly existing between Akh·en·Aten and Tut·ankh·Amen is studied, the more interesting grows the light thrown on contemporary history and ancient sociology.

This affinity may have been derived either directly through Akh·en·Aten or indirectly through Queen Tyi. The peculiar physical traits exhibited both in Akh·en·Aten and Tut·ankh·Amen are not to be found in the preceding Amen·hetep and Thothmes family, but they are noticeable in certain more intimate, as distinguished from more conventional, portraits of Queen Tyi, from whom Akh·en·Aten seems to have inherited his physical peculiarities. It is possible therefore that Tut·ankh·Amen may also have inherited them from the same source, and may even have been a grandson of Queen Tyi through some other offspring. But on this point of apparent blood-relationship of the two kings, the following letter from among the cuneiform correspondence found at El Amarna, seems to throw considerable light :

From Dushratta (King of Mittanni, Upper Mesopotamia) to Napkhuria (Akh·en·Aten, King of Egypt).

To Napkhuria, the King of Egypt, my brother, my son-in-law, who loves me and whom I love, has spoken thus Dushratta, the King of Mittanni, thy father-in-law, who loves thee, thy brother : I am in health. Mayst thou be in health ! To thy houses, (to) Teie, thy mother, the mistress of Egypt, (to) Tatuk-hepa, my daughter, thy wife, to thy other wives, to thy children, to thy great ones, to thy chariots, to thy horses, to thy warriors, to thy land and to everything, that belongs to thee, may there be health in a very high degree.[1]

Throughout Egyptian history, with rare exception, such as the offspring of Rameses II, the recognized children are generally confined to the issue of the chief wife—called " The Great Royal Wife "—who in the case of Akh·en·Aten would be the children of The Great Royal Wife, Nefertiti. For this reason only Nefertiti's children—all daughters—are recorded on the monuments, and the reference to Akh·en·Aten's " other wives," in the letter quoted, has hitherto been assumed to be merely a conventional presumption on King Dushratta's part.

Judging from the precedent of other Egyptian monarchs, there is every reason to believe that Akh·en·Aten had other wives, and that the phrase " Thy other wives," is something more definite than a conventional presumption. Further, in these circumstances one cannot but feel that, unless there be

[1] Knudtzon, " El-Amarna-Tafeln," 28 (= W. 24).

115

evidence to the contrary—negative evidence being no proof—this view must be accepted, especially as we know that the Mesopotamian king in question had been closely allied by marriage for several generations with the Egyptian royal house.

Thus, since **Queen Nefertiti** had no son, it is not improbable that a son by a less important marriage may have been selected as co-regent and successor, and his marriage to the eldest living official daughter would follow as a matter of course.

That either Tut·ankh·Amen was a son of Akh· en·Aten or grandson of **Queen Tyi** from other issue seems to be, for the moment, the only possible explanation of this very perceptible affinity between the two men.

There is one point more of great interest: the king's head shows that, through the convention of the period, the finer contemporary representations of the king upon the monuments, beyond all doubt, are accurate portraits of Tut·ankh·Amen.

Upon the king's neck there were two kinds of symbolical collars and twenty amulets grouped in six layers, and between each of these layers were numerous linen bandages. A " Collar of Horus " in chased sheet-gold (Plate LXXIX,B) covered the neck and formed the uppermost layer. It was attached to the neck by means of beaten gold wire, having a tag or counterbalance at the back. Among the Egyptian forms of personal ornament, such collars or collarettes were perhaps the most prevalent and certainly predominant. But that they also had a much deeper significance than mere personal adornment becomes manifest from the important part they play in this royal burial, as well as in burial ceremonial generally.

As will be seen from this and many other examples to come, they had attached to them a sort of tag acting as a kind of counterbalance at the back, which was called *mankhet* (Plate LXXVI,B). According to instructions in the Pyramid texts, the coffin texts of the Middle Kingdom, and in the rubric of the " Book of the Dead " of the New Empire, these collars with their tags were to be placed upon the deceased's neck or on his breast. They were to be of many kinds, of different materials and of different workmanship—a custom thoroughly illustrated in this burial.

The second layer or group of objects comprised four amulets, held round the neck by gold wires and placed over the throat in the following order, commencing from right to left : a red jasper *Thet*, an inscribed gold *Ded*, a green felspar *Uaz* sceptre, and a second gold *Ded* inlaid with faience (Plate LXXVIII,A). Immediately beneath this group and forming the third layer were three amulets : on the right and left side of the neck, two curious palm-leaf-like symbols in gold, and between them, tied on the same cord, a serpent *Zt* of thin chased sheet-gold (Plate LXXVIII,C). An amulet of *Thoth* in green felspar, a serpent's head in red carnelian, Horus in lapis lazuli, Anubis in green felspar, and an *Uaz* sceptre also in green felspar, formed the fourth layer (Plate LXXVIII,B). Each amulet of this group was bound to the neck by gold wire. The amulets of the fifth layer were all made of sheet-gold and chased. They were eight in number and fastened around the neck-bandages by strings (Plate LXXVIII,D). Among these eight symbols there were four distinct types : one human-headed winged serpent, one uræus, one double uræus, and five vultures, which were distributed over the throat, one partly covering the other, the human-headed winged serpent on the extreme right, the uræus and Nekhebet vulture on the left side. The texts found upon coffins dating before the New Empire give different names for each of these symbols where it is stated they should be placed " at his head." Two of the vultures seem to be of the Mūt type (*gyps fulvus*, Gm., the griffin vulture), the other three of Nekhebet. Their frailness shows that they were not intended for actual use in lifetime, but designed purely for sepulchral purposes. Below these symbols, tied round the last few bandages and forming the sixth layer, was a small sort of dog-collar formed of four rows of beads (Plate LXXVII,B).

This profusion of amulets and sacred symbols placed on the neck of the King are of extreme significance, suggesting as they do how greatly the dangers of the Underworld were feared for the dead. No doubt they were intended to protect him against injury on his journey through the hereafter. The quality and quantity of these protective symbols would naturally depend on his high rank and wealth, as well as upon the affection of his survivors. The actual meaning of many of them is not clear, nor do we know the exact nomenclature, nor the powers ascribed to them. However, we do know that they were placed there for the help and guidance of the dead, and made as beautiful and costly as possible.

In accordance with the rubric of the " Book of the Dead," whoever wears the *Ded*—the emblem of Osiris—may " enter into the realms of the dead, eat the food of Osiris, and be justified." The symbol seems to represent " Firmness," " Stability," " Preservation " and " Protection." The sacred book also states that it should be of gold and placed on the neck of him whom it is supposed to protect, and thus enable him " to enter in through the gates of Amduat . . . rise up as a perfect soul in the Underworld." He on whom the *Thet* symbol—the girdle of Isis—is hung, will be guarded by Isis and Horus, and be welcomed with joy into the Kingdom of Osiris. The book further instructs that it must be " of red jasper," that " it is the blood, incantations and power of Isis " —a charm " for the protection of this mighty one, protecting him from doing of what to him is hateful." The *Uaz* sceptre, of green felspar, seems to represent " Verdure," " Fertility " and " Eternal Youth," to which it was hoped the deceased might attain in the Underworld. The serpent's head in carnelian may have been a talisman for protection against obnoxious reptiles, with which the tunnels of Amduat were supposed to abound.

We learn also from the " Book of the Dead " that, when these mystic emblems were placed on the deceased, the magic spells associated with them were to be uttered " in solemn voice." In the case of the amulets and symbols found upon the king, there were traces of a small papyrus that bore a ritual, written in white linear hieroglyphs, but too decayed and disintegrated to allow of practical conservation, though here and there names of gods, such as Osiris and Isis, were with difficulty decipherable. I am therefore of the belief that this diminutive document, disintegrated beyond recovery, possibly pertained to such spells.

Symbols of certain divinities were duplicated, and often two were combined, especially those of Nekhebet and Buto—were they thus rendered more effective ?

These ornaments of a mystic and personal nature

upon the king, are so numerous that a full description of each in detail would far exceed the limits of this volume. I shall, however, endeavour to convey briefly the principal facts and point out their more striking features. As we have already seen, they all have a particular meaning, being seldom, if ever, placed upon the mummy for the sake of mere beauty and effect. In them will be found great ingenuity. The principles of ornamental art and symbolism have been combined with a result that they have both meaning and effect. Their details, when studied, are not mere crude imitation of nature, but natural objects, selected by symbolism and fashioned by symmetry into ornaments, with only here and there objects of purely geometrical type.

Those of the head and neck have been mentioned, and we next come to the objects found upon the body and arms.

Covering the thorax—that is from the neck down to the abdomen—were thirty-five objects, disposed in seventeen groups which formed thirteen layers, included in a complicated series of bandaging that enveloped the whole of the body.

The first of these groups was a series of four gold collars extending well below the clavicles, covering the shoulders but pendent from the neck by means of wire, and having the usual *mankhet* at the back. Each collar was placed so as only partially to cover the other. The uppermost, on the right, takes the form of the Nekhebet vulture, with open wings (Plate LXXIX,B); the second, over the left side, combines both the winged serpent Buto and the vulture Nekhebet (Plate LXXIX,A); the third, still farther over the left shoulder, is of the serpent Buto alone, but with full-spread wings (Plate LXXIX,A) ; the fourth and outermost, slightly right of the centre of the chest, takes the form of the collar of " The Hawk," which represents an ordinary collarette of tubular beads, with heads of " The Hawk " for shoulder pieces (Plate LXXIX,B). Below these different collars, dependent from a long gold wire, reaching as far down as the umbilicus (Plate XXX,Q), was a large black resin scarab, mounted upon a gold *funda* and having inlaid upon its wing-cases, in coloured glass, a *Bennu* bird (Plate XXVI,C). Inscribed upon the base of the scarab is the *Bennu* text.

The *Bennu* is a bird of the heron family *Ardeidæ* and, from the numerous existing vignettes in colour, probably *Ardea cinerea*, Linn., the common heron. This bird, which is often identified with the heart, is one of the many forms the deceased takes when he " comes forth as a soul living after death ; " it is also connected with the Sun-god. From certain corrupt representations it might be mistaken for one of the night species of herons, but as the " Book of the Dead " (Chap. XIII) mentions : " I enter as a Hawk and come forth as a Bennu at Dawn," there can be little doubt that the common heron, one of the earliest of risers among all birds, is intended.

Next to this rather meagre substitute for the well-known heart scarab, came a large pectoral-hawk-collar in chased sheet-gold (cf. Plate LXXIX,B) ; its body covering the whole of the lower part of the thorax, its wings extending upwards under the arm-pits. In the texts of the world beyond the grave it is called " The Collar of Horus," but whatever may be its powers, from the æsthetic point of view it is far surpassed by a magnificent collar of similar form,

121

found immediately underneath and almost exactly similarly placed—a pectoral-collar of Horus entirely made up of inlaid gold plaques fashioned in the manner of cloisonné work (Plate LXXX,A). This beautiful specimen of jeweller's craft forms the first of a series of three similar collars, and as the other two follow but a few layers down, I will in due course describe them together. Over this collar of cloisonné work was placed a plain sheet of papyrus paper, and under it, over the middle of the thorax, another collar of " The Hawk " (cf. Plate LXXIX,B), of chased sheet-gold, like that in the first group over the shoulders and upper chest. On either side, parallel with the right and left arms, was a gold amuletic knot (Plate LXXXIII, A), of unknown meaning. On the right and left of the lower part of the thorax, there were three amuletic gold bangles (Plate LXXXII,A): two of which bear large barrel-shaped beads of lapis lazuli and carnelian respectively, the third, an emblematic Eye-of-Horus, in iron, making the second of three examples of this rare and all important and, I might say here, historical metal found upon the king. In the *Urs* head-rest found near the king's head, this *Uzat* bracelet, and in a third and far more important example I have yet to describe, we have our first decisive proof of the introduction of that very import-ant metal, iron, into Egypt—a metal whose proper-ties, as Ruskin says, play, and have played, so import-ant a part " in Nature, Policy and Art."

By removing several more thicknesses of linen wrappings we reached the eighth layer, which con-sisted of a very large pectoral-collar of the serpent Buto, also of chased sheet-gold (cf. Plate LXXIX,A). It covered the whole of the lower part of the thorax, its huge wings extending over the shoulders, the tips of its flight feathers being bent round the neck bandages. Like the other collars of this kind it had the usual tag or *mankhet*, fastened by wire at the back. This latter specimen was the last of a series of eight of the simple metal collars found upon the neck and chest of the king, all obviously of purely amuletic nature designed for eternal inertia. Concealed under it, with just a slip of plain papyrus between, were two magnificent collars or breast-plates, one covering the other, but of a totally different workmanship. These were in the form of the two goddesses, Nekhebet and Buto, but made up of numerous gold plaques of cloisonné work, like the " Collar of Horus " just mentioned.

These breast-plates, or to call them by their real names : " The Collar of Horus," " The Collar of Nekhebet," and " The Collar of Nebti " (i.e. Nekhebet and Buto), are devised in such a unique manner as to merit special attention. Each is composed of a very large number of separate gold plaques, engraved on the back and minutely inlaid on the front with opaque coloured glass in the manner of cloisonné work ; the glass imitating turquoise, red jasper, and lapis lazuli stones. " The Collar of Horus " (Plate LXXX,A) is composed of thirty-eight plaques ; that of Nekhebet (Plate LXXX,B) of 256 pieces ; and of Nebti 171 pieces (Plate LXXXI,B). Each plaque is fundamentally similar in make, differing only in modification of form and colour, in accordance with the feathers of the " district " of the wing it belongs to, or, as the case may be, the particular feather or part of feather it represents. These plaques are divided up into groups which form the principal " districts " of the wing, i.e. the primaries, secondaries, coverts, lesser coverts, and the so-called " bastard wing " ; each plaque of cloisonné of the group or " district " having tiny eyelets on their upper and lower margins by which they were threaded together with bead borders. The various parts of the wings being thus firmly held together, make both gorgeous, intricate, and at the same time flexible collars.

We now arrive at the eleventh and twelfth layers of objects, which comprise a series of more personal jewellery. Hanging over the upper part of the chest and secured around the neck by means of lapis lazuli and gold flexible straps, was a small pectoral ornament fashioned to represent a sated vulture (Plate LXXXIV,A). This exquisite example of goldsmith's work, perhaps the finest of all found upon the king, inlaid with green glass, lapis lazuli and carnelian, seems with little doubt, to be intended to symbolize the Southern goddess—Nekhebet of El Kab; for the characteristics of the bird, so beautifully rendered here, are certainly those of the sociable vulture, and are identical with the vulture insignia of Upper Egypt belonging to the diadem (Plate LXXVI,A). The clasp of its suspending straps takes the form of two miniature hawks, but even more charming is the finely chased under surface of the pectoral itself, where, as a sort of *quid pro quo*, around the neck of the bird goddess, in high relief, a tiny pectoral is represented in the form of the king's cartouche. Still lower on the chest of the mummy was another pectoral, in form, three scarabs of lapis lazuli, supporting above the symbol of heaven, disks of the sun and moon (Plate LXXXIV,c). Their posterior legs hold the *Neb* emblems of sovereignty upon a horizontal bar, from which marguerites bloom and lotus flowers pend.

The beetles here, no doubt, have some mysterious connexion with the solar and lunar disks they hold in their fore-legs. The association of the scarab with the disk is a common occurrence in religious texts. In all probability the lunar disk—in this case the older orb growing out of the younger crescent—symbolizes the god Thoth, who personifies the moon. Both disks were in great part the original sources of Egyptian mythology, and no matter what system of religious worship on the part of those ancients prevailed, behind that veil or cult the sun was always the principal, not alone with the living, but even more with the dead. In the "Book of the Dead" (Chap. xv) we find : " O thou Radiant Orb, who arisest each day from the horizon, shine thou upon the face of Osiris [the deceased] who adoreth thee at Dawn, and propitiateth thee at the Gloaming."

We have in such specimens of private jewellery, the culminating style of the Eighteenth Dynasty in ornamental art—natural forms and symbolism associated to gratify and attract. In this case, and in other examples to come, the execution of the beetles is remarkable to a degree. Though conventionally treated, each essential detail of the insect is observed and its most striking features shown : the horny prothorax, and elytra (wing-cases) are rendered in deliberate manner ; the *clypeus* or shield, that is the edge of the broad flat head, is notched with angular teeth arranged in a semicircle ; the fore-legs, bow-shaped, are properly armed on the outside with five strong teeth, and like the four long and slender hinder limbs, are carved free ; the last pair, slightly bowed,

end with their sharp claw. Even the articulation of
the underparts of this famous dung-beetle are shown,
and their different functions equally realized.

Immediately below, under bandages of gossamer
thickness, were three more pectorals (Plate LXXXIV,B),
one placed over the centre of the thorax, and one
on each side, slightly lower down. The two outer
ones were suspended from the neck by gold chains
terminating with lotus flowers, carnelian beads, and
heart-shaped pendants at the back, below the nape of
the neck. The central pectoral, also hung from the
neck, had, at the ends of its three-string necklace of
faience and gold beads, a small pectoral-shaped clasp
of *Ded* and *Thet* symbols. The pectoral on the right
side takes the form of a solar-hawk of gold—the body
of open-work enclosing a peculiar green stone. That
of the left side, also of gold and brilliantly inlaid,
seems so devised as to incorporate a play upon the
king's name: it is composed of a winged scarab
beetle holding in its fore-legs a lunar disk and crescent, in its posterior legs the plural determinatives
and the *heb* festival sign; thus reading, "Kheperu·heb·
Aah" in place of "Kheperu·neb·Re." The central
pectoral, an *uzat* eye, having in heraldic fashion the
uræus of Buto in front and the vulture Nekhebet
behind, has its under surface of finely chased gold
and upper surface inlaid with lapis lazuli and an
unidentified stone of pale green colour somewhat
suggestive of epidote. All these pectorals show traces
of actual wear such as would be caused by use during
lifetime, and were, no doubt, personal ornaments.

The heart pendants of carnelian encased in gold
and minutely inlaid with the king's name, recall the
chapter in the "Book of the Dead" upon the heart "of

carnelian," where it says : " It is granted to the soul of Osiris [the deceased] to come forth upon the earth to do whatsoever his genius willeth." From the disposition of the latter three pectorals—that of the eye in the centre, the solar orb on the right, and the lunar disk on the left—it is tempting to connect them with the " Pair of Eyes " considered as the Sun and Moon, attributed to Osiris as well as Re and other deities : " His right eye is the Sun and his left is the Moon." I should also mention here that the lunar disks on the jewellery of this tomb are always of gold-silver alloy, in contradistinction to the gold solar disks which have a copper alloy.

Below these five pectorals came the lowest layer of all, next to the flesh, though not in actual contact with it ; for there were several thicknesses of linen underneath, charred almost to powder. This last layer consisted of an elaborate collarette of minute blue glass and gold beads, threaded after the manner of a bead mat, and having all the appearance of a bib. In design it was so made that the gold beads, worked into the blue glass beads, formed yellow chevrons or waves of water upon a blue background ; the collarette having flexible golden hawk clasps as shoulder-pieces, a border of gold sequins and an outer margin of gold drop pendants.

Included in the wrappings of the thorax and abdomen were two groups of finger-rings : over the wrist of the right hand a group of five, and beside the wrist of the left hand, a group of eight rings. These were of massive gold, lapis lazuli, cloudy-white and green chalcedony, turquoise, and one of black resin (Plate LXXXV). Often, even when the devices upon the bezels included the king or his cartouches, his name was also engraved on either side of the loop of the ring, or on the under surface of the bezel; a distinguishing mark by which finger-rings may be identified as personal property of the Pharaoh. This suggests an early form of the hall-mark.

Before dealing with the several objects that were placed upon the abdomen, I will next describe the arms, forearms and hands, which, though included in the bandages of the body, were first separately wrapped. The forearms were flexed over the upper part of the abdomen, the left being placed slightly higher than the right. The right hand was over the left hip, the left hand reaching the lower right side of the thorax (Plate XXXIII). Enclosed in the wrappings of the arms were two quite small amuletic bangles, which broke away with the decayed fabric during our examination of the mummy, but from the positions in which they fell, on either side, they had evidently been placed just above the elbows. That of the right arm took the form of a thick gold wire bracelet bearing a large rough green stone bead, and six finely made *uzat* eyes of various materials (Plate LXXXII,A). The one, belonging to the left arm, was a small gold bangle with swivel joint secreted under three beads and, on the opposite side of the circle, an exquisitely carved carnelian *Ment* bird (Plate LXXXII,A). This *Ment* bird, with the solar orb upon its rump, probably represents one of the mythical transformations of the Sun-god, mentioned in the " Book of the Dead " (especially in Chap. LXXXVI), " whereby one assumeth the form of a swift." There can be little doubt that this *Ment* bird is of the family of the swifts (*Cypselidæ*), though it is sometimes confused in those religious texts with the *wr* bird, of the family of swallows and martins (*Hirundinidæ*), but it could never be of the genera of doves and pigeons (*Columbidæ*), as I have seen mentioned. Though it is not dissimilar to the little grey swift (*Cypsellus parvus,* Licht.) of the southern provinces of Egypt, in all probability it is intended to represent the ordinary Egyptian swift (*Cypsellus pallidus,* Shelley). The peculiar feature of the Egyptian swift is that it makes its abode in large colonies in the cliffs, far back in the hills that border the desert plain, whence it comes down to the Nile Valley at early morn and returns late in the evening. For the reason that it comes forth screaming at sunrise and returns, with even shriller notes, when the sun sinks, it may be that the ancient Egyptians connected it in some way with the transformation of the Sun-god, or the souls of the departed which came forth by day with the sun and return at night. The chapter says : " I am the *Ment* bird . . ." and at the end, " If this chapter be known he will re-enter after coming forth by day."

Both the forearms were smothered from elbow to wrist with magnificent bracelets (Plates xxxiii, lxxxvi), seven on the right and six on the left forearm, composed of intricate scarab devices, granular gold-work, open-work carnelian plaques, rich gold and electrum work ; some having wrist-bands of flexible bead-work, others of elaborate geometric and floral design, inlaid with semi-precious stones and polychrome glass. Their diameter shows that they had encircled a very small arm, none of them was of sepulchral nature, but all were obviously once personal ornaments that had been worn during life.

Each finger and thumb having been primarily wrapped in fine strips of linen, was enclosed in a gold sheath. Upon the second and third fingers of the left hand was a gold ring : upon the bezel of one is the lunar barque on a deep blue ground, upon the bezel of the other, that of the second digit, the king, minutely engraved in intaglio, is represented kneeling and offering the figure of Truth (Plate LXXXV).

We now come to the abdomen, distributed over which, in almost as many layers, were ten objects which I will record in the order they were found, beginning with the uppermost layers. At the left flank, within the first few outer bandages, was a curious Y-shaped amulet of sheet-gold and an oval gold plate (Plate LXXXIII,A), placed one immediately above the other. The meaning of the Y-shaped amulet is not clear. A similar object depicted in the Middle Kingdom coffin texts carries the name *abt* or *abet*, which seems to convey something of the nature of a baton, but as this symbol forms in shape part of the hieroglyphic determinative *mnkh* for clothing or linen, it would seem more likely to have some reference to the bandages, or bandaging of the mummy, the more so, as the second object—the oval metal plate found with it—has direct relation with, and was intended to cover, the incision in the left flank of the mummy, through which the embalmers removed the internal organs for separate preservation. The next object in sequence was a T-shaped symbol (Plate LXXXIII,A) made of sheet-gold resembling a draughtsman's T-square. It was placed in the wrappings over the left side of the abdomen and extended down the upper part of the left thigh. So far as I am able to judge it has no parallel and its meaning is unknown. Encircling the waist, the two front ends as low as the hips, was a narrow chased gold girdle

(Plate xxxiv), to which, in all probability, belong a ceremonial apron and a dagger found over the thighs, the description of which will be given later. Then came a plain dark blue faience collar made up of minute beads, which had been included in the wrappings over the left side of the abdomen, as high up as the umbilicus, and reaching down over the pudenda. It has semicircular shoulder-pieces, but its distinctive name is difficult to identify among the painted texts devoted to collars on the Middle Kingdom coffins; although it is of dark blue faience it may possibly be intended to take the place of the " Collar of Lapis Lazuli," which apparently can have either rounded or hawk-headed shoulder-pieces. Over the middle of the abdomen was a circlet, such as an armlet or anklet, of gold, inlaid with coloured opaque glass. It belongs to a series of eight of similar kind (four pairs) (Plate LXXXII,B), varying only in their inlay, found elsewhere on the mummy, mostly over the thighs down to the knees. They are of purely sepulchral nature.

Having carefully removed the above objects found upon the abdomen, together with a few more layers of bandaging which were in a very decayed state, another chased gold waist-band or girdle was exposed (Plate xxxiv). Tucked under it obliquely—the haft to the right of the abdomen, the point of the sheath over the upper part of the left thigh—was a most interesting and handsome dagger (Plate LXXXVII,A) that certainly calls for admiration. It has a handle ornamented with bright yellow granulated gold decoration, encircled by alternate bands of cloisonné work of semi-precious stones and glass, and terminating at the hilt with a rich chain-scroll, applied in gold wire with rope pattern border. In contrast to its ornate handle, the blade of the dagger, of especially hardened gold, is simple and of beautiful form. Its surface is unadorned save for deep grooves down its centre, which converge at the point, and are surmounted with a finely engraved lily " palmette " design below a narrow band of somewhat archaic geometric pattern. The blade is housed in a richly ornamented gold sheath. On the front it has a frieze of " palmette " ornament, and the whole of the field covered with a feather-pattern in cloisonné fashion, which terminates at the lower point with a jackal's head of embossed gold (Plate LXXXVIII,A). The design on the back is in many ways more attractive; for it has embossed in high relief on its gold surface, an extremely interesting scene of wild animals, suggesting that the dagger was for the chase (Plate LXXXVIII,B). Here the subjects are : below a frieze of inscription and scroll-pattern, a young male ibex attacked by a lion; a male calf galloping with a slughi hound upon its back, biting its tail; a cheetah (tail annulated) having sprung on to the shoulders of an adult male ibex, is mauling its neck, whilst from underneath a lion attacks the antelope; below, is a galloping bull worried by a hound; and lastly a quite young calf is represented in full retreat. Between the exquisitely rendered animals, are various plants treated conventionally; the scene terminating at the bottom by an ornate floral device which, like the whole scheme of decoration upon the dagger and sheath, suggests affinity to the art of the Ægean or Mediterranean islands. However, the character of the hieroglyphs of the king's cartouche upon the knob, and of the short legend " the Good God, Lord of Valour, Kheperu·neb·Re " (Tut·ankh· Amen) upon the frieze of the sheath, as well as the general treatment of detail, and of the animals in the attempt at the picturesque and ornamental, suffice to show that this admirable piece of workmanship is the handiwork of an Egyptian and not of an alien, whatever the influence may be. In this superficial study it may suffice here to say that those islands, once governed by the Egyptians of the fifteenth century B.C., and called by them " The-islands-in-the-midst-of-the-sea," formed the link between the art of the Nile, Asia Minor and European civilizations.

The girdle (Plate XXXIV) under which the dagger was tucked is similar in type to the first example already mentioned, save for difference of the pattern chased upon it. It had attached to the front fastening or name-plate, stamped with the king's cartouche, an apron composed of some twenty strings of different faience and glass beads, connected at intervals by gold spacers or connectors. The beads had to a large extent fallen away from their decayed threads, but from our photographic records and notes, their original order can be recovered. On the centres of the backs of the two girdles are projecting cylinder-like attachments for ceremonial pendent tails, such as you see depicted hanging from the waist-bands of kings on the monuments, and which, in this case, were actually discovered under the mummy extending down between the legs. Unfortunately, by being the lowest of all the objects in the coffin, these most interesting ritualistic tails suffered considerable damage by becoming embedded, like a fossil in its matrix, in the thick hardened mass of congealed unguents that was poured over the mummy. They had to be extricated by means of hammer and chisel and, as they are composed of beads—one of them of a close mesh of minute faience beads woven over a core of fibre—restoration to their original state will be a very difficult task. They appear to be quite similar to those found by Mace and Winlock ("The Tomb of Senebtisi," p. 70 ff.) and in this case both the examples of girdles, the apron and the tails, seem to have been made for tomb use only, though there can be little doubt that they are replicas of those used for ceremonial purposes during life.

Coinciding with the lowest layer of ornaments—the last three pectorals and the bib-like bead collarette—found on the thorax, and in reality belonging to that group, were two more pieces of jewellery : (1) a pectoral in the form of an *uzat* eye of brilliant blue faience, suspended by a necklace of equally bright blue faience, plain yellow gold and red granulated gold cylindrical beads, which from their brilliance have an almost barbaric effect ; and (2) around the waist a girdle of closely strung cylindrical and discoid beads in gold and faience, which has yet to be cleaned and remounted. The interest of this latter peculiar segmented worm-like bead girdle, is that it interprets the use of the quantities of beads prominent among the famous discoveries of Egyptian jewellery of the Middle Kingdom at Dashur and Lahûn.

Having seen the material that decked the king's head and neck, body and arms, we have now to see what was placed over his legs. The first object revealed to us, while removing piece by piece the masses of padding and bandages that the embalmers found necessary to pack and bind the thighs into orthodox mummy form, was the ceremonial apron (Plate LXXXIII,B) belonging, in all probability, to the first chased gold girdle that we found around the waist. This is made up of seven gold plates inlaid with opaque polychrome glass, the plates being threaded together by means of bead borders. It extended from the lower portion of the abdomen down to the knees, corresponding in position and size to the aprons depicted on the dress of Egyptian monarchs pictured upon the monuments. Beside the apron, along the right thigh, and I believe also belonging to the same girdle as the apron, was an extraordinarily fine and unique dagger (Plate LXXXVII,B) housed in a gold scabbard (Plate LXXXVIII,C). The haft of the dagger is of granulated gold, embellished at intervals with collars of cloisonné work of coloured stones, and is surmounted with a knob of turned rock crystal ; but the astonishing and unique feature of this beautiful weapon is that the blade is of iron, still bright and resembling steel !

This astounding and historical fact, to digress from the main subject, marks one of the first steps in the decline of the Egyptian Empire—the greatest empire of the Age of Bronze. This metal, iron, of which we have found three examples upon the king's mummy, was in all probability introduced by the Hittites into Egypt from Asia Minor at the time of Tut·ankh·Amen, probably in small quantity when, no doubt, it was looked upon as a speciality. Rather more than a century later, when iron began to overtake bronze in Syria, a tablet records how one of the Hittite kings undertook to supply Rameses the Great with a shipment of that metal, and that a sword of iron was sent as a gift to the Pharaoh. With regard to Egypt, iron is one more indication of foreign influence at this period. If the history of Egypt be studied, from that moment gradual foreign intrusion becomes more and more noticeable, ending eventually in foreign domination. Bronze could not fight against the superiority of iron, and as bronze took the place of copper, so iron took the place of bronze—just as in our day iron has been superseded by steel.

Both daggers—that found on the abdomen and this specimen—like those of Aah·hetep and Kames in the Cairo Museum, dating from the beginning of this dynasty, are foreign in shape. They are of a style introduced into Egypt during the Hyksos invasion. Before then the handle of the dagger was of a different style. It was held between the second and third fingers, the knob against the palm of the hand, and therefore thrust instead of being used, as was the later form, with a downward stroke from the elbow.

Tucked in the hollow of the left groin was a broad barrel-shaped wristlet or anklet (Plate LXXXII,B), typical of those ornaments represented on the wrists and ankles of figures in the mural decorations of private chapel and tomb. This was the only specimen of its kind found on the king, whereas, judging from the mural paintings, one would have expected, at least, one or three pairs, for the arms, forearms and ankles.

It was here we found the royal insignia of the diadem. That of Upper Egypt, the Nekhebet vulture head, on the right thigh near the knee, and that of Buto, the uræus of Lower Egypt, along the left thigh ; they, as heretofore mentioned (p. 110), being placed (Plate XXX,R, S) in correct orientation in accordance to the country to which they belong. The remainder of the ornaments, disposed over the legs, were seven circlets (Plate LXXXII,B) included in three distinct layers of wrappings over and between the thighs, and four collarettes of cloisonné work (Plate LXXXI,A) which were folded and crushed over the knees and the shins. The single circlet found over the abdomen with these seven specimens makes up a series of eight, i.e. four pairs ; the four collarettes with their tags or *mankhets* make two pairs of a kind, each pair differing only in the number and system of cloisonné plates of which they are made up. They answer in the lists upon the coffins of the Middle Kingdom, to those which have a metal basis worked in cloisonné inlay of semi-precious stones, though in this case, they being of the New Empire, opaque coloured glass imitates and takes the place of the real stones.

Lastly, upon the feet were gold sandals (Plate XXXV,A), made out of sheet metal, embossed to imitate rush-work. Each digit was enclosed in a separate gold stall, having details, such as the nails and first joints of the toes, engraved upon them. Around the right ankle was a gold wire bangle of somewhat crude workmanship (Plate LXXXII,B).

These last items complete the 143 objects that were carefully disposed over the head, neck, thorax, abdomen, and limbs of the young king, in 101 separate groups.

I have described them, beginning with those on the head downwards, ending with the feet, and have dealt in each case with the uppermost object first, and have ended with the lowest nearest the mummy itself last. But it must be remembered that in the original order of sequence of the wrapping of the mummy, the lowest objects, that is those nearest the king, were the first placed upon his mummy, and those included in the uppermost wrappings last.

The objects may be divided into two categories :

those which are real and personal property ; and those which are purely religious and amuletic. Those of a personal character are of a much finer and more permanent nature ; the others, in general, are of less permanent make and of simpler kind—they were for sepulchral use only and amuletic in meaning.

The beautiful pectorals (Plate LXXXIV), possibly the finer examples of the cloisonné collars (Plates LXXX, LXXXI), the majority of the rings (Plate LXXXV) and bracelets (Plates XXXIII, LXXXVI), the daggers (Plate LXXXVII) and diadem (Plate LXXV), were—there is little doubt—personal jewellery ; while the various other collars and amulets of chased sheet-gold, the inlaid amulets, the bead collarettes, the toe and finger stalls, the sandals, the apron and the symbolical tails, were only intended to be beneficial for the dead king.

The beautiful objects give us a vivid insight into the work of the skilled craftsmen of Thebes. The Theban Court artisans were naturally picked men, and here, in this discovery, we can discern the refinement of their art. I say refinement, for the actual technique in many ways is perhaps not so fine as regards finish or simplicity as that of the Middle Kingdom jewellers, but if the technical skill be not so good, the taste displayed surpasses all our expectations. Especially when we remember that we are dealing with material belonging to the very end of the Eighteenth Dynasty. A certain ornateness and lack of high finish that may be here visible, are but steps in decadence creeping in with iron and other foreign influences. Nevertheless it would tax our best goldsmiths and jewellers of to-day to surpass the refinement which is found in those royal ornaments.

From the mass of material upon the mummy, of

which space has only allowed a cursory description, we can begin to realize the profusion of wealth with which it seems to have been customary to adorn the mortal remains of the ancient Pharaohs buried in the Valley. It impressively conveys to us the inner feelings of that ancient people for their dead—feelings which, though in many ways latent, are exhibited from time to time, among the fellahîn to-day. The dead are generally first in their thoughts at all their festivals. They assemble in the early morning after prayer to visit the graves of their relatives, especially on the occasion of the commencement of *El Eed E' Sugheiyir* (The Small Festival), the first day of the month of *Showwal*, after *Ramadân* (the month of abstinence) when they carry, as I have witnessed at Thebes, palm-branches to lay upon the tombs, and are also provided with various foodstuffs to distribute to the poor in honour of their dead. Later, clad in their best and newest clothes, they visit their living friends.

Before I bring this narrative to a close I should mention that the charred remains of the mummy itself show no traces of the cause or causes of the young king's death, but the masses of swathings, ornaments and amulets, at least conveyed to us the care that was taken with his mortal remains and for his future life. A feeling, a sense and a care, that cannot be better expressed than in the words of Sir Gardner Wilkinson, who did so much wonderful research work in Egypt during the early half of the last century :

" Love and respect were not merely shown to the sovereign during his lifetime, but were continued to his memory after his death ; and the manner in which his funeral obsequies were celebrated tended to show, that, though their benefactor was no more, they retained a grateful sense of his goodness, and admiration for his virtues. And what, says the historian [meaning Diodorus], can convey a greater testimony of sincerity, free from all colour of dissimulation, when the person who conferred it no longer lives to witness the honour done to his memory ? "

APPENDICES

APPENDIX I

REPORT UPON THE EXAMINATION OF TUT·ANKH·AMEN'S MUMMY

By Douglas E. Derry, M.B., Ch.B., Professor of Anatomy, Egyptian University

IN the Museum of Antiquities in Cairo may be seen the mummies of many of the most famous Pharaohs of ancient Egypt, kings who left behind them great monuments, magnificent temples and colossal statues, and whose names have become as familiar as those of modern monarchs, though separated from them in time by some thirty to forty centuries. Little was it expected that a king of obscure origin with a short and uneventful reign should one day attract the attention of the whole world, and that, not on account of fame attaching to himself, but to the single fact that while the tomb of every other Pharaoh yet discovered had been rifled in ancient times, that of Tut·ankh·Amen was found practically intact. In the confined space of this small tomb was contained an assemblage of royal possessions such as had never before been seen. What then must have been the contents of the tombs of Seti I, of Rameses III, and others, in one of whose halls alone all the wealth of the tomb of Tut·ankh·Amen might have been stored? But the tomb of every one of these monarchs had been entered by thieves, and that not once or twice, but over and over again until not a shred of the original tomb furniture remains.

The wrappings of the royal mummies had been torn open in search of jewels and in some cases much damage had been done to the body itself. Most of the royal mummies were rewrapped at least once by the priests, many of them more than once, but the persistence of the robberies eventually necessitated the removal of the bodies of many of the kings and queens to special hiding-places which were only discovered in recent times owing to the perpetration of fresh robberies, and the mummies were then brought to the museum in Cairo. As a result of these frequent disturbances it is not surprising that some doubt exists as to the identity of certain of the mummies which had been removed from their own coffins and reburied in others often of later date. With one or two exceptions none of the Pharaohs has been found in his original tomb, few in their own coffins, and none except Tut·ankh·Amen has ever been seen in the wrappings, coffins, sarcophagus and tomb in which he was originally laid to rest.

A word may fittingly be said here in defence of the unwrapping and examination of Tut·ankh·Amen. Many persons regard such an investigation as in the nature of sacrilege, and consider that the king should have been left undisturbed. From what I have said as to the persistent robberies of the tombs from the most ancient times up to the present, it will be understood that when once such a discovery as that of the tomb of Tut·ankh·Amen has been made, and news of the wealth of objects contained in it has become known, to leave anything whatever of value in the tomb is to court trouble. The knowledge that objects of immense value lay hidden a few feet below ground would certainly invite the attempt to obtain them,

Appendix I

and while the employment of a strong guard might suffice for a time to prevent any such attempt meeting with success, any remission of vigilance would be instantly seized upon, and objects which are now safely housed for all time in the Museum of Antiquities would have been destroyed, while others would reappear in a more or less dilapidated state in the hands of dealers through whom they would soon be dispersed to all parts of the civilized world. The value of the intact collection to scientists is incalculable, while the instruction and delectation provided for the public by the exhibition of these ancient works of art is in itself an argument of immense weight in favour of their preservation in a museum. The same argument applies to the unwrapping of the king, whose person is thus spared the rude handling of thieves, greedy to obtain the jewels massed in profusion on his body. History is furthermore enriched by the information which the anatomical examination may supply, which in this case, as will presently be detailed, was of considerable importance.

The preservation of the dead body, brought to its highest pitch by the ancient Egyptians in the art of mummification, has always excited the greatest interest. Much has been written on the subject and the methods employed at different periods have been investigated by Professor Elliot Smith [1] in the royal mummies preserved in the Museum of Antiquities, as well as in a number of mummies of priests and priestesses of the Twenty-First Dynasty.[2] From these and other researches we have a tolerably clear

[1] "Catalogue Général des Antiquités Egyptiennes du Musée du Caire, The Royal Mummies."

[2] "A Contribution to the Study of Mummification in Egypt" (Mémoires de l'Institut Égyptien, tome V, fascicule I, 1906).

picture of the manner in which the embalming process was carried out. Nevertheless there can be little doubt that a large measure of its success is due to the peculiarly dry climate of Egypt, apart from which it is questionable whether the most perfectly embalmed body would have persisted unchanged, as some have, for nearly four thousand years. The vast majority of mummies examined prove to have had the internal organs removed through an opening made in the abdominal wall. By this means the most decomposable parts were got rid of, and the subsequent immersion of the body in a saline bath seemed to account sufficiently for the excellence of the results obtained. But recently a series of the most perfect mummies yet examined has been described by Mr. H. E. Winlock and myself from the tombs in the vicinity of the Eleventh Dynasty Mentu·hetep Temple at Deir el Bahari, in which there is no abdominal or other incision, and from which none of the organs whatever has been taken away. Such perfect preservation without mummification is also exhibited in the remains of some of the predynastic race in Egypt, but these people were usually buried in sand without coffins and the rapid desiccation so produced, by heat and the favourable draining properties of sand, is understandable. The case of the Eleventh Dynasty mummies just referred to is at first sight entirely different, as they were bandaged with great care and placed in coffins and sarcophagi, and so might be expected to have suffered from the effects of enclosed humidity, nevertheless, as already said, they are amongst the most perfect examples of artificial preservation yet seen, and a careful examination of all the facts seems to point to the extreme dryness of the area in which they were discovered as the principal factor in attainment of this result.

Such methods, or lack of them, are however rare and in the following dynasty, the Twelfth, as exemplified in the mummies of certain nobles discovered at Sakkara, the removal of the viscera through an opening made in the abdominal wall was already practised, and there is evidence that it existed even earlier. The mode of preserving the body in the Eighteenth Dynasty, to the end of which period Tut·ankh·Amen belongs, has been described by Professor Elliot Smith in the catalogue to which reference has been made. This observer examined most of the kings of the Eighteenth Dynasty and among them some of the ancestors of Tut·ankh·Amen.

Unfortunately much doubt exists as to the accuracy of the identification of the mummy said to be that of Amen·hetep III, the grandfather of Tut·ankh· Amen. Professor Elliot Smith points out that the methods employed in the preservation of this king, and in particular the curious practice of packing materials of various kinds beneath the skin of the limbs, trunk, neck, etc., with the object of restoring as far as possible to the dead body some resemblance to its appearance in life, was not introduced until the Twenty-First Dynasty nearly three centuries later. It is possible, therefore, that this is an example of the mistakes which were apt to be made, when, owing to the frequent robberies of the tombs and desecration of the bodies, the priests undertook the removal and rewrapping of the mummies. The mummy in question was in a coffin of much later date bearing the names of three kings, amongst which was that of Amen·hetep III, hence the identification, but it is probably that of a person of a later period.

This statement receives further confirmation in the examination of Amen·hetep's descendants, for it is improbable that had this method been introduced in the time of Amen·hetep III, it would have been discarded in that of his immediate successors. The remains we now have of his son Akh·en·Aten consist, it is true, of little else than the bones, but had his body and limbs been packed in the manner described by Professor Elliot Smith for his supposed father, some indication at least would assuredly have remained of the process. In the case of Tut·ankh·Amen as we shall see, the methods employed were those in vogue in his dynasty and agree very closely with the descriptions given by Professor Elliot Smith for other undoubted mummies of the period. We must therefore regretfully conclude that, so far, the mummy of Amen·hetep III has not been identified.

The examination of the mummy of King Tut·ankh·Amen was begun on November 11, 1925, in collaboration with Dr. Saleh Bey Hamdi. When first seen the mummy was lying in the coffin to which it was firmly fixed by some resinous material which had been poured over the body after it was placed in the coffin. Over the head and shoulders, and reaching well down on the chest, was the beautiful gold mask which is an effigy of the king's face, head-dress and collar. This could not be removed as it also was stuck to the bottom of the coffin by the resin, which had dried into a mass of stony hardness. The mummy was enclosed in a sheet which was held in position by bandages passing round the shoulders, hips, knees and ankles. At the outset it was clear that no sort of orderly unwrapping was possible, as the bandages were in a state of extreme fragility and crumbled at a touch. This seems to have been due to the inclusion of some humidity at the time of interment, as well as the decomposition of the unguents, which generated a high temperature and thus brought about a sort of spontaneous combustion which carbonized the wrappings. This has frequently been observed and has given rise to the idea that mummies so affected have been burnt. Other facts, already pointed out by Dr. Carter, bear witness to the same effect of damp. Had the tomb been absolutely dry the textile fabrics would have been in perfect condition.

As all operations had to be conducted with the mummy *in situ*, Dr. Carter suggested that the upper layers of bandages might be strengthened with melted paraffin wax in order that they might be incised and turned back with less disturbance to the original arrangement. This was done and, when the wax had set, an incision was carried down the middle line of the mummy wrappings from the lower edge of the mask to the feet. This penetrated only a few millimetres and the two flaps so produced were turned outwards. A number of objects came to view included in the layers of bandages, and hereafter it became necessary to remove the latter piecemeal in order to expose the objects, so that they might be numerically recorded and photographed before being touched. Throughout the course of this part of the work, which was necessarily slow, the increasing state of disintegration of the wrappings was noticeable. These in many places were reduced to dust, and in no case could any length of bandage or sheet be removed intact. Thus it was impossible to follow the system of bandaging, as may be easily done when the condition of the mummy wrappings is such as to allow of the removal layer by layer of the bandages, sheets or actual clothing, which may have been employed in the final stages of the ritual of mummification. So far as could be ascertained the general principles of bandaging with which we are familiar in mummies, and which have been described in detail by Professor Elliot Smith in his Catalogue of the Royal Mummies in the Museum of Antiquities in Cairo, were followed in the case of Tut·ankh·Amen. Numerous wads of linen were so placed as to fill up the inequalities produced by the objects which were included in the bandages, in order to enable the embalmer to apply the bandages smoothly round the body and limbs.

Some of the linen used in the wrapping of the king was of the nature of the finest cambric, notably that first encountered when the examination was commenced and again immediately next to the body itself. The intermediate bandages were of coarser make, and at one stage folded sheets of linen were placed along the front of the body as far as the knees and retained in place by transverse bandages. The practice of using immense quantities of linen in the form of folded sheets appears to have been common in the Twelfth Dynasty, one such sheet, removed by myself from the mummy of a noble, measured 64 feet in length by 5 feet in width, this being folded to produce a covering eight layers thick. In his account of the removal of the bandages from the mummy styled Amen·hetep III (*loc. cit. supra*) Professor Elliot Smith notes the presence of several folded sheets, as well as " a number of rolls of bandage . . . in front of the body, apparently left there inadvertently." These latter may well have been employed originally to fill up the spaces and inequalities existing between the limbs and body, a practice frequently seen in mummies of all periods, and with the same object as in the case where they were used in connexion with the funerary ornaments placed on the body. Over the thorax the bandages were made to pass alternately in crossed and transverse layers, the crossed bandages being carried over one shoulder then round the body returning over the opposite shoulder.

In the crutch the crossed arrangements of the bandages was easily visible, though the method used to produce this could not be followed out, both on account of the fragility of the wrappings and the fact that the body could not be moved at this stage from the coffin.

All the limbs were separately wrapped before being enclosed by the bandages which enveloped the body as a whole. The upper limbs were so placed that the king lay with his forearms across his body, the right forearm resting on the upper part of the abdomen with the hand on the crest of the left hip bone. The left forearm lay higher up over the lower ribs, with the hand lying on the right side of the thorax, between the latter and the right upper-arm. Both forearms were loaded with bracelets from the bend of the elbow to the wrist. All fingers and toes were bandaged individually and gold sheaths (Plate xxxv,A) were then adjusted over each before the bandage covering in the whole hand or foot was applied. In the case of the feet gold sandals (Plate xxxv,A) were put on at the same time as the toe-sheaths and after the first few layers of bandage had been applied, in order to allow the bar of the sandal to be adjusted between the great and second toes— the whole being then enclosed in a bandage.

When first exposed, the upper part of the bandaged head was seen to be surrounded by a double fillet which overlay a bandage encircling the head. This fillet, which somewhat resembled a Bedouin head-rope, but of a much smaller diameter, was composed of some sort of vegetable fibre around which twine had been tightly wound (p. 110, Plate xxv). The circular bandage in its turn held in place a sheet which passed over the head and face. Beneath this sheet the bandages passed alternately across the head and transversely round the head and face. When the face was finally exposed some resinous material was found plugging the nostrils, and a layer had been placed over the eyes and between the lips.

General Appearance of Head (Plates xxxi, xxxii). The head appears to be clean-shaved and the skin of the scalp is covered by a whitish substance probably of the nature of fatty acid. Two abrasions on the skin covering the upper part of the occipital bone, had probably been caused by the pressure of the diadem which was enclosed by the tightly-wound head bandages. The plugs filling the nostrils and the material laid over the eyes were found by Mr. Lucas to consist of some woven fabric, impregnated with resin. Mr. Lucas also examined some whitish spots on the skin over the upper part of the back and shoulders, and these proved to be composed of " common salt with a small admixture of sodium sulphate " in all probability derived from the natron used in the embalming process. The eyes are partly open and had not been interfered with in any way. The eyelashes are very long. The cartilaginous portion of the nose had become partially flattened by the pressure of the bandages. The upper lip is slightly elevated revealing the large central incisor teeth. The ears are small and well made. The lobes of the ears are perforated by a circular hole measuring 7·5 mm. in diameter.

The skin of the face is of a greyish colour and is very cracked and brittle. On the left cheek, just in front of the lobe of the ear, is a rounded depression, the skin filling it, resembling a scab. Round the circumference of the depression, which has slightly raised edges, the skin is discoloured. It is not possible to say what the nature of this lesion may have been.

The head when fully uncovered was seen to be very broad and flat topped (platycephalic) with markedly projecting occipital region. Even allowing for the shrinkage both of the scalp and the posterior muscles of the neck, this prominence is still remarkable. There is pronounced bulging of the left side of the occiput and the post-bregmatic region is depressed. The general shape of the head, which is of a very uncommon type, is so like that of his father-in-law, Akh·en·Aten, that it is more than probable there was a close relationship in blood between these two kings. Such a statement made in regard to the normal type of Egyptian skull might justly be considered to have little weight, but the reality of the comparison is accentuated when it is recalled that the remarkable shape of the skull of King Akh·en·Aten, led Professor Elliot Smith who first examined it in 1907, to the conclusion that the heretic king had suffered from a condition of hydrocephalus. Subsequent examination has not confirmed his theory, chiefly because the flattening of the cranium in Akh·en·Aten contrasts markedly with the shape of the head in known cases of hydrocephalus. In these the pressure of fluid in the brain acting upon the yielding walls of the cranium naturally produces a globular shape, particularly in the frontal region, which is quite the reverse of the condition observed in the skull of Akh·en·Aten.

When, therefore, we find that Tut·ankh·Amen exhibits an almost exact reproduction of his father-in-law's head it not only disposes finally of the theory of hydrocephalus, but makes the argument in favour of a very close relationship extremely convincing. This argument receives still greater weight when we compare the measurements of the two skulls. A breadth of 154·0 mm. in Akh·en·Aten is, as pointed out by Professor Elliot Smith, " quite an exceptional breadth for an Egyptian skull " yet in his son-in-law we have a breadth of 156·5 mm. When allowance is made for the thickness of the scalp, over which in the case of Tut·ankh·Amen, all measurements were necessarily made, and which by a special instrument was found to be not more than 0·5 mm. in thickness, the breadth of the actual skull is 155·5 mm. exceeding therefore that of his father-in-law, which as we have seen is " quite exceptional." Corresponding measurements in the two skulls, so far as these may be justly compared under the different conditions of examination, show a remarkable similarity, and make the probability of blood relationship almost a certainty.

The effigy of Tut·ankh·Amen on the gold mask exhibits him as a gentle and refined-looking young man. Those who were privileged to see the actual face when finally exposed can bear testimony to the ability and accuracy of the Eighteenth Dynasty artist who has so faithfully represented the features, and left for all time, in imperishable metal, a beautiful portrait of the young king.

The skull cavity was empty except for some resinous material which had been introduced through the nose in the manner employed by the embalmers of the period, after they had extracted the brain by the same route.

The right upper and lower wisdom teeth had just erupted the gum and reached to about half the height of the second molar. Those on the left side were not so easily seen but appeared to be in the same stage of eruption.

General Appearance of Body and Limbs. The cracked and brittle state of the skin of the head and face, already referred to, was even more marked in the body and limbs. The abdominal wall exhibited a marked bulging on the right side. This was found to be due to the forcing of the packing material across the abdominal cavity from the left side where the embalming incision is situated. This opening, which had a ragged appearance, is roughly 86 mm. in length and is placed parallel to a line drawn from the umbilicus to the anterior superior iliac spine and an inch above this line. This was only exposed after the removal of a carbonized mass of what was apparently resin, and the length of the incision may therefore have been greater than is now apparent, as the hardness of the adherent mass made it difficult to define the limits of the wound. The lips of the wound are inverted owing to the forcible packing of the abdomen with a mass of linen and resin, now of rock-like hardness. The plate of gold or wax so frequently found covering the embalming wound was not present, but an oval plate of gold was found on the left side during the removal of the wrappings included amongst the layers of bandages and in the neighbourhood of the opening in the abdominal wall (p. 130, Plate xxx). The incision is situated somewhat differently from that described by Professor Elliot Smith in the royal mummies he examined ; in these it was usually placed more vertically and in the left flank, extending from near the lower ribs to the anterior superior iliac spine. At a later period the incision was more often made in the lower part of the abdominal wall, parallel with the line of the groin, but always on the left side, but there were occasional reversions to the older site and it seems questionable whether the position had any significance. There was no pubic hair visible, nor was it possible to say whether circumcision had been performed, but the phallus had been drawn forward, wrapped independently, and then retained in the ithyphallic position by the perineal bandages.

The skin of the legs, like that of the rest of the body, was of a greyish-white colour, very brittle and exhibiting numerous cracks. Examination of a piece of this showed that it consisted not only of the skin but of all the soft parts down to the bone, which was thus laid bare when such a piece came away, the whole thickness of skin and tissues in this situation being not more than two or three millimetres. The fractured edges resembled glue. There is little doubt that this was produced by the combustion referred to. The left patella (Plate xxxv,B) and skin covering it could be lifted off and the lower end of the femur was thus exposed, showing the epiphysis which was found to be separate from the shaft and freely movable. The term epiphysis is applied to that part of a bone which ossifies separately and which eventually becomes fused to the main bone. In the limb bones the epiphyses form the chief part of the upper and lower ends. During early life they are attached to the main bone by cartilage which finally becomes completely converted into bone and growth then ceases. The average date of union of all the epiphyses is known, hence the approximate age can be estimated in any case where union is still incomplete.

The limbs appeared very shrunken and attenuated, but even when due allowance is made for the extreme shrinking of the tissues, and the appearance of emaciation which this produces, it is still evident that Tut·ankh·Amen must have been of slight build and perhaps not fully grown at the time of his death.

Direct measurements made him about 5 feet 4¼ inches in height, but this is almost certainly less than his stature during life, owing to the shrinkage referred to. An estimate of living height from the measurements yielded by the principal limb bones calculated according to the formulæ devised by Professor Karl Pearson[1] gives a stature of 1·676 metres (5 feet 6 inches), which is probably very near the actual truth. With the assistance of Mr. R. Engelbach, the writer measured the two wooden statues of the young king, now in the Museum of Antiquities, which stood on either side of the sealed door leading to the Burial Chamber, and which represent him as he appeared in life. Measurements were made from the root of the nose to the sole of the foot, the nasion being the only anatomical point on the heads of the statues which could be located with any degree of accuracy,

[1] "Phil. Trans. of the Royal Society," Vol. 192, pp. 169–244.

as the actual height of the head is obscured in the statues by the head-dress. In the two statues this measurement gave 1·592 metres and 1·602 metres respectively, as the height from sole of foot to root of nose. It was then necessary to add to this the calculated height from this point to the top of the head. This was estimated by measurements from the actual photographs of the king, as well as from a series of observations on Egyptian skulls, to amount to between 8 and 9 cm., which, added to the height of the statues already given, yields a result within a few millimetres of the calculated statue from the bones.

The evidence for the age of the king at the time of his death was obtained from the extent of union or otherwise of the epiphyses. As already mentioned, the cracked condition of the skin and tissues overlying the femur permitted a clear view of the lower ununited portion. This part unites with the shaft about the age of twenty. At the upper end of the thigh bone the prominence known as the great trochanter was almost entirely soldered to the main bone, but on its inner side a definite gap showing the smooth cartilaginous surface where union was still incomplete, could be well seen. This epiphysis joins about the eighteenth year. The head of the femur was fixed to the neck of the bone, but the line of union was clearly visible all round the articular margin. This epiphysis also unites about the eighteenth or nineteenth year. The upper end of the tibia was also ununited, but the lower end appeared to be quite fused. As this latter portion of the tibia is generally found to fuse with the shaft about the age of eighteen, Tut·ankh·Amen, from the evidence of his lower limbs, would appear to have been over eighteen but below twenty years of age at the date of his death.

But we are not limited to these bones for evidence of age. It was possible to examine the upper limbs. Here the heads of the humeri, or upper-arm bones, which join about twenty, are still not united, but the lower ends are completely joined to the shaft. In modern Egyptians of seventeen years of age the lower end is seen to be quite fused to the shaft as well as the epiphysis capping the internal condyle, when examined by X-rays, so that if what obtains in Egypt to-day can be applied to the young king, Tut·ankh· Amen was evidently over seventeen when he died.

The lower ends of the radius and ulna in modern Egyptians show little or no union in most cases until the age of eighteen, after which date they fuse fairly rapidly. The union begins on the inner side of the ulna and proceeds laterally, gradually involving the radius. In Tut·ankh·Amen fusion appeared to have begun in the ulna, but the distal end of the radius is entirely free, no bony union whatever having commenced between the shaft and its epiphysis. From the state of the epiphyses above described it would appear that the king was about eighteen years of age at the time of his death. None of the epiphyses which should unite about the twentieth year shows any sign of union. There is evidence that in Egypt the epiphyses tend on the average to unite somewhat earlier than is the rule in Europe.

Mention has already been made of the epiphysis of the internal condyle of the humerus which in Egypt is joined completely to the shaft by about seventeen years of age, and of those of the lower end of the radius and ulna which begin to unite at about eighteen.

N   159

The absence of any ossification here might be taken as evidence that Tut·ankh·Amen was less than eighteen at death, but against this we have the complete union of the lower end of the tibia, usually about eighteen, as well as the condition of affairs at the upper end of the femur where the great trochanter, which also joins about eighteen years of age, is, with the exception of a very small portion, fused to the main bone and the head of the same bone, although the line of union is clearly visible all round, is nevertheless joined to the neck.

There is thus little room for doubt as to the approximate age of the king, but it should be borne in mind that the dates given represent the average and that it is permissible to add or deduct about a year, so that Tut·ankh·Amen might be any age between seventeen and nineteen, but with the balance of evidence strongly in favour of the middle date, viz. eighteen.

The following table illustrates the similarity between the measurements made on the skull of Akh·en·Aten and those from the head of Tut·ankh·Amen.

	AKH·EN·ATEN.		TUT·ANKH·AMEN.
Length of skull . . .	190·0	..	187·0
Breadth ,, ,, . . .	154·0	..	155·5
Height ,, ,, . . .	134·0	..	132·5
Forehead breadth . . .	98·0	..	99·0
Height of face: Upper . .	69·5	..	73·5
,, ,, : Total . .	121·0	..	122·0
Breadth of jaw . . .	99·5	..	99·0
Circumference of head . .	542·0	..	547·0
Height calculated from limb bones	1·66 metres (5ft. 5¼ in.)		1·68 metres (5ft. 6 in.)

Although the examination of the young king afforded no clue to the cause of his early death, the investigation has added something at least to the few facts already known of the history of the period. The age of Tut·ankh·Amen at the time of his decease, and the likelihood that he was a blood relation of Akh·en·Aten, are important evidence in the reconstruction of the events of the time, and will play their part when the history of that time comes to be written.

APPENDIX II

THE CHEMISTRY OF THE TOMB

By A. Lucas, O.B.E., F.I.C.

IT is proposed to describe from a purely chemical aspect the materials used in the construction of the tomb and the composition of some of the objects found. The description will be as non-technical as possible, and although a very large number of chemical analyses have been made, the citing of percentage compositions will be avoided, the results being given instead in the form of conclusions derived from a careful consideration of the analyses, and from a long and varied experience of materials in general and of Egyptian materials in particular.

The tomb, including the steps leading down to it, is cut out of the solid rock. This rock is a white, amorphous limestone containing flint and flinty masses, often of considerable size, and also occasional veins of calcite.

The outermost doorway of the tomb, as also three inner doorways, were all closed with irregular-shaped blocks of limestone put together without mortar, but thickly covered on the outside with a light-coloured grey plaster that is still very hard and durable and corresponds in composition to plaster of Paris; the grey colour is due to the presence of a little unburned fuel.

A considerable amount of misconception exists concerning the nature of the plaster employed by the ancient Egyptians and it is generally wrongly described, often as lime plaster. It is, however, crude gypsum simply burned and powdered. Gypsum occurs largely in Egypt and is worked at the present time in the vicinities of both Cairo and Alexandria, and in the district stretching south from Cairo to Beni Suef. There are also small local deposits in other places, but whether any such occur in the neighbourhood of Thebes is not known.

In addition to its use as a plaster, gypsum was also employed in ancient Egypt as mortar, for example in the construction of the Giza pyramids and in the temples of Karnak, and no evidence whatever has been found of the use of lime in Egypt for any purpose before the time of the Roman occupation.

In addition to the plaster on the doorways there is a considerable amount of other plaster in the tomb, thus it was employed to fill up cracks and irregularities in the walls of the stairway, of the sloping entrance passage and of the Antechamber; it was also used to repair several of the steps, as well as the doorway at the bottom of the steps, where these had been cut away in order to admit objects too large for the entrance as originally made; it covered the wall at the north end of the Antechamber, built to close off the Burial Chamber, as also the four walls of this latter, where it was used to smooth the surface before it was painted upon. All this plaster is crude gypsum, similar to that made and used in Egypt at the present time. On the east wall of the Antechamber there is a little clay plaster covered with a thin coating of carbonate of lime, that is to say it has been whitewashed to make it resemble the rest of the plaster, and a similar whitewash occurs on the wooden lintel of the first doorway.

A marked feature of the Antechamber is the pink colour seen everywhere, not only on the walls, but also on the ceiling and even on the floor. This pink colour, although it occurs particularly on the plaster is not confined to the plaster, but is also present on the rock surfaces which are unplastered. On the rock, however, the pink occurs only in occasional patches, and in a few places where there are veins of calcite the colour is scarlet. This colour is not original nor intentional, as is evidenced, for instance, by its presence on the floor, and is due to chemical changes that have taken place in the iron compounds on the surface of the plaster and stone.

When the objects from the tomb were examined it was found that many of them had undergone changes and deterioration that could only have occurred in the presence of heat and moisture. The tomb therefore must have been both hot and damp at some period. Unfortunately, circumstances did not allow of either the temperature or humidity being determined when the tomb was first opened, and although a few observations were made subsequently, these did not necessarily bear any relation to the conditions either when the tomb was closed originally or when it was opened in 1922.

The humidity may easily be accounted for. In the first place, the plaster on the walls and on the doorways was necessarily used wet, and any moisture in excess of that required for chemical combination would evaporate into the atmosphere and, as the tomb which consists of four small rooms only, would be closed before the plaster had time to dry, this alone would cause considerable humidity ; secondly, the moisture from the lungs and skins of the men engaged in preparing the tomb, in erecting the shrines and in carrying in and arranging the objects cannot have been negligible; thirdly, there would be a small evaporation of moisture from organic materials, such as wood and fabrics; and fourthly, the tomb is at the lowest level of the Valley and near the surface of the rock, which may possibly have been damp from the heavy rains that occur about once in every decade. There is no evidence, however, that actual water penetrated into the tomb at any time.

The heat of the tomb is a natural consequence of its position in the Valley, where the temperature is generally high and in the summer very high.

So far as can be ascertained no life of any kind, even of the lowest form, existed in the tomb when it was first found. Thus the morning after the sealed doorway of the Burial Chamber was opened, sterile swabs were taken into the extreme corner of the chamber near the back of the shrines, some six yards beyond where anyone had trod for more than 3,000 years, and were wiped on the walls, on the bottom of the outer shrine and under some reeds on the floor. These swabs, which were kindly supplied by Dr. A. C. Thaysen of the Bacteriological Laboratory of the Royal Naval Cordite Factory, near Wareham, were examined at that laboratory by Mr. H. J. Bunker, and out of five swabs from which cultures were taken, four were sterile and the fifth contained a few organisms that were undoubtedly air-infections unavoidably introduced during the opening of the doorway and the subsequent inspection of the chamber, and not belonging to the tomb, and it may be accepted that no bacterial life whatever was present. The danger, therefore, to those working in the tomb from disease germs, against which they have been so frequently warned, is non-existent.

Not only was bacterial life absent, but life in any form. Fungus growths occur on the walls of the Burial Chamber, where they are so plentiful as to cause great disfigurement, and they occur also, though only to a slight extent, on the walls of the Antechamber and on the outside of the sarcophagus, but in every instance the fungus is dry and apparently dead. Insects also occur, but these too are dead. As a matter of scientific interest specimens were collected and were submitted to Mr. E. W. Adair, entomologist to the Ministry of Agriculture, Cairo, who passed them to Mr. A. Alfieri, entomologist of the Royal Agricultural Society, Cairo, by whom they were identified. They proved to be chiefly small beetles such as feed upon and destroy dead organic matter, and they are all of kinds common in Egypt at the present day, and 3,000 years have not brought any change or modification in their size or structure. Spider-webs, and the remains of small spiders, were also found. Various wooden objects, too, contain holes manifestly made by insects and, judging from the debris present, the damage had evidently occurred while the objects were in the tomb.

The most important materials in the tomb that have been examined up to the present will now be considered and, for the sake of convenience, this will be done in alphabetical order.

Adhesive materials were well represented and included glue, resin, beeswax, and gypsum.

Glue was well known in ancient Egypt and a specimen recently examined may be described. This was found some years ago by Dr. Howard Carter in a rock chamber over the mortuary temple of Queen Hat·shep·sût at Deir el Bahari : it had been cast and was originally rectangular in shape, but now it is shrunken and distorted owing to desiccation ; in appearance it cannot be distinguished from modern glue, and it still responds to the usual tests.

From an examination of the objects from the tomb it is evident that glue was employed in ancient Egypt exactly in the same manner as by the modern joiner, being used to fasten wood together, and to fix ebony and ivory veneer and inlay in place. It was also used mixed with whiting to form gesso (a special kind of plaster employed for covering wood before gilding and generally before painting), to attach gesso to its base and to fasten gold-foil to gesso.

Resin was another adhesive largely employed and was used to lute on the lids of alabaster vases and to fasten inlay of stone, glass or faience into the setting. Sometimes the resin was mixed with whiting and such a mixture is employed by jewellers to-day ; resin is also the principal ingredient in many of the cements that are used to fasten on the handles of modern knives and forks. When this cement was used with inlay the effect was enhanced by the cement being tinted the same colour as the inlay, thus blue inlay had a blue cement and red inlay a red cement. In the same way inlay of transparent quartz, or of translucent calcite, was fastened in place with a red cement, which considerably improves the appearance of the stones, imparting to them the semblance of carnelian.

Beeswax was another adhesive found and was used to lute on the covers of several alabaster vases ; still another adhesive was **gypsum,** which has already been described in connexion with plaster and mortar, but it was also used as a cement and was employed to repair the lid of the sarcophagus, which had been broken anciently, and also to fix on the cover of a pottery jar.

Alabaster is the name applied to two very different materials, which happen to be much alike in appearance though totally unlike in chemical composition, one being sulphate of lime and the other carbonate of lime ; which of the two has the prior claim to the name will not be discussed. Although the ancient Egyptians occasionally used sulphate of lime for making small objects, and examples of this occur in the tomb, the name alabaster in Egyptology always means carbonate of lime, or as it is termed geologically, calcite, and it is this material that was so extensively employed for sarcophagi, statues, vases, and other objects. Alabaster is fairly soft and may readily be cut, it was therefore an easy material to work ; it occurs plentifully in Egypt, principally in the eastern desert, the Hat·nub quarries behind Tell el Amarna having been specially noted for the quality of their product. This stone, like many others used in Egypt in antiquity is not now worked.

Faience was well represented in the tomb in the form of vessels of various kinds, inlay on jewellery, inlay on furniture, beads, necklaces and rings. This material, which is peculiar to ancient Egypt, consists of a highly siliceous body coated with a coloured glaze, which latter is a soda-lime silicate made from the same materials and in the same manner as glass, from which it only differs by always being applied to the surface of another material, whereas glass was used independently.

The material of the body of faience consists of

angular grains of quartz showing all the signs of having been artificially crushed and is therefore some form of powdered quartz, probably quartz sand or quartz rock, though it is not unlikely that different forms of quartz were used at different times or in different places, that particular form being chosen that was most easily obtained locally. An interesting problem is how such a material, which is without any natural coherence, was held together while being shaped and glazed. It is generally stated that sufficient clay was added for this purpose, but both chemical analysis and microscopical examination prove that clay is absent and no other binding material is disclosed. This raises the presumption that possibly some substance of the nature of gum or glue, which burned away during the firing of the glaze, might have been employed, and there is some slight evidence for such an addition. One investigator escapes the difficulty by stating that the material is not artificial, but is simply sandstone carved into the many shapes found. Ingenious as is this solution there are many objections to it, any one of which is fatal: firstly, the material is often too friable to have been carved ; secondly, sandstone corresponding in texture and quality to the siliceous body does not exist, and thirdly, the material has certainly been artificially powdered.

Glass so far found in the tomb, with the exception of a few small cups and vases, has been entirely in the form of inlay and beads. This, as is the case with ancient Egyptian glass generally, is very similar in the nature of its constituents, though not in the proportion in which they occur, to modern glass of ordinary quality, and corresponds in composition to what would be obtained by fusing together a mixture of siliceous sand, containing carbonate of lime as an impurity, and natron (natural soda), both of which occur plentifully in Egypt.

One great difference between ancient and modern glass is that the latter is largely employed to transmit light and is therefore often transparent, whereas the former, not having been required for that purpose, was at most semi-transparent and more generally opaque.

The colours of the glass found in the tomb are white, red, blue, green, yellow and black.

Of white glass there is very little, namely a small vase that is translucent, several rings and a few beads that are opaque, in which the white is alternated with black. This latter probably owes its whiteness to the presence of oxide of tin, which is a suitable material for the purpose and one known in Egypt at the time, but there has not yet been an opportunity of confirming this by analysis.

The red glass is all opaque and was made to imitate red jasper. From the appearance alone it is possible to say that the colour is almost certainly due to red oxide of copper, and this has been proved by chemical analysis.

The blue glass is generally opaque, though in some instances translucent, and is of several shades of colour, namely dark blue, imitating lapis lazuli; light blue, imitating turquoise, and greenish blue. The chemical interest in this glass is in the nature of the colouring matter employed, and analysis proves that all three shades generally owe their colour to copper compounds, but that the dark lapis lazuli blue is occasionally coloured by means of cobalt, which was found in one specimen among many examined from the tomb, the rest being coloured by copper.

Cobalt is found in Egypt, but only in very minute quantity as an impurity in other minerals, and there is no evidence, and very little probability, that this occurrence was known to the ancient Egyptians, the cobalt required being almost certainly imported. Cobalt is the usual colouring matter employed for blue glass at the present day.

One noticeable feature of the dark blue glass was the manner in which it had often deteriorated, frequently having lost its colour and become grey and sometimes entirely perished, being reduced to the condition of powder. The light blue and the red glass on the other hand were generally in a good state of preservation, though there were occasional instances where these too had deteriorated. There can be little doubt that the deterioration in all cases had been largely brought about by damp.

The green glass from the tomb is all opaque. A green colour in glass may be due either to copper or to iron, the colour of the modern green bottle glass, for example, being produced by iron. It is to copper however that the green of the ancient Egyptian glass is usually due.

No record of the nature of the yellow colour in the earlier ancient Egyptian glass can be traced and no yellow glass from the tomb has been analysed, but a specimen belonging to the Nineteenth Dynasty kindly supplied by Dr. Howard Carter was examined, and the colour was found to be due to a compound of antimony associated with lead, which had previously been reported only for Egyptian glass of Persian and Arab times.

The black glass found in the tomb was not available for analysis, and the nature of the colour therefore cannot be stated.

Although glass probably originated in Egypt, which was long renowned for the quality of this ware, it is not now made in the country, only a few kinds of simple objects being fashioned from broken glass of foreign make that is remelted.

Gold. One of the most striking features of the tomb was not only the number of objects of gold, culminating in a gold coffin, but also of wood covered with gold, some being coated with sheet-gold and others being only gilt, the gilding however being much thicker than that of the present day. In the specimens measured the gold varied in thickness from one-hundredth of a millimetre, which was that of the thinnest gilding, to rather more than half a millimetre, which was the thickest sheet-gold. Beneath the gold when it occurs on wood, there is as a rule a coating of white plaster termed " gesso," which consists of whiting to which a little glue has been added to make it cohere. This is identical with the material used by modern picture-frame makers for plain gilt mouldings, gesso being employed instead of plaster of Paris because this latter is not sufficiently hard to permit of the burnishing of gold. In a few cases copper or bronze objects in the tomb were gilded, the thin covering of gold having been put on with some adhesive soluble in water, probably gum or glue.

One very noticeable feature of the gold was the varied colour it presented, sometimes in patches and sometimes over the whole surface. The colours comprised bright yellow, dull yellow, grey and red of various shades, including reddish brown, light brick colour, blood colour, dull purple (plum colour), and a very remarkable rose colour, all except the last named manifestly being fortuitous, and due to chemical changes that had taken place during the time the objects had been in the tomb. The bright yellow gold is evidently fairly pure and doubtless corresponds to the " fine gold " referred to in the ancient records. The dull and tarnished yellow gold contains small proportions of other metals, such as silver and copper, which on the surface have undergone chemical changes and thus caused the tarnishing. The gold that has become grey contains a large proportion of silver that on the surface has become converted into chloride, which has then darkened in the manner usual with this compound ; it also contains a little copper and a trace of iron. Such gold corresponds to the naturally-occurring alloy of gold and silver— termed *electron* by the Greeks and *electrum* by the Romans—that was largely employed by the ancient Egyptians. The proportion of silver in these alloys varies considerably ; they are always lighter in colour than pure gold, and when the proportion of silver is high they are silver-white.

Although very few references to the occurrence of any sort of red colour on gold can be traced, the dark red of old gold is not uncommon, and even the characteristic rose colour may be seen on several small objects in the Cairo Museum, although there is no certain reference to it in the description of the objects. The reddish-brown colour gives the tests for iron, silver and copper, and is evidently due to iron and copper in the gold that have oxidized. In some instances a red or purple colour proved to be a staining of the gold by organic matter, since it was not soluble

173

either in acids or in organic solvents, but could readily be removed by heating. The rose colour can be proved by chemical analysis not to be due to any colloidal modification of the gold, nor to any sort of organic lacquer or varnish, and the gold can be made red-hot without the colour being removed or diminished, but in some instances rather enhanced. The coloured film, however, is so extremely thin, being probably less than one hundred-thousandth of an inch in thickness, that without more material than it is desirable to use, chemical analysis becomes very difficult. A trace of iron is the only metal found so far, and since it is well known that native gold is sometimes reddened by being coated with a translucent film of oxide of iron, it is suggested that the colour in question is probably due to oxide of iron, but in what manner it was produced is not known, as it occurs on both sides of most of the objects on which it is present. This suggests that the object may have been dipped in a solution of an iron salt and then heated. That this colour is intentional is shown by its regular and systematic distribution on certain objects, or on certain parts of objects.

The gold nails that fastened on the lid of the gold coffin, as also the gold heads of the silver nails of both the first and second coffins, were found on assay by the touchstone method, which however can only be regarded as an approximation, to be between eighteen and twenty-one carats in fineness—the alloy being chiefly silver with a small proportion of copper.

The metals found in the tomb besides gold were silver, copper or bronze, iron and lead, all however in small amount.

The silver comprised small portions of several

articles of jewellery, the tongues and nails that fastened the lid of the second coffin to the shell, the nails of the first coffin and probably also the tongues, though these have not yet been examined, and the metal cores of the flail and crook held in the gold hands that were on the outside of the mummy. The nails of the two coffins, which had gold heads soldered on, were found by the touchstone method of assay to consist approximately of 80 per cent. silver, the rest being principally copper.

The copper or bronze objects have not yet been analysed and therefore it is impossible to state with certainty of which of the two metals they consist, but as bronze was well known in the Eighteenth Dynasty the probability is that they are bronze; the objects so far found comprise many of the tongues of the shrines that surrounded the sarcophagus (the others being of wood), hinges, bolts and other fastenings for wooden objects, a few arrowheads and a small serpent (gold-inlaid) from one of the chariots.

The iron objects are only three in number, namely a dagger-blade, part of an amuletic bracelet and a miniature head-rest, all of wrought iron.

The lead consisted of one small piece.

All these metals, except the silver cores of the crook and flail mentioned, although tarnished, were in good condition.

Leather. Originally there had been a considerable amount of leather in the tomb, for example, for horse trappings, for the seats of stools and for sandals, but when found most of this leather was unrecognizable except from its position and by chemical analysis, as it had become a black brittle, pitch-

o   175

like mass, parts of which at some period had been viscous and had "run," and in several instances had dropped on to objects below, which it had cemented together. Judging from its position, what had been raw hide had perished more completely than tanned leather, thus the soles of sandals were in a worse condition than the upper parts. This destruction of the leather had been brought about by the combined heat and humidity of the tomb. Four specimens of this leather have been kindly examined by Dr. R. H. Pickard, F.R.S., Director of The British Leather Manufacturers' Research Association, and it was found that the specimen from the seat of a stool was unquestionably goat-skin and that from the sandals was possibly calf-skin.

Oils and fats, being very susceptible to influences causing decomposition, do not come down from ancient times in an unaltered condition, but when found generally consist, wholly or chiefly, of solid bodies of an acid nature known as fatty acids, the principal being stearic and palmitic acids, which have resulted from the chemical changes that have taken place. This decomposition makes recognition of the original oil or fat very difficult.

A number of alabaster vases from the tomb were found to contain fatty matter or in some cases fatty matter mixed with other material, which has not been identified, and an anointing substance that had been poured both over the mummy and over the gold coffin and, to a small extent, on the foot-end of the outermost coffin, also contained fatty matter. The fatty matter from the vases in one instance smells like rancid coco-nut oil, which, however, is a well-known result of decomposition and not the original smell of the substance, and does not in any way indicate that coco-nut oil was present ; in another case the smell is suggestive of valeric acid, which again is the result of decomposition. The analytical work on these samples has not yet been finished, but of two specimens kindly examined by Dr. R. Thomas, F.I.C., one was probably originally castor oil and the other, possibly, beef fat.

Castor oil was well known in ancient Egypt, and the castor-oil plant grows plentifully in the country. Beef fat would also be well known.

A trace of oil which was extracted from the linen wick and metal container of one of the *ankh* torch-holders consisted of a yellowish, viscous, oily liquid of acid character, but unfortunately the amount was too small for identification to be possible.

The anointing material mentioned which contained fatty matter was black and lustrous and in appearance closely resembled bitumen or pitch ; where the layer was thin, as on the lid of the gold coffin, the material was hard and brittle, but between the gold coffin and the next outer one and under the mummy, where a thicker layer had accumulated, the interior of the mass was still soft and plastic. When cold there was little or no smell, but when warmed a strong penetrating, not unpleasant, but rather fragrant smell was evident. A detailed chemical analysis has not yet been possible, but the material contains fatty matter and resin, and is entirely free from bitumen or mineral pitch. One specimen examined contained 46 per cent. of fatty matter (now largely or wholly fatty acids), 19 per cent. of a brown resin and a black, brittle organic residue that has not been identified.

The fatty acids resulting from the decomposition

of the original oil or fat of this anointing substance, have been the cause of considerable deterioration of the inlay of the trappings from outside the mummy and of the jewellery on the mummy, partly from their action on the cement with which the inlay was fastened in place and which frequently consists of a mixture of resin and whiting, and partly from a direct action upon some of the stones like calcite and lapis lazuli, and upon the glass—more especially that of a dark blue colour—though occasionally also upon the light blue and the red.

Pigments. Ancient Egyptian pigments are often as bright to-day as when they were fresh, which is due to the fact that, with the exception of black, they are all of mineral origin. These pigments have frequently been analysed and in some instances with apparently conflicting results. The fact, however, that one analyst has found one ingredient, and another analyst a different ingredient in a similarly-coloured pigment, and even belonging to the same period, is not necessarily antagonistic, since the specimens examined were not the same and different substances were doubtless employed for the same purpose, and certain colours were produced in more than one way in ancient Egypt, just as at the present day. The colours of the pigments from the tomb are white, red, blue, green, yellow and black.

The white pigment of the ancient Egyptians generally consisted of whiting, though the use of powdered gypsum has also been recorded. In the present case all the specimens examined have been whiting. The red pigment has been variously stated to be red ochre, hæmatite and burned yellow ochre. Since however red ochre is merely a soft variety of hæmatite containing a little earthy matter, generally of a clayey nature, the colouring matter of both being due to oxide of iron, there is very little real difference between the two. Both occur naturally in Egypt and it is little wonder, therefore, that one analyst reports one and another analyst the other. Yellow ochre also occurs in Egypt, and if calcined produces red ochre, and one instance is recorded where yellow ochre on a tomb wall has been changed to red as the result of incendiarism in the chamber. All the red pigment in this tomb consists of ochre.

With regard to the ancient Egyptian blue pigment it is stated by some authorities that the colour is due to copper and by others to cobalt. Like the blue colouring matter of glass, which has already been dealt with, it is sometimes due to one and sometimes to the other, but much more often to copper than to cobalt. In the former case the material is an artificial frit consisting of a definite crystalline compound of silica, lime and copper. This has been investigated by many chemists beginning with Sir Humphry Davy, in 1815, and was later successfully reproduced by Dr. W. T. Russell and others. It is, as stated, a frit, the temperature at which it was made not having been sufficiently high to result in complete fusion, which would have given glass. A large piece of this frit found by Dr. Howard Carter in the Valley of the Tombs of the Kings, and dating from the New Empire, and also several small pieces from the present tomb have been analysed and all were found to consist of lime-copper-silicate, as also was all blue paint from the tomb that has been examined. Cobalt however is recorded as the colouring matter of the blue paint in the tomb of Perneb, dating from about 2650 B.C.

It is generally accepted that the green pigment of the ancient Egyptians owes its colour to copper, but the nature of the copper compound is not so certain and it is frequently stated to be malachite, a natural copper ore that occurs in Egypt. This is so in the case of the green pigment from earlier periods, but in the present tomb all the green paint so far examined has been an artificial frit similar in composition to the blue compound already described, and a small piece of this frit was also found and analysed.

Of yellow paint two kinds were employed in ancient Egypt, one a dull brownish shade and the other a bright canary colour. The former has frequently been analysed and is generally accepted as being a natural yellow ochre, the colouring matter of which is due to hydrated oxide of iron. The bright yellow pigment from the tomb, of which one specimen from a wooden box was examined, proved to be orpiment (sulphide of arsenic), and in another instance a similar-looking pigment, with which the incisions of an inscription on a box had been filled, but which was not available for analysis, was probably also orpiment. In this latter case the pigment had been coated with beeswax, doubtless as a measure of protection, and this having deteriorated partly masks the yellow colour and causes it to appear almost white. At one time orpiment, originally as the naturally-occurring mineral and afterwards as an artificial product, was largely employed in Europe as a pigment, but its use was discontinued on account of the very poisonous nature of the artificial product. The natural mineral, however, is not poisonous and there is little doubt that it was this that was employed in ancient Egypt, and, since it does not occur in the country, it must have been imported.

The black used as a pigment was always carbon, generally soot, though possibly, occasionally, powdered charcoal. The specimens of this pigment from the tomb that have been examined were not in a sufficiently fine state of division to be soot, unless in a very impure condition, and were probably powdered charcoal. In this connexion a black coating on various funerary objects may be mentioned, as it has all the appearance of being a paint, though it is not a paint but a black varnish. This black is a thin lustrous coating on various wooden objects and has generally been applied directly to the wood, though it is occasionally found on gesso. In the past every black material having any resemblance to bitumen or pitch has been called one or the other, and this black varnish is no exception, though it is neither bitumen nor pitch but resin. It has, however, not become black from age and chemical change like so many materials, but was naturally and originally black and is of a similar nature to the black varnish resins which occur in India, China and Japan, and are used as lacquers. Whether such a resin is found nearer to Egypt than India, in the Sudan for instance, is not known.

Much discussion has taken place concerning the nature of the paint vehicles employed by the ancient Egyptians. The pigments could not have been used in the dry state, but must have been mixed with some medium. In modern practice the two principal paint media are oil (frequently boiled linseed oil, thinned with turpentine), and water in which a little glue (size) is dissolved to make the pigment adhere.

In ancient Egypt oil was never used for mixing with paint and turpentine was unknown, and so by exclusion, since no other medium can be suggested, water was employed. Although several of the pigments, especially red and yellow ochres, would adhere to some extent if mixed with water alone, they would not be satisfactory, and it seems highly probable that some binding material was employed. The nature of this is not known, and gum, white of egg and glue (size) have all been suggested. Gum has been reported as having been found on one occasion, but this has not been confirmed. As for the white of egg (albumen), it is doubtful whether there is any test by means of which it could be identified after such a lapse of time, since it undergoes change and becomes denaturalized, and its presence has never been proved. With regard to glue there is also a difficulty, as this material was probably used as a sizing to fill up the pores of the ground to be painted upon before applying the colours; hence the finding of glue on a painted surface would not prove that it was used as a binder in the paint. Either gum or glue, however, seems the most likely material to have been employed.

Varnish, having all the appearance of modern varnish, was largely employed in ancient Egypt and examples of its use occur in the tomb. It has not been possible to examine this varnish chemically, but other ancient Egyptian varnishes that have been analysed consist, like modern varnish, of resin, though the particular kind of resin has not yet been identified. Before resin can be applied as a thin coating to any surface it must be in liquid form, and in present-day varnishes solvents such as boiled linseed oil, turpentine and alcohol are employed to dissolve it. These materials, however, were all unknown to the ancient Egyptians, and no other solvent likely to have been used can be suggested. The varnish, too, shows no evidence whatever of oil having been used in its preparation : it is insoluble in turpentine but readily soluble in alcohol. Wine has been proposed as the solvent, but even strong wine does not contain a sufficient proportion of alcohol to dissolve resin. The alternative, therefore, seems to be a resin that did not require an extraneous solvent, which means a naturally-occurring resin already in liquid form. Such resins do exist and are termed " oleo-resins," the solvent being a natural oil which evaporates on exposure. These oleo-resins however, although liquid, are at the best of a thick syrupy consistency, too viscous at ordinary temperatures to admit of application as a thin coating and therefore if they were used, they would probably require heating first in order to thin them down. It has also been suggested that the resin was applied in the form of a fine powder which was then heated, but this does not appear probable.

Ancient Egyptian varnish, other than the black varnish mentioned, is now always yellow or reddish, but there can be no doubt that originally it was colourless or practically so, since there are many instances where a white painted surface, partly varnished and partly unvarnished, is now yellow in the former case and white in the latter, the edges of the varnished portions being irregular and unsightly. This can only be explained on the assumption that the varnish was colourless when it was applied and so did not show.

Resin. One of the substances most commonly

found in connexion with burials in Egypt is resin. Resin is not now one of the products of Egypt and whether it ever was produced is doubtful, since it seems probable that in ancient Egypt—in historical times at any rate—as to-day, trees were never very plentiful. Certain kinds of small resin-bearing trees, however, that do not now grow in the country may have existed at one time and have been destroyed. Resin occurs plentifully in the Sudan and in other parts of Africa, as also in Asia, and could readily have reached Egypt from any of these sources.

As the word resin is frequently used very loosely and often as a synonym for gum—which is a substance of totally different properties—it may be well to explain that while both are excretory products of trees, the exudation being either natural or produced by incisions made for the purpose, and while both are very similar in appearance, they differ considerably both in composition and properties. Thus resins generally are neither soluble in, nor softened by water, but are soluble in alcohol and many other organic solvents, while gums are insoluble in alcohol and organic solvents and either dissolve in water or take up sufficient water to form a mucilage.

Resin was found in the present tomb in many forms, which included large pieces, coarse powder, small balls of incense, beads, a ring, two large scarabs, cement, varnish, both the black kind on funerary objects, and the ordinary kind covering and protecting painted surfaces, and also mixed with fatty matter, as the anointing material poured over the mummy. The botanical sources of the various kinds of resin used have not been identified.

The stones used for jewellery, amulets, personal

ornaments and inlay comprised amethyst, calcite, carnelian, chalcedony, green felspar, red jasper, lapis lazuli, crystalline limestone, malachite, obsidian and turquoise. Few of these stones would be regarded as " precious " at the present day, but such stones as the diamond, ruby, and sapphire were unknown in ancient Egypt, and the pearl did not come into use until Ptolemaic times. For inlay, however, even of jewellery, both glass and to less extent faience, were often employed in the New Empire onwards.

Textiles. One of the disappointments of the tomb was the very bad state of preservation of practically all the textile fabrics. These, most of which had been white originally, varied in colour when found from light yellowish brown, to very dark brown, almost black and were generally in very poor condition, the darker the colour the worse the condition ; the best preserved were fragile and tender, and the worst had become a mass of black powder. The material of the fabrics is probably linen in every case, though this has only been confirmed by microscopic examination in a few instances. The discoloration and disintegration were not uniformly distributed even on the same fabric, and it was quite common to find one portion of a fabric much discoloured and badly decayed, and another portion of the same fabric exposed to apparently similar conditions, less discoloured and in a much better state of preservation. Even folded articles exhibited a similar irregularity, and both on the outside and inside there were often patches of the material in good condition and others in bad condition. The mummy wrappings were in the same disintegrated condition, and have all the appearance of having been partly burned. This disintegration seems to be the result of some kind of slow spontaneous combustion in which, almost certainly, fungoid growth plays a part. The precise nature of the phenomenon has not yet been determined, but it is suggested that it commenced with a fungoid attack induced by the warmth and humidity present, and that after a time chemical changes took place.

Not only were the wrappings of the mummy black and disintegrated, but the mummy itself was black. Such a condition has often been noticed before in mummies and has led to the erroneous statements either that the body had been burned or that it had been soaked in bitumen. Neither of these statements, however, is justified by the facts, which all point to a combined fungus and chemical action on the organic matter both of the tissues and of the bones.

The Wood from the tomb was on the whole in excellent condition, being very well preserved. The nature of the woods will not be discussed as their identification is not a chemical problem. Egypt is, and always has been, very poorly provided with timber, and it has always been necessary to import a large proportion of that required.

Stopping. One striking feature seen when handling the wooden objects was that in order to cover up defects in the wood and to hide joints, stopping was employed in the same way as is done to-day. This stopping consists of a mixture of whiting and glue and is generally coloured to match the wood on which it is used.

From the foregoing description of the nature of the materials from the tomb it will be evident that the ancient Egyptians had a considerable knowledge of chemical processes, and the question naturally arises as to the extent of their knowledge. The answer is not in doubt. So far as the science of chemistry was concerned there is neither evidence nor probability that this was in any way understood, but of the art of chemistry a very great deal was known, probably more than is generally allowed. The ancient Egyptians were skilled in the arts of making glaze, glass, and pottery ; in the preparation and use of vegetable dyes ; in the extraction and working of gold, copper and lead ; in the making of bronze, which latter involved the use of tin ; in the fermentation industries, as evidenced by their beer and wine ; in the extraction of various naturally-occurring mineral pigments and in the manufacture of others, particularly some very remarkable blue and green frits ; in the making of varnish, glue and plaster ; in the extraction and use of vegetable oils ; in the preparation of leather, paper (papyrus) and ink. These operations were all " of the nature of manufacturing processes, empirical in character and utilitarian in result."

There is no doubt about the Egyptian craftsman being an empiricist, in which, however, he was not alone, as empiricism was the rule in most manufacturing processes all the world over until recently, and even now is not entirely extinct. As the result of long practice and many failures, he doubtless knew how best to choose his materials and what precautions to take in his operations in order to secure the desired results, which, even judged by present-day standards, are often marvellous. The methods employed were probably trade or family secrets and jealously guarded.

As the objects from the tomb were all very dirty,

and in some instances broken or in a bad state of preservation, a certain amount of cleaning, repairing and preservative treatment was necessary to enable them to be handled, photographed, packed and transported. The treatment given on the spot was entirely preliminary, since neither the time nor the means were available for anything further to be done. This subject has already been dealt with in a previous volume, and only a very brief reference to the chemical aspect of it will be made. Before an object can either be cleaned or preserved, its nature, and also the nature of any change or deterioration that has taken place, must be known, as also something of the properties of materials in general, since, on this knowledge, must be based the treatment required. The aid chemistry can render to archæology, therefore, is not limited to analyses made for the purpose of the identification of unusual materials so as to enable them to be correctly described, or so that the substances used in their manufacture may be known, but includes problems of cleaning and preservation. This is now becoming generally recognized, and the chemist will ultimately take a place as a necessary member of the staff of all museums and archæological expeditions, as he has done in this case for the first time.

APPENDIX III

REPORT ON THE FLORAL WREATHS FOUND IN THE COFFINS OF TUT·ANKH·AMEN

By P. E. Newberry, M.A., O.B.E.; Sometime Brunner Professor of Egyptology at the University of Liverpool; Hon. Reader in Egyptian Art at the University of Liverpool; Fellow of King's College, London; etc.

FROM time immemorial it has been the custom to decorate the bodies of the dead with wreaths of flowers. When, in 1881, the mummies of the Kings Ahmose I, Amen·hetep I, and Rameses II were discovered in the vault of a king of the Twentieth Dynasty at Deir el Bahari many floral wreaths were found in their coffins. Some of these were in an astonishing state of preservation, and Dr. Schweinfurth, who examined them shortly after they were brought to light, remarked that in some instance even the colours of the flowers were admirably preserved. Adorning the mummy of the Princess Nesikhensu, which was also found at Deir el Bahari, was a garland made of willow leaves, poppy flowers and cornflowers; of the poppy flowers Dr. Schweinfurth said that " rarely are such perfect and well-preserved specimens of this fragile flower met with in herbaria; the colour of the petals is maintained in a high degree, as in dried specimens of the present day."

The wreaths found by Dr. Carter in the coffins of Tut·ankh·Amen are, unfortunately, not in such good preservation as were those which Dr. Schweinfurth examined from the Deir el Bahari cache, but they are, nevertheless, in a sufficiently good state to enable us to determine nearly all the kinds of plants that were used by the king's florists. Most of the leaves of which the wreaths were made were too brittle to handle when taken from out of the coffins, so they were soaked in lukewarm water for a few hours before being examined. Two or three flowers fell into dust on being touched, but other specimens were selected from better-preserved portions of the wreaths and these were sufficient for me to determine their genus and species. In all, three wreaths were found.

I. A Small Wreath (Plate XXII). This was tied around the vulture and uræus insignia on the forehead of the king's second coffin. It is composed of the leaves of the olive (*Olea europea*, L.), petals of the blue water-lily (*Nymphœa cœrulea*, Sav.), and flowers of the cornflower (*Centaurea depressa*, M. Bieb.). In the manufacture of this wreath a strip of papyrus pith served as a foundation ; over it were folded leaves of the olive which served as clasps for the cornflowers and water-lily petals ; the olive leaves were securely fastened together in a row by two thinner strips of papyrus pith, one placed over, the other under, alternate leaves. The leaves were arranged so that one leaf had its upper surface outwards, the next with its under surface outwards, this arrangement giving the effect of a dull green leaf beside a silvery one. This wreath was probably the king's " Wreath of Justification." A special chapter of the " Book of the Dead " (Ch. XIX) was devoted to this kind of wreath, and a magical formula is preserved which was to be recited when such a wreath was placed upon the coffin. These " wreaths of justification " were common from the Twenty-second Dynasty to the Græco-Roman period.

II. A Pectoral Garland (Plate xxii). This garland was made in four bands which were arranged in semicircles on the breast of the second coffin. The first and second bands are composed of the olive (*Olea europea*, L.) and cornflowers (*Centaurea depressa*, M. Bieb.). The third is of leaves of a willow (*Salix safsaf*, Forsk.), cornflowers, and petals of the blue water-lily. The fourth and lowest band is of olive leaves, cornflowers and leaves of the wild celery (*Apium graveolens*, L.). In the making of this wreath the willow leaves are folded over narrow strips of papyrus pith and serve as clasps for the cornflowers, water-lily petals and sprigs of wild celery.

III. The Floral Collarette (Plate xxxvi). This Floral Collarette, found upon the third coffin, is composed of the leaves, flowers, berries and fruits of various plants, together with blue glass sequin beads, arranged in nine rows and attached to a semicircular sheet of papyrus pith. It is one of a type that is only known from examples [1] of Tut·ankh·Amen's reign and it is especially interesting as showing the actual kinds of leaves, flowers and fruits upon which the faience pendant-bead collarettes of the latter half of the Eighteenth Dynasty were modelled. Dr. Carter has published a photograph of one of these many faience collarettes in Plate xxxix of the first volume of this book.

The first three and the seventh rows of this collarette are similar; they are composed of blue glass sequin beads and berries of the woody nightshade

---

[1] Theodore Davis in 1908 found in the Valley of the Tombs of the Kings several objects belonging to the funerary furnishings of Tut·ankh·Amen. Among these were some floral collarettes very similar to the one here described; they are now in the Metropolitan Museum of Art, New York, but have not yet been published.

(*Solanum dulcamara*, L.) strung on thin strips of the leaves of the date palm. The sequins and berries are arranged in groups alternately, twenty to twenty-four sequins and four berries. The fourth row is of leaves of the willow and of a plant as yet unidentified, arranged alternately and serving as clasps for petals of the blue water-lily; these are all bound side by side with strips of papyrus pith going over and under the leaves. The fifth row consists of berries of the woody nightshade strung on a strip of the leaf of the date palm. The sixth row is composed of the leaves of a plant not yet identified, flowers of the cornflower, and of *Picris coronopifolia*, Asch., with eleven fruits of the mandrake (*Mandragora officinalis*, L.)[1] placed at regular intervals along the row. The fruits of the mandrake have been sliced in .half lengthwise and the calices cut away; they were then sewn on to the collarette. For the seventh row see the description of rows one to three. The eighth row is composed of leaves of the olive and of an unidentified plant arranged alternately. The ninth and outermost row is made up of the leaves of the same unidentified plant as were used in rows six and eight, together with flowers of the cornflower.

Remarks on the Plants identified. The wild celery (*Apium graveolens*, L.). This plant was already known from ancient Egypt from two sources. A very beautiful wreath composed of its leaves and of petals of the blue lotus was discovered in a tomb of the Twenty-second Dynasty at Thebes in 1885 and is now preserved in the Cairo Museum. Another somewhat

---

[1] For the identification of the mandrake fruits I am indebted to Mr. L. A. Boodle of the Jodrell Laboratory, Royal Gardens, Kew, and to Mrs. Clement Reid.

similar wreath was found by Schiaparelli in the tomb of Amen·hetep III's architect Kha at Deir el Medineh (now in Turin). Wild celery (σέλινον) was also a favourite plant among the chaplet-makers of Greece and Rome (Anacreon, 54; Theocritus, 3, 23); the victors of the Isthmian and Nemean games were crowned with garlands made of its leaves (Pindar, O., 13, 46; Juvenal, 8, 226); and such garlands were also hung on tombs, whence σελίνου δεῖται was said of persons dangerously ill (Plutarch, 2, 676 D). It is interesting to note here that some wild celery seeds from an Egyptian tomb are preserved in the museum at Florence (No. 3628), and that seeds of this plant were one of the ingredients used in embalming the bodies of kings by the Scythians (Herodotus, iv, 71).

The cornflower (*Centaurea depressa*, M. Bieb.). This was one of the commonest flowers used in wreath-making by the ancient Egyptian florists, and many specimens of it have been preserved in garlands dating from the Eighteenth Dynasty to Græco-Roman times. It is not a native of Egypt but must have been introduced from Western Asia or the Greek mainland probably at first as a cornfield weed,[1] and then cultivated in the gardens of Thebes. At the present day there are no localities for it in Syria or Palestine, but it occurs in Arcadia and in the Attic plain, where it flowers in April.

The mandrake (*Mandragora officinalis*, L.) is not a native of the Nile Valley but was certainly introduced in ancient times from Palestine where it is a common plant, especially in marshy plains. It is the love-apple of *Genesis* xxx. 14 ff., and *Canticles* vii. 13; its fruit was, and still is, considered in the Near East to

---

[1] Newberry in Petrie's " Hawara, Biahmu and Arsinoe," p. 49.

possess aphrodisiac properties and to promote conception. In wall-paintings of several Theban tombs of the Eighteenth Dynasty baskets of this fruit are represented, and sometimes women are depicted smelling or eating it at banquets.[1] The plant with its leaves and fruit is figured in a Theban tomb.[2] Tristram[3] says that it is a very striking plant which at once attracts the attention from the size of its leaves and the unusual appearance of its blossoms. He notes that he found it in flower in Palestine at Christmas in warm situations, and gathered the fruit in April and May. The wheat harvest is, therefore, the period of its ripening. The fruit is of a pale yellow colour, soft, and of insipid and sickly taste. The Arabs believe it to be exhilarating and stimulating even to insanity, hence their name for it, *tuffah el jinn*,—the apple of the jinn.[4] It is probable that it is the *didi*-fruit (*cp.* Hebrew *dudaim*, " mandrake "), often mentioned in Egyptian inscriptions of the New Kingdom ; it is said to have been gathered at Elephantine and was sometimes mixed with beer to produce unconsciousness. It is interesting to note that the Carthaginian general, Maharbal, is recorded as having captured or slain a host of rebels whom he had contrived to drug with a mixture of mandragora and wine.[5] An extraordinary amount of folk-lore has grown up around this plant ; it has been collected and discussed by Sir James Frazer in the second volume of his " Folk-Lore in the Old Testament," pp. 372–397.

[1] N. de G. Davies, " The Tomb of Nakht," Plates x and xvii.
[2] Wilkinson, " Manners and Customs of the Ancient Egyptians," 2nd Ed., Vol. ii, p. 413, No. 5.
[3] " Natural History of the Bible," p. 468.
[4] Thomson, " The Land and the Book," Vol. ii, p. 380.
[5] Frontinus, " Stratagem," ii, 5, 12.

The blue water-lily (*Nymphœa cœrulea*, Sav.) was the celebrated lotus of the ancient Egyptians and it was used by them for chaplet-making from the Pyramid age onwards. It is a native of the Nile Valley but is now chiefly found in ditches and stagnant pools of the Delta where it generally blooms from July to November.

The olive (*Olea europea*, L.). This tree is only cultivated in a very few gardens in Upper Egypt at the present day, but there is good evidence that it must have been more widely distributed throughout the Nile Valley in ancient times.[1] It is mentioned in the inventory of plants grown by Inena in his Theban garden in the time of Queen Hat·shep·sût, and Theophrastus, Pliny and Strabo refer to its being grown in Upper Egypt. The first-named writer expressly states (iv, 2, 9) that it grew in the Theban province in his day.

The *Picris coronopifolia*, Asch., is a small composite plant which is very common on the outskirts of the desert at Thebes and elsewhere in Upper Egypt. It flowers in March and April.

The willow (*Salix safsaf*, Forsk.) still occurs in the wild state on the banks of the Nile in Nubia, but in Egypt proper it was considered by Dr. Schweinfurth as only a riverine fugitive whose real home is in the south.

The woody nightshade or bitter-sweet (*Solanum dulcamara*, L.). Only the berries of this plant have been found in Egyptian tombs; they are always threaded on to thin strips of the leaves of the date palm. Berries of this nightshade are often found in the wreaths of the Græco-Roman period.[2] Pliny

[1] *See* Newberry in " Ancient Egypt," 1915, pp. 97–100.
[2] Newberry in Petrie's " Hawara, Biahmu and Arsinoe," p. 51.

(H.N., xxi, 105) mentions the nightshade being used by the garland-makers of Egypt.

Note on the Season of the Burial of Tut·ankh: Amen. From the blossoms and fruits found in these wreaths it is possible to indicate the season of the year at which King Tut·ankh·Amen was laid to rest in his tomb. The cornflower flowers at about the harvest time in March or April, and it is just at this time that the mandrake and woody nightshade fruits ripen. The small *Picris* also flowers in March and April. Although the water-lily blossoms in the ditches and stagnant pools of Lower Egypt from July to November, it is very probable that being cultivated in garden tanks at Thebes it would flower much earlier in the year. We may therefore safely say that the season of the year when Tut·ankh·Amen was interred was from the middle of March to the end of April.

APPENDIX IV

NOTES ON OBJECTS FROM THE TOMB OF KING TUT·ANKH·AMEN

By Alexander Scott, F.R.S., Sc.D. (Camb.), D.Sc. (Edin.), Director of Scientific Research, British Museum

THE following notes relating to objects in and from the tomb of King Tut·ankh·Amen may prove of interest, and are supplementary to the more systematic report of Mr. A. Lucas. Some of the experiments were made on the spot in January, 1924, with only very rudimentary chemical apparatus, and minute quantities of material.

A. The Pall and other Textile Fabrics. The fabric of the pall which was within the outer shrine, but which covered the second shrine, was very frail yet possessed quite enough strength to withstand weak tensile strains such as would be involved in attempting to wind it on a roller. To render it strong enough to stand any kind of manipulation beyond this it seemed essential to strengthen the threads with some flexible material which would bind the fibres together. Various solutions were tried which, from their known properties, seemed likely to prove suitable for this purpose. The most promising were :

I. " Duroprene." This, as sold, is too viscous to admit of ready application and is not readily or rapidly absorbed. When this was diluted with an equal volume of xylol and this solution applied to the fabric with a soft brush and then dried, the desired result seems to have been attained at once. Although the interstices of the fabric were completely filled up when the solution was applied, on drying, these connecting films of liquid—dried in such a manner that all the dissolved matter was left in the threads so that no glistening films showed anywhere—the fabric looked practically unchanged in colour and structure. A second application of the " Duroprene " solution to a portion of the pall which had been already treated and dried, did not seem to effect any real improvement or increase in strength. Solutions still more dilute, such as one-third and even one-quarter of the original, have been found very useful.

II. Celluloid in Acetone.—The results obtained by the application of a solution of celluloid in acetone (2½ per cent. strength) were similar to those obtained with " Duroprene " solution. The toughness, although much increased, was not equal to that imparted by the " Duroprene ", whilst the flexibility of the treated fabric was notably less.

III. Collodion.—Collodion was also tried but, unlike the two solutions just described, its liquid film dried in such a way as to leave a solid film extending from thread to thread. This gave a glossy, almost silvery appearance to the treated fabric which alone rendered it unsuitable for the purpose. Naturally it did not add so much to the tensile strength of the fabric as the other solutions did.

Solutions of " Duroprene " were therefore used in the attempts to preserve the pall, and xylol was used as the diluent in preference to either benzol or toluol, on account of the high outside temperature in front of the tomb of Seti II which was utilized as a laboratory. THREE TEXTILES were examined and these differed notably in their structure as is shown by the enlarged photographs shown on Plate XXXVI,A. All are magnified fifteen times.

All were of pure flax and contained no trace of cotton. For this information (in which all agreed) and that the fibres were those of *Linum usitatissimum* I am indebted to Dr. A. W. Hill, Director of Kew Gardens, Dr. A. W. Crossley, Director of the Cotton Research Association, and to Dr. A. C. Thaysen, Head of the Bacteriological Laboratory at the Royal Naval Cordite Factory at Holton Heath, all of whom kindly examined these ancient fabrics. No traces of bacteria or moulds could be detected in any of the pieces of cloth submitted to them.

B. A Brown Powder found at the bottom of the Bundle of Ceremonial Batons (Plate VIII).

Some of the wooden sticks which were enveloped in the much-decayed linen wrapping (Plate VIII, B) showed that they had suffered from the attacks of insects. At the lower end of the linen wrapping was a quantity of a fine brown powder resembling ordinary snuff in appearance. Everything suggested that this fine brown powder resulted from the attack of the wood by some insect. The powder when heated on platinum foil, gave off inflammable gases without melting or agglomerating in any way and then burnt away leaving a white ash. This entirely corroborates the above conclusion.

Examination under the microscope indicated that the powder was the result of attack by a boring insect which did not pass the borings through its system. The particles were very small and consisted of fragments of cells, medullary rays and fragments of larger vessels on which well-marked characteristics (such as pitted vessels) still remained. Along with these minute particles there were much larger sausage-like agglomerations which were evidently the true excreta of the insect and were usually of a dark brown colour. When ignited these also left a pure white ash retaining the form of the sausage-shaped lumps.

Alcohol seemed to extract very little except a trace of resinous matter ; ammonia solution also dissolved some resinous substance which, on drying, left a brownish film marked by well-defined cracks. Alcohol did not seem to have any appreciable effect on the dry ammoniacal extract.

C. Brown Spots on the Painted Walls of Burial Chamber.—Spots of a dark brown colour varying in size from that of a threepenny-piece to that of half a crown were observed all over the paintings in the sepulchral chamber. They were quite independent of the colour and did not seem to occur more closely or to show any preference for any particular colour. This seems to indicate that the substance on which the moulds depended for their growth was the size employed in the lime-wash underlying the painted surface or in the paint itself. A few well-defined spots were found on the unpainted walls of the Antechamber. All that could be seen pointed to these spots having been produced by moulds, fungoid growths, or bacteria of some sort which found nutriment in the glue (or albumen) used for sizing.

These brown patches were entirely superficial and flaked off on being touched by a knife-blade, no trace of colour being visible below the surface. Many of these patches showed what appeared to be well-defined crystals in the middle of each patch. These sparkled brightly under a strong light as if they had brilliant plane facets, and when examined with a hand lens suggested crystals of selenite. Heated on platinum foil they intumesced strongly, the swollen mass being white or pearl-like and this, on being heated, still more strongly charred, after which the black mass burnt like tinder and left a pure white ash. The ash dissolved with effervescence in dilute hydrochloric acid.

A brown patch placed on platinum foil and moistened with a drop of hydrochloric acid gave a strong effervescence, due to the plaster below and a yellow solution which was viscid, but in which no mycelia or mould-like structure could be detected. On evaporating the liquid to dryness a white residue was left which, when heated, also intumesced strongly, charred and burned, leaving a white residue with a few particles of carbon.

When examined under a low-power microscope the spots seemed to be glossy and gelatinous all over, the appearance recalling that of an ordinary brown seaweed. No sporangia, or anything resembling them, could be found on any of the spots. Some spots were taken and placed in water (which detached the greater part of the plaster backing), then to the liquid some dilute gelatine solution was added. Some of this was left in a beaker in the pure atmosphere of the Valley of the Kings, but after several days no brown or coloured growths were found, but only grey spots of Penicillium. A thin layer of gelatine solution was spread on a white earthenware pot into which a piece of a brown spot was placed to see if anything would grow. Here also nothing could be detected except a yellow or orange stain round the spot. Dr. Thaysen, with all the resources of a properly equipped bacteriological laboratory and great experience in such work, was likewise unable to obtain any growths or any evidence of live bacteria or of moulds or their spores. With regard to what have been described as crystals it ought to be pointed out that Dr. Thaysen does not agree that they are really such. He says, " they appear to me to be merely an exudation of the size or binding material used to convert the calcium carbonate of the wall-rendering into a plastic compound." The binding material is soluble in water and nitrogenous in nature.

Having had the great advantage of observing these bodies in large numbers *in situ*, I still feel convinced that they are true crystals, probably of the calcium salt of an organic acid formed by the action of some form of life on the material used as a size.

The importance of what has been gone into arises from the fact that it gives a clue to, and an explanation of, the peculiar tarnishing of the gold leaf covering the shrines. Gold of good quality should not tarnish in any ordinary atmosphere, and much less so in an atmosphere such as that of a tomb excavated in a pure limestone. Moreover, the discoloration did not look like the usual tarnishing of a metallic surface. Examination under the microscope showed that the gold was covered with the same brownish seaweed-like substance as on the wall, spots with similar crystal-like bodies but smaller in size and of the same amber tint. When the gold, tinted red in this way was heated, exactly the same phenomena of intumescence, etc., were observed, and on blowing off the white ash, the gold was seen to be of its usual brilliant yellow colour. The explanation suggested by these observations is that some of the gesso-material (calcium carbonate and glue) was allowed to remain on the gold when the gold leaf was stuck on to the shrine, and that the same chemical changes occurred as took place on the walls with the same substances and through the same agencies.

D. A Glossy (Resinous) Material on the Bronze Tongues of the Shrine. The appearance of the substance coating the bronze tongues at once suggested a resin melted on the bronze by heat. The surface was glossy all over and unscratched or broken in any way. Why was it on the lower parts of the bronze tongues and not on the alternate wooden ones ? Why only on the lower parts ? Why has it the appearance of being melted on ? What is its use ?

Some was scraped off and tested to see if it was related in any way to the black resin so much used on various objects. The powder was of a pale reddish-brown colour. It fused easily to a dark brown liquid which readily solidified on cooling. When more strongly heated on platinum foil, it gave off inflammable gases and burnt away, leaving only a trace of ash. It dissolved readily in alcohol and left a brown residue on evaporation of the solution. Water precipitated the resin from the alcoholic solution.

The black resin when powdered behaved very differently. This on heating on platinum foil gave off much gas, with a smell almost like that from heated india-rubber. It burnt away but left as an intermediate product much bulky charcoal and a trace of ash. It hardly dissolved in alcohol, but what did dissolve left a brown resinous residue. The same phenomena characterized both some of the black resin which had been applied to wood and a lump of unused resin which broke with a conchoidal fracture.

A clear resin of a brownish colour which was in

spherical-shaped lumps of the size of a small walnut, gave a lighter coloured powder which dissolved in alcohol. This powder also fused, but gave off much more gas than that from the bronze tongues and also a much lighter coloured solution in alcohol.

The resin from the tongues behaved in every way like shellac ; none of the others did.

E. Black Coating on Staples on Doors of Shrine. The staples of metal into which the ebony bolts slide, and by means of which the doors of the shrines were closed, were found to be covered by a black coating which scaled off easily. When removed this coating was seen to be of a metallic nature. Examination with the microscope showed it to be highly crystalline and brilliantly white on the edges and other broken surfaces. As the metal was not easily fusible it was clearly neither tin nor lead, and it was not tarnished by being made red-hot. These simple tests pointed to the metal being silver of a high degree of purity. This conclusion was con-firmed by its dissolving completely in nitric acid with the exception of a few black flakes (gold ?) and the silver nitrate formed being of a sparkling whiteness with perhaps a trace of greenish hue at one spot. This might indicate a trace of copper, but even if this were so, it might have come from the bronze staple. No trace of a blue colour could be detected when ammonia solution was added in excess.

Heated with strong sulphuric acid until it fumed strongly, it gave a distinct brown colour to the acid as if the coating contained organic matter. When heated thus, one side became clean and bright but the other remained black. In spite of the evolution of sulphur dioxide the black substance remained strongly adherent and, when examined under the microscope, showed many cracks. These may have been caused by flattening out the original rounded surface. The black coating did not seem to be loosened or affected in any way by either pyridine or caustic soda solution.

There is no real evidence that the silver was coated with black paint of any ordinary kind, and it does not seem probable that, if the staples were to be painted, they would have been coated with silver as the bronze would have taken the paint just as well.

It is interesting to note that the silver originally applied in the form of a thin malleable sheet had become highly crystalline and brittle, merely by the lapse of time.

F. The Metal Band round the Base of the outer Shrine. This band was thought to be pure copper from its general appearance when cleaned by scraping with a knife or by means of nitric acid. That it was not *pure* copper was evident from its much greater hardness and that, when cleaned with nitric acid, a brown stain was left behind, easily rubbed off with the finger, as is the case with many varieties of bronze.

When dissolved in nitric acid and evaporated to dryness, the residue of tin oxide had a purplish tint, which was probably due to a trace of gold.

Analysis showed the composition of the alloy to be :

							Per cent.
Copper	.	.	.	.	.	.	97·2
Tin	.	.	.	.	.	.	2·5
Silver	.	.	.	.	.	.	0·3
							100·0

No evidence of the presence of lead could be found. The metal was covered with a dark green coating which suggested that it had been painted (especially in view of the discovery of a broad line painted a similar dark green around the base of the stone sarcophagus). Unfortunately the bending and twisting of the metal in detaching it from the wood of the shrine had removed almost the whole of this coating. One piece when heated in a glass tube seemed to show a blistering of the coating as if it contained an oily admixture. Alcohol dissolved a little of something which charred with strong sulphuric acid. From what remained, caustic soda seemed to dissolve nothing, even in the presence of alcohol, as the solution gave no trace of precipitate, or even opalescence, on being made acid with sulphuric acid, and this solution on evaporation to dryness and heating showed no traces of charring.

It is probable, therefore, that this metallic strip was originally painted dark green, although it can hardly be said that this has been *proved.*

G. Examination of Cosmetic contained in Calcite Jar. The cosmetic jar (pp. 34, 35, Plates L and LI) of calcite was found to contain a large quantity of a fatty substance intended evidently for use as the cosmetic. This unguent was sealed up completely from the atmosphere by the substance itself having reacted with the carbonate of lime of the jar and with the outside air, so forming a continuous crust of stable substances round the lid. Consequently a unique opportunity was provided for studying the behaviour of a natural fat kept at a relatively high air temperature for over 3,000 years, even if the fat should prove on examination to be mixed with neutral substances.

The cosmetic was examined very thoroughly by Dr. H. J. Plenderleith at the Research Laboratory of the British Museum, but owing to the decomposition of the material no crucial tests could be applied so as to determine, with any degree of certainty, what was the original source of the fat or even to decide whether it was of animal or vegetable origin. In order to make the most of this exceptional material at our disposal, Mr. A. Chaston Chapman, F.R.S., when applied to, most kindly agreed to give us the benefit of his very wide experience and knowledge of fats and oils, and also quite independently made a complete investigation of the cosmetic. These two investigations furnish a very searching chemical examination of this material and illustrate the value of pure research in arriving at sound conclusions with regard to the problems, often of extreme difficulty, presented by the archæologist.

The cosmetic was contained in a wide-mouthed jar of what is often wrongly termed *alabaster* but is really *calcite*, a form of calcium carbonate, whereas alabaster, strictly speaking, is hydrated sulphate of lime. This difference here is of some importance, because calcite can be, and is, readily attacked by the weakest acids, while true alabaster is not. When opened by Dr. Carter the contents of the jar were found to weigh about 1 lb. (450 grams) and were of a somewhat sticky nature, with a smell recalling that of coco-nut. They presented the appearance of a heterogeneous mixture of yellowish nodules with a chocolate-coloured substance. At a temperature as low as that of the hand, the substance softened and tended to melt in part at least, and the odour became stronger but still suggested coco-nut to almost everyone who smelt it. It has also been described as resembling that of the flowers of the broom, or as being valerianaceous in character. The smell could be described as decidedly fatty, but this was certainly not that characteristic of advanced rancidity. A careful microscopic examination failed to reveal any traces of vegetable or any other organized structure.

It is interesting to note in this connexion that a fat found in Egyptian jars protected by thick mud layers, has been described by Petrie and Quibell.[1] It dates from a much earlier period of Egyptian history, and possesses the external characters at least of the specimen under discussion. The Nagada fat, however, was found to contain vegetable fibre when examined under the microscope. Although the histological examination of the debris proved wholly inconclusive in the hands of Dr. Thiselton-Dyer at Kew, these investigators seem convinced that the presence of fibre in the fat is indicative of its vegetable origin—a conclusion which is not beyond question, in consideration of the fact that it is stated on the best authority that fats were preserved by the Egyptians by rolling them in vegetable fibre. While Petrie and Quibell state that the nature of their specimen is not yet certain, they conclude that the only source known for it would be one of the vegetable butters—the shea or the oil palm. It seems unlikely, however, that the fragrant constituents of such oils or fats would be stable enough to withstand the action of oxygen and moisture for such a prolonged period. It should be mentioned that excavators are decided in stating that this smell of coco-nut is often noticeable in specimens freshly excavated, and this suggests that it might be

[1] "Naquada and Ballas," 1896, p. 39.

Appendix IV

due to an odorous product of decomposition of such substances as fats, resins or balsams.

The specimen, when submitted to a systematic analysis, proved to be organic in nature, although when burnt it left a residue of 2 per cent. of its weight in the form of calcium carbonate. This resulted from the combustion of the salts formed by the acids in the fat attacking the calcite of which the jar was made. The cosmetic was free from compounds containing nitrogen or sulphur. As the following analysis shows, the fatty matter soluble in ether amounted to almost 88 per cent. : the total glycerine, free and combined, was almost exactly $5\frac{1}{2}$ per cent.

GENERAL PROXIMATE ANALYSIS

	Per cent.
Fatty matters soluble both in light petroleum and in ether	59·1
Fatty matters soluble in ether but practically insoluble in light petroleum . .	28·6
Matters soluble in alcohol, but insoluble in ether	0·9
Matters soluble in water, but insoluble in alcohol	4·4
Matters insoluble in any of the foregoing solvents	4·7
Moisture (loss on drying at 105° C.) .	2·3
	100·0

An exhaustive qualitative and quantitative examination of the relative amounts of the acids of the stearic acid series and those of the " oxidized " acids derived from those of the oleic acid series, points to the conclusion that the fatty constituent was more probably of animal than of vegetable origin. Owing to the slow and prolonged oxidation by atmospheric oxygen, all the more characteristic but unstable constituents of animal, as contrasted with vegetable fat, had disappeared.

Summing up the results of their investigations Chapman and Plenderleith say:[1] " On the whole we are inclined to regard the chemical evidence as supporting the view that the fat was of animal character, since it does not seem probable that any vegetable fat with the small proportion of olein this appears originally to have contained, would have been available. The chemical evidence, generally, would seem to exclude coco-nut or palm kernel oils. Having regard to all the results it appears probable that the cosmetic consisted of about 90 per cent. of a neutral animal fat with about 10 per cent. of some resin or balsam."

H. Analysis of Silver Nail with Gold Head— (from the Second Coffin). The diameter of the gold head (which was distinctly pale in colour) was $10\frac{1}{2}$ millimetres. The nail itself was $49\frac{1}{2}$ millimetres in length, with a diameter of $4\frac{3}{4}$ at the head gradually tapering to 2·9 at the point when it was abruptly rounded off. It was almost black in colour and, when washed with ammonia solution, gave a liquid which became strongly opalescent on the addition of pure nitric acid. This gave an explanation of the tarnishing in that it proved the presence of chlorine, no doubt from the common salt in the perspiration of the ancient artificers who fashioned it. The specific gravity of the silver alloy was 10·52. Analysis showed the substance of the nail to consist of :

	Per cent.
Silver	90·2
Gold	5·1
Copper	4·5
Lead	0·2
	100·0

[1] *Jour. Chem. Soc.*, Vol. cxxix, pp. 2614–2619.

Appendix IV

I. Analysis of the Gold Nail—(from the Gold Coffin). The gold nail was pale in colour and the metal brittle. It became dark brown on being made red-hot in air, thus indicating a notable amount of copper in the alloy from which it was made. The diameter of the head was 8½ millimetres, and that of the body of the nail, 5 millimetres. Its length was 25 millimetres or almost exactly one inch. Its specific gravity was as nearly as possible 14·5. There was a well-marked flaw in the metal close to the point, but the specific gravity of the nail as a whole agreed exactly with that of the sample taken for analysis which had been fused into a bead and then flattened by hammering.

Analysis showed the composition of the alloy to be :

								Per cent.
Gold	.	.	.	.	.	.	.	67
Silver	.	.	.	.	.	.	.	25
Copper	.	.	.	.	.	.	.	8
								——
								100

J. Brown Fluffy Material from Outside of Sarcophagus. This is of great interest as it is the only object from the tomb in which undoubted mould growths or any of the lower forms of life have been detected. The single tuft of what looked like a tiny patch of cotton-wool was found on the outside of the sarcophagus, beginning just above and continuing over the incised line of hieroglyphics around the upper part. It was noticed at the time that what seemed to be some fungus hyphæ spread over the red-coloured figures, but avoided those coloured yellow, keeping sharply, when it came in contact with them, to the uncoloured stone which lay between the individual figures. This was an additional proof that these hyphæ had been alive, the poisonous nature of the yellow sulphide of arsenic preventing their growth as soon as they reached it.

From my own microscopic examination of this fluff I was convinced that it consisted of fungus hyphæ, on which were several spherical masses of a clear rather transparent brown, which I hoped might prove to be sporangia and so give a clue to the identification of this particular mould.

I therefore sent all the material to Dr. A. W. Hill, Director of Kew Gardens, to whom and to Miss E. M. Wakefield, who made the actual examination, I am much indebted for the following careful report:

Brown Fluffy Material from Sarcophagus.

Fungus hyphæ were found in this, but no fructification, hence identification is impossible. The hyphæ are colourless, but they are coated with an amorphous brown substance, suggesting an irregular encrustation of gelatine or gum. Where branching occurs this substance is sometimes collected in large rounded or oblong drops, which I take to be the bodies referred to as possible reproductive organs. When treated with very dilute solutions of potassium hydrate the brown substance disappears, leaving the hyphæ scarcely visible. It is dissolved also, but more slowly, by lactic acid.

It is unfortunate that no information is given as to what may have been the substance on which the fungus was growing. If it was on paint which had been mixed with gelatine, it is possible that the gelatine was liquefied by the fungus and thus was able to form a coating along the hyphæ. Or possibly a gum may have been acted on similarly. It has not been possible to find out the nature of the brown substance, partly because of ignorance as to what changes may have been undergone in such a long period of time, and partly because of the impossibility of applying chemical tests, such as Millon's for proteid, in the case of such minute quantities of material so readily soluble in both acids and alkalis.

Note. It ought to be mentioned for the information of those interested that a complete account of the chemical examination of the cosmetic is published in the *Journal of the Chemical Society* for 1926, Vol. cxxix, pp. 2614–2619.

APPENDIX V

REPORT ON THE EXAMINATION OF SPECIMENS FROM THE TOMB OF KING TUT·ANKH·AMEN

By H. J. Plenderleith, M.C., Ph.D.

British Museum Research Laboratory,
July, 1926.

(1) Reed Torch (from Floor Rubbish of Burial Chamber). The pith is impregnated with a black gum-resin which has probably been poured into the reed in the molten condition. It is readily soluble in alcohol and largely soluble also in ether. The small insoluble portion on extraction with water yields a trace of gum. The acid value for the original product is 137·9. The gummiferous portion is slightly dextrorotatory in aqueous solution. Microscopic examination of the residue insoluble in alcohol, revealed the pitted vessels characteristic of coniferous woods, and the solutions had a decided odour of pine.

The experimental evidence suggests that this specimen is a pine resin of some kind, possibly from juniper.

(2) Red Resin (from Kiosks, Plate LIII,B). This was red and very powdery. About 93·9 per cent. was soluble in alcohol and 6·1 per cent. soluble in water. It gave a terebenthinate smell on being heated. Its acid value was 137·7. It was practically insoluble in benzene and in ether. The qualitative evidence from solubilities suggests shellac, but for this the acid value is much too high. It is possibly Angola copal.

(3) Material from mending of Sarcophagus. This on examination proved to be a mixture of gum-resin with calcium carbonate and sand. The yellow colour is due, apparently, to superficial darkening.

(4) A Fragment of Cement from the Tomb. This was found to consist of calcium sulphate with a small quantity of limestone grit and sand.

(5) A Greyish Powder (from Kiosks, Plate LIII,B). This powder is mainly organic in its nature, and is largely soluble in water but not appreciably soluble in alcohol. The aqueous solution is strongly alkaline. It contains carbonates and sulphates, sodium and potassium, with traces of copper and nitrogen.

The powder contains also the remains (elytra) of many beetles of a length of from 3 to 5 millimetres which, together with small pieces of bark, are readily observed floating in the aqueous solution. There is not enough detail left in the insect remains to determine the exact specimens, but there is no doubt that they are members of the Cigarette family of beetles which live on species such as cinnamon and pepper as well as tobacco.

This substance therefore seems to consist of the residue of a gum or spice of some kind.

(6) Examination of " Consecration Fluid." The mixture was not uniform. An average portion treated by extraction gave :

		Per cent.
A. Matters soluble in alcohol	. . .	56
B. Matters insoluble in alcohol	. . .	44
		100

A. Matters soluble in Alcohol. The evaporated residue from this fraction was completely soluble in carbon disulphide, benzene, chloroform, turpentine and pyridine and gave a turbid ethereal solution. It was moderately soluble in acetone, insoluble in water but largely soluble in caustic soda. On heating, the substance melted approximately at 130° C. (softening from about 110° C.), and emitted a characteristic resinous odour resembling that of myrrh and possibly bdellium.

B. Matters insoluble in Alcohol. This black residue was completely soluble in carbon disulphide, benzene, chloroform, turpentine and pyridine, but only slightly soluble in ether and in acetone. It melted about 70° C. and had a decided odour of pitch.

It is evident that odoriferous resins have been melted with pitch and used as a consecration fluid. The question as to whether mineral pitch or wood pitch is here employed must remain doubtful, as this is determined by the relative solubility of the pitch in alcohol; a figure which is not obtainable here as alcohol had to be employed to remove the resinous portion in the first instance.

Efforts to separate the resin from the pitch (1) by the difference in melting points and (2) by freezing, powdering and the slight difference in specific gravity proved ineffectual.

APPENDIX VI

DESCRIPTION OF THE OBJECTS

(A) THE KING, SEATED IN HIS CABINET, POURING PERFUME ON THE
HAND OF THE QUEEN

In his left hand he holds a lotus blossom and fruits of the mandrake.

(*See* pp. 14, 193)

(B) THE KING, ACCOMPANIED BY HIS QUEEN AND LION-CUB, SHOOTING
WILD DUCK

(*See* pp. 14, 15)

PLATE 1

(A) A SKETCH UPON A SPLINTER OF LIMESTONE

Depicting the king, aided by his slughi hound, slaying a lion with a spear.

(See p. 16)

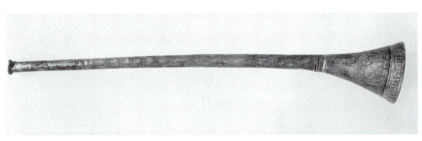

(B) A SILVER TRUMPET

Embellished with gold and dedicated to the legions of Re, Amen and Ptah.

(See pp. 19, 30)

PLATE II

Plate III

TUT · ANKH · AMEN HUNTING LION

The young king in his chariot, drawn by prancing steeds gorgeous in their trappings, and accompanied by his slughi hound, is here represented slaying lions and lionesses. The scene in miniature painting, wherein the agonized shaft-pierced beasts are portrayed with splendid power, is from a painted casket (No. 21) found in the Antechamber.

(*See* p. 18, Vol. I, Plate XXI)

PLATE IV

INTERIOR OF THE BURIAL CHAMBER

Here will be seen the first (outermost) shrine with roof removed, and the linen pall supported upon wooden struts over the second shrine within. On the (North) wall behind (from right to left) we see the upper portions of the painted scenes: (A) King Ay presiding over the obsequies of Tut·ankh·Amen; (B) Tut·ankh·Amen before the goddess Nūt; (C) Tut·ankh·Amen followed by his "Ka" embracing Osiris; and (D) on the West wall (left-hand side) is the upper part of vignettes selected from chapters of the Book of Amduat.

(See pp. 28, 29, 33, Plates V and LIV)

PLATE V

INTERIOR OF THE BURIAL CHAMBER

Here, placed between the First (outermost) shrine and the North wall, are (183–192) ten magic oars to ferry the king's barque across the waters of the Nether World; at the far end (193) are two small black kiosks in wood varnished with black resin, and, in the N.E. corner (194), is an Anubis emblem, hanging upon a pole, and covered with linen. (See p. 32, Plates VI and LIII)

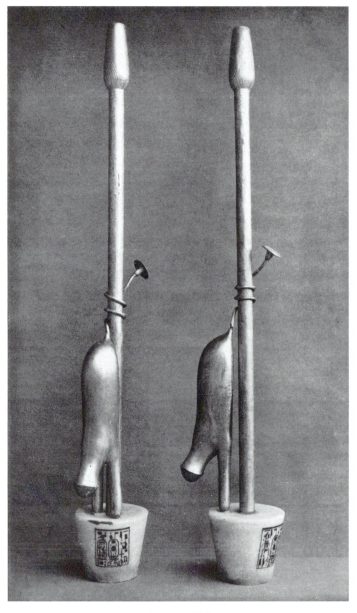

PLATE VI

TWO ANUBIS EMBLEMS

Two curious emblems of the god Anubis, in the form of animal skins, hung
upon lotiform poles, stood in alabaster (calcite) bases, and placed in the N.W.
and S.W. corners of the Burial Chamber. They stand some 5 to 6 feet in height.
are carved of wood, and covered with gesso-gilt. (See p. 32, Plate V, 194)

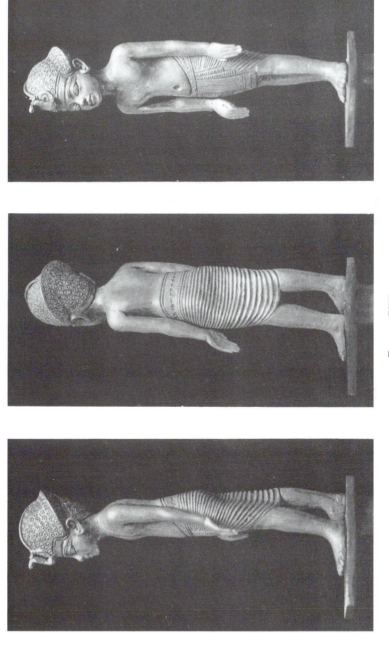

PLATE VII

THE GOLD STICK

One of a pair of ceremonial gold and silver sticks shown from three points of view. The statuettes in solid metal, some 3½ inches in height upon tubular shafts about 4 feet in length, represent Tut-ankh-Amen at about 12 years of age, when he ascended the throne.

(See pp. 35, 36, 95)

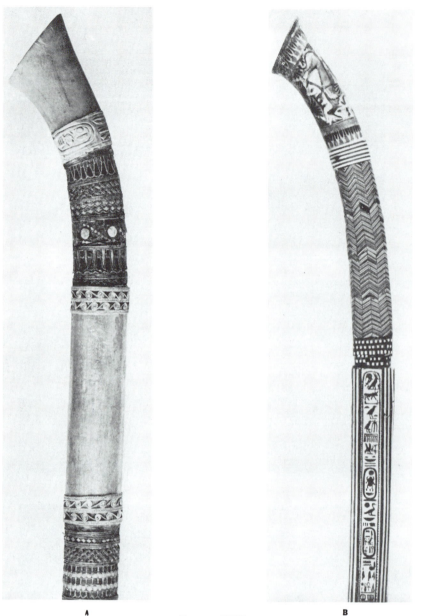

A   B

PLATE VIII

CEREMONIAL BATONS

(A) Red wood, elaborately decorated with minute marquetry of variegated barks,
iridescent elytra of beetles, broad bands of burnished gold, and applied gold wire-work.

(B) Red wood, veneered with intricate ivory and ebony geometrical patterns and,
at the ends, carved ivory tips.   (*See* pp. 35, 36)

PLATE IX

PREPARING THE GUARDIAN STATUES FOR TRANSPORT
TO THE LABORATORY

(See pp. 25, 39, 41)

PLATE X

DEMOLISHING THE PARTITION WALL DIVIDING THE ANTECHAMBER
FROM THE BURIAL CHAMBER

(*See* pp. 39, 41)

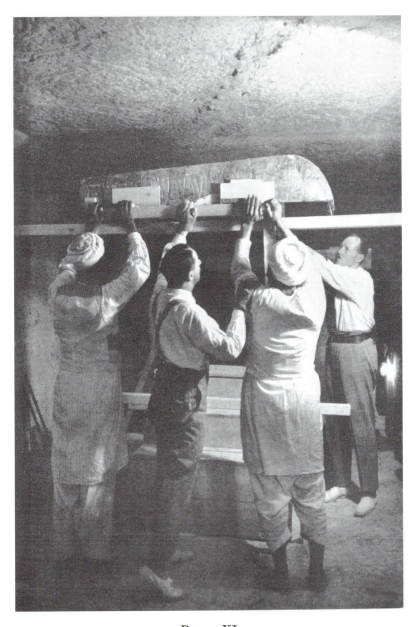

PLATE XI

A ROOF SECTION OF THE FIRST (OUTERMOST) SHRINE BEING REMOVED
TO THE ANTECHAMBER

(See p. 42, Plate LIV)

PLATE XII

OPENING THE DOOR OF THE SECOND SHRINE

(See p. 44, Plate XIII)

PLATE XIII

OPENING THE DOORS OF THE FOURTH (INNERMOST) SHRINE

(See p. 45, Plate XII)

PLATE XIV

FIRST GLIMPSE OF THE SARCOPHAGUS FILLING THE ENTIRE AREA OF
THE FOURTH (INNERMOST) SHRINE

(See p. 45, Plates LXIV and LXV)

PLATE XV

THE ROOF OF THE FOURTH (INNERMOST) SHRINE

On slings ready to be removed to the Antechamber.

(*See* p. 47, Plates LVIII and LIX)

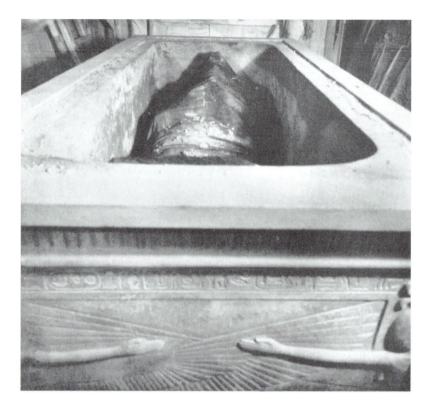

PLATE XVI

RAISING THE LID OF THE SARCOPHAGUS
The first coffin within the sarcophagus covered with linen shrouds.
(*See* p. 51, Plates LXVI and LXVII)

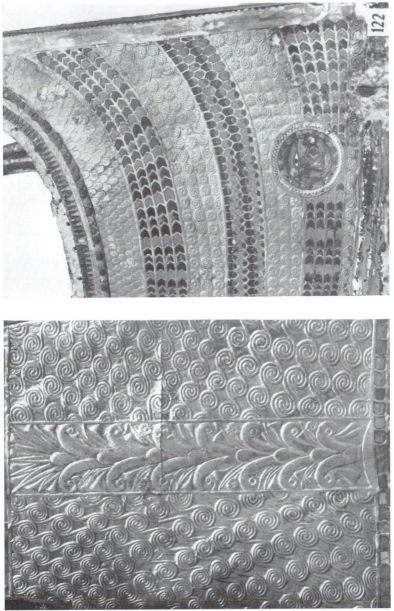

122

PLATE XVII

(A) ORNAMENTATION ON THE FIRST STATE
CHARIOT

(B) ORNAMENTATION ON THE SECOND STATE
CHARIOT

(See pp. 61, 62, Plates XXXVII and XXXVIII)

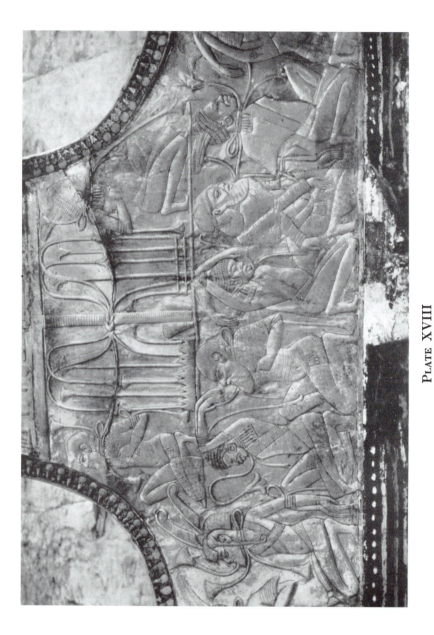

PLATE XVIII

DECORATION ON THE INTERIOR OF THE FIRST STATE CHARIOT

In the centre is a symbol of the "Union of the Two Kingdoms," to which alien foes are bound.
(See p. 61, Plates XIX, XX and XXXVII)

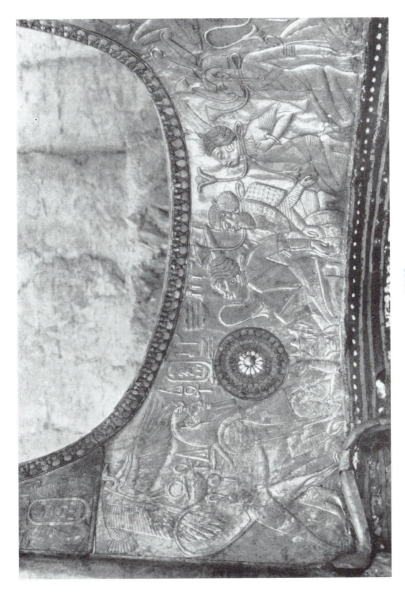

PLATE XIX

DECORATION ON THE INTERIOR OF THE FIRST STATE CHARIOT (LEFT SIDE)

Alien foes before Tut·ankh·Amen, in the form of a human-headed lion, crushing Egypt's enemies.

(See p. 62, Plates XVIII, XX and XXXVII)

PLATE XX

DECORATION ON THE INTERIOR OF THE FIRST STATE CHARIOT (RIGHT SIDE)
Alien foes before Tut-ankh-Amen, in the form of a human-headed lion, crushing Egypt's enemies.
(See p. 62, Plates XVIII, XIX and XXXVII)

A

B

C

PLATE XXI

ORNAMENTS ON THE STATE CHARIOTS

(A) An open-work design between the upper rims of the Chariots.
(B) A head of the god Bes on the first State Chariot.
(C) A jewelled boss on the second State Chariot.

(See pp. 61, 62, Plates XXXVII and XXXVIII)

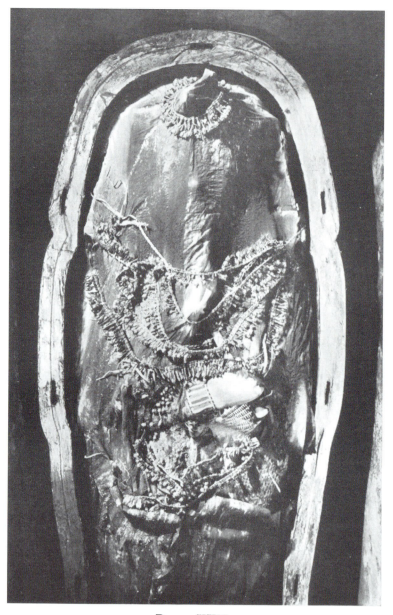

PLATE XXII

A WREATH AND GARLANDS OF FLOWERS AND LINEN SHROUD COVERING
THE SECOND COFFIN

(*See* pp. 72, 190, Plates XXIII, LXVIII and LXIX)

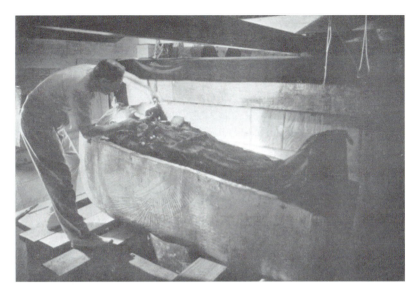

(A) ROLLING BACK THE LINEN SHROUD THAT COVERED THE SECOND COFFIN

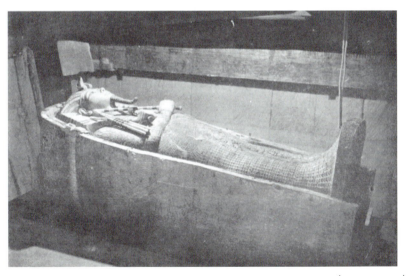

(B) SECOND COFFIN AS IT LAY IN THE SHELL OF FIRST (OUTERMOST) COFFIN. (*See* pp. 73, 74, Plates XXII, LXVIII and LXIX)

PLATE XXIII

PLATE XXIV

THE THIRD (INNERMOST) COFFIN OF GOLD

Covered with linen shroud and floral collarette, as it lay in the shell of the second coffin.

(*See* p. 77, Plates XXXVI, LXX–LXXII)

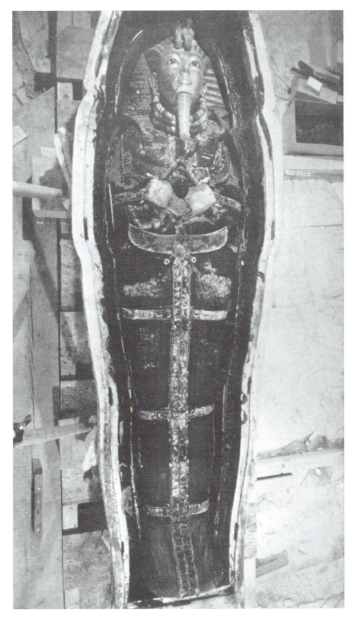

PLATE XXV

THE MUMMY OF THE KING WHEN FIRST DISCLOSED
(*See* pp. 82, 83, Frontispiece and Plates XXVI, XXVII and LXXIII)

C

A

B

PLATE XXVI
(A) BLACK RESIN SCARAB FROM THE EXTERIOR TRAPPINGS OF THE KING'S
MUMMY
(B) *BA* BIRD FROM THE EXTERIOR TRAPPINGS OF THE KING'S MUMMY
(C) BLACK RESIN SCARAB FROM WITHIN THE WRAPPINGS OF THE KING'S
MUMMY

(*See* pp. 83, 121, Plates XXV, XXVII and XXX, Q)

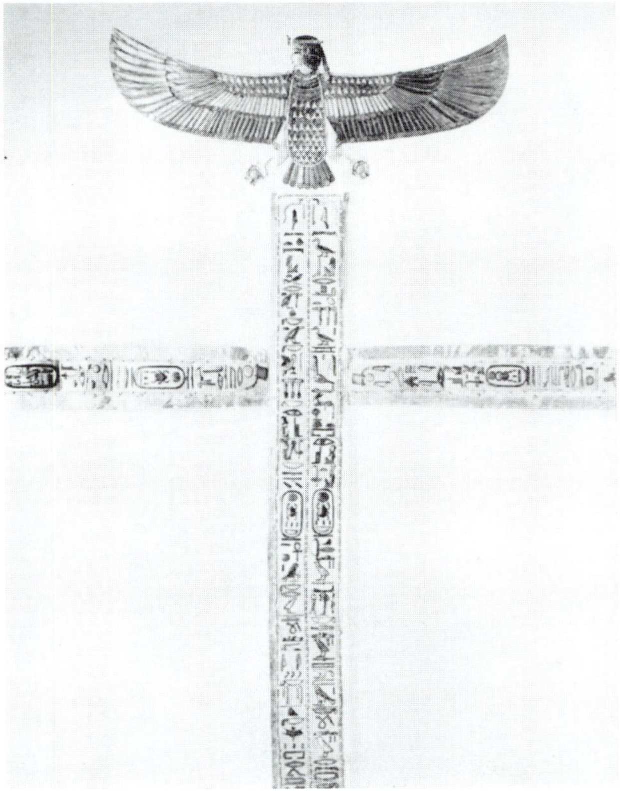

(A) Longitudinal and transverse trappings dependent from a *Ba* bird.

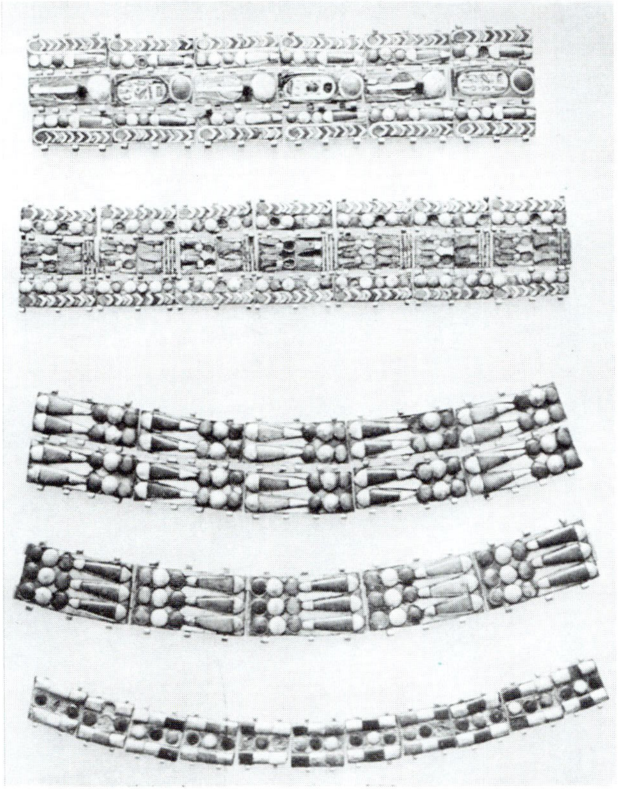

(B) Side straps and festoons from between the transverse trappings.

PLATE XXVII

DETAILS OF THE EXTERIOR TRAPPINGS OF THE KING'S MUMMY

(*See* pp. 83, 84, 85, Plates XXV, XXVI)

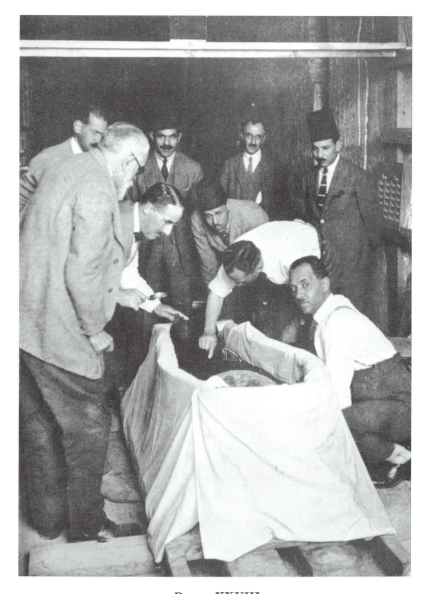

PLATE XXVIII

THE EXAMINATION OF THE ROYAL MUMMY

The Committee present: Dr. Derry making the first incision in the wrappings.

(See pp. 106–108, Plate XXIX)

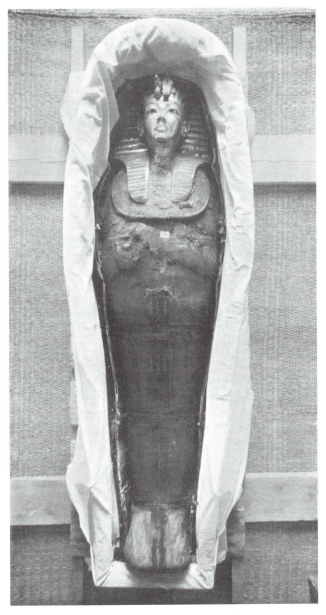

PLATE XXIX

THE ROYAL MUMMY WITHIN ITS COFFIN
The external trappings have been removed

(*See* pp. 107, 148, Plate XXVIII)

PLATE XXX

A RECORD OF OBJECTS FOUND WITHIN THE WRAPPINGS

This is one of a large series of photographic records that were taken of the objects *in situ* during the process of examination of the mummy.

(*See* pp. 109, 110, 120, 136,

Plates XXVI, XXXIII, XXXIV, LXXII, LXXIX, LXXXIII and LXXXVII)

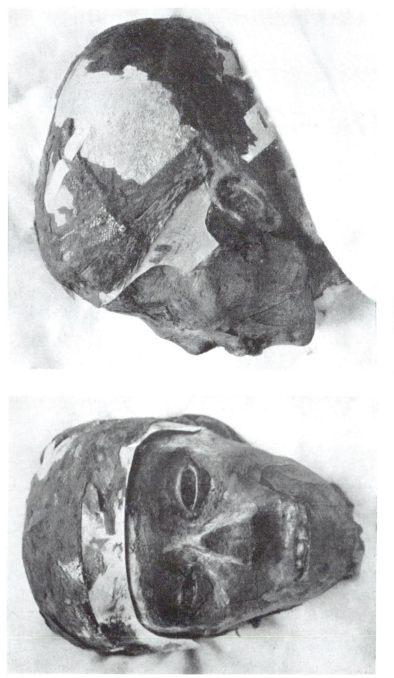

PLATE XXXI

TUT·ANKH·AMEN : THE HEAD OF THE KING'S MUMMY AS FIRST REVEALED

Remark the unusually elongated cranium, the well-formed features, especially the clearly marked lip and pierced ears so noticeable in his portrait mask. Upon the head are the remains of a skull cap (Plate XXXII) and a temple-band (Plate LXXVII, A)

PLATE XXXII

THE BEAD-WORK DEVICE OF THE SKULL CAP

The cartouches upon the uraei are the later forms of the Aten cartouches.

(*See* p. 113, Plate XXXI)

PLATE XXXIII

BRACELETS (*IN SITU*) ON THE KING'S FOREARMS

(*See* pp. 128, 129, Plates XXX, LXXXVI)

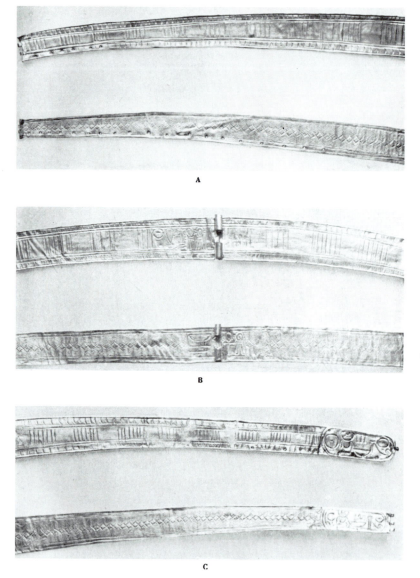

A

B

C

PLATE XXXIV

CHASED GOLD GIRDLES FROM THE WAIST OF THE MUMMY

(*See* pp. 131, 133, Plate XXX)

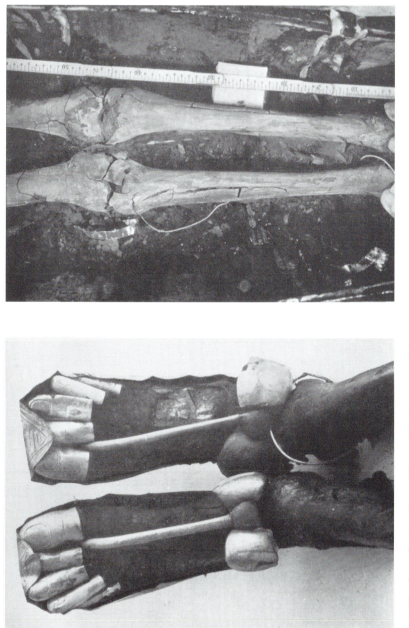

(A) The feet, showing the gold toe sheaths and sandals.   (B) The legs, showing left *patella* removed.

PLATE XXXV

DETAILS OF THE MUMMY

(*See* pp. 137, 151, 156)

Plate XXXVI

A FLORAL AND BEAD COLLARETTE, *IN SITU,* UPON THE THIRD (INNER-MOST) COFFIN

(*See* pp. 78, 191, Plates XXIV, LXX–LXXII)

(A) The Pall which covered the second shrine. It was dark brown in colour and its texture was the coarsest of the three.

(B) The wrapping cloth for the bundle of ceremonial staves (Plate VIII) found within the first shrine. Its colour was a very dark brown, almost black. It shows two threads in one direction to one in the other.

(c) The veil which was thrown over the guardian statues at the entrance to the sepulchral chamber (Vol. I, Plate I). In colour it was much lighter than the other two, being of a dark cream colour, and its texture was of a filmy lightness.

PLATE XXXVIA

ENLARGED (15 TIMES) MICROSCOPIC FRAGMENTS OF FABRICS

PLATE XXXVII

THE BODY OF THE FIRST STATE CHARIOT

Built of bent-wood and completely overlaid with burnished thin sheet-gold upon gesso. The margins, etc., are encrusted with semi-precious stones and polychrome glass.

On the front (A) the embossed ornament comprises: the names of Tut-ankh-Amen, a central vertical band of floral design, and side panels of elaborate coil-pattern. On the interior (B) is a panel of cartouches of the king with the symbolical "Union of the Two Kingdoms" to which underneath are bound captives of the North and South. Below is a magnificent frieze of alien prisoners, with arms lashed behind them, kneeling before the all powerful human-headed lion (sphinx) Tut-ankh-Amen. Upon the foot-rail are collars of encrusted gold-work, and at either side at the juncture of the framework of the "body" are highly ornamented bosses surmounted by grotesque heads of the god Bes.

(*See* p. 61, Plates XVII, A, XVIII–XX, XXI, B)

A

B

PLATE XXXVII

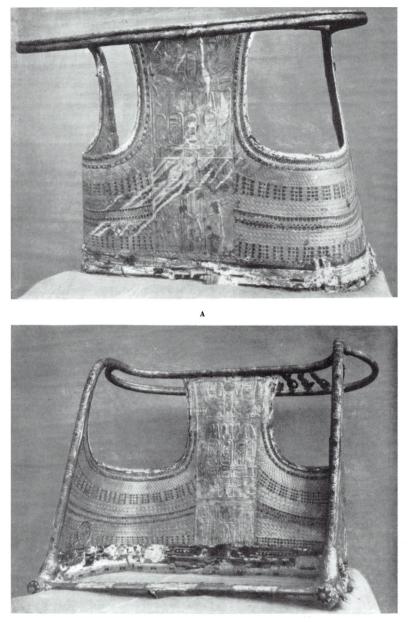

A

B

PLATE XXXVIII

PLATE XXXVIII

THE BODY OF THE SECOND STATE CHARIOT

Built of bent-wood and overlaid with gold upon gesso. The margins of the panels and upright rails of the " body " are encrusted with semi-precious stones and polychrome glass.

On the front surface (A) in the centre and embossed upon the sheet-gold is a solar-hawk, the cartouches of the king, the *Rekhyt* (i.e. the people), and the symbolical " Union of the Two Kingdoms," to which are tied alien captives. Upon the sides are embossed and inlaid feather, ox-eye and coil-patterns.

On the inside surface (B) the ornamentation is almost exactly similar to that on the front. The uprights of the " body " are encrusted with an hieroglyphic device incorporating the king's prenomen, and at the junctures of the upright rails and base are jewelled bosses.

(*See* p. 61, Plates XVII, B, and XXI, A and C)

PLATE XXXIX

THE AXLES OF THE STATE CHARIOTS

These axles are made of a strong (?) wood, having their exposed parts overlaid with sheet-gold upon gesso. As will be seen from the illustrations (A and B), the overlaid portions have at intervals collars and bands of heavier gold-work which are richly encrusted with hieroglyphic and floral devices in glass and semi-precious stones—the central piece forms (?) a sort of foot-plate.

(See p. 62)

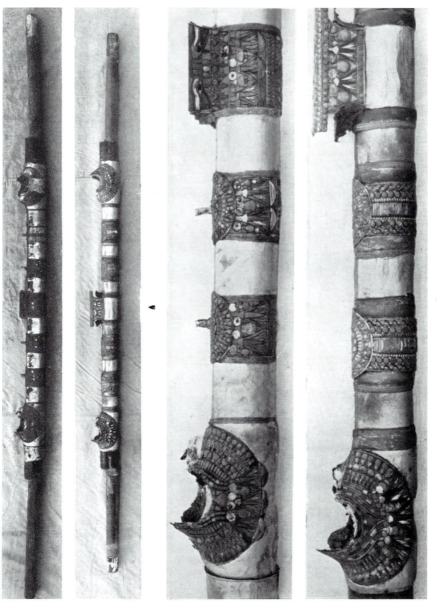

PLATE XXXIX

PLATE XL

PLATE XL

THE WHEELS OF THE STATE CHARIOTS

The felloes, 6 radial bars, the naves and flanges, are made of different kinds of woods and are overlaid with sheet-gold upon gesso. For further description and probable construction, *see* pp. 57, 62. The tyres were of leather.

Plate XLI

THE YOKES OF THE STATE CHARIOTS

(A) These yokes, which were fixed to the pole of the chariot, are made of bent-wood, are overlaid with sheet-gold and have their " bearings " furnished with leather. Their curved ends terminate with knobs of opaque calcite.

The yoke of the first State chariot has, in addition to the terminating stone knob, a figure (B) of a Northern prisoner, and a figure (c) of a Southern prisoner, devised to form the curved ends.

(*See* pp. 59, 63)

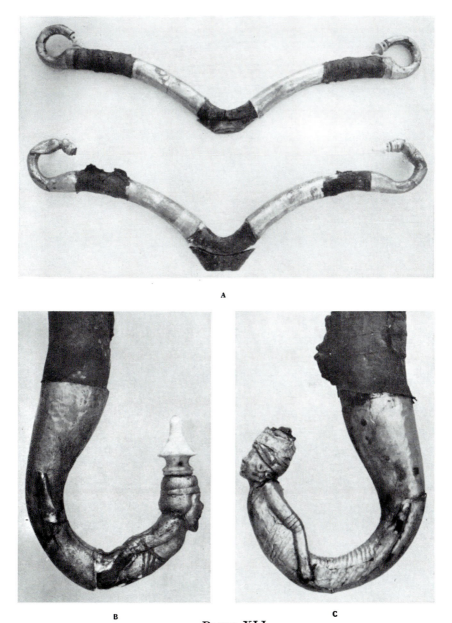

A

B   C

PLATE XLI

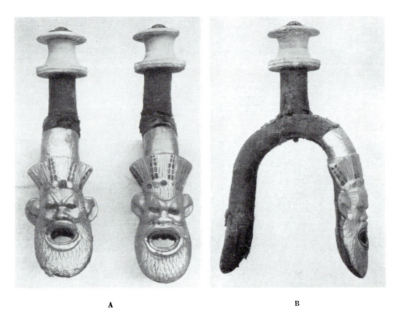

A　　　　　　　　　　　　B

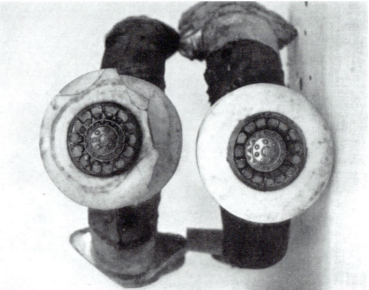

C

PLATE XLII

Plate XLII

HARNESS SADDLES BELONGING TO THE STATE CHARIOTS

(A and B) These saddles are made of bent-wood and were covered with leather. The end of the near-side of the left saddle and the end of the off-side of the right saddle takes the form of the head of the god Bes. These heads are overlaid with gold upon gesso, and are inlaid with polychrome glass—their widely opened mouths are devised to receive the girth straps. The calcite reels (C) on the tops of the saddles are ornamented with granular gold-work and are encrusted.

(*See* p. 63)

R

A

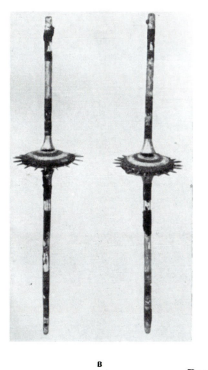

B

C

PLATE XLIII

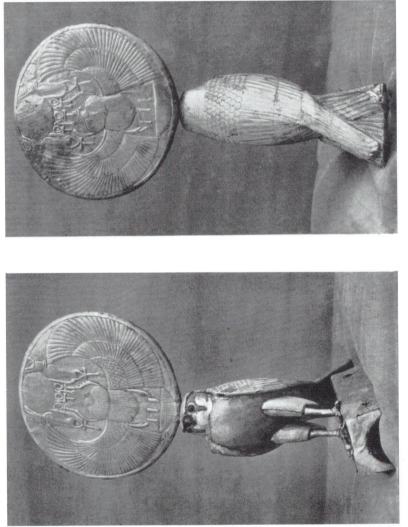

A B

Plate XLIV

PLATE XLIV

A SOLAR-HAWK FROM THE POLE OF A STATE CHARIOT

(A and B) Front and back view of one of the solar-hawks from the poles of the State chariots, which served as a kind of cockade of the Royal Household.

These hawks are carved of wood and are completely overlaid with sheet-gold. The device upon the front and back of the solar-disk fixed on the head of the hawk, incorporates the king's prenomen, and suggests his supposed solar origin.

(*See* pp. 60, 62)

Plate XLV

AN ALABASTER (CALCITE) LAMP

A palace lamp of chalice form upon a trellis-work pedestal, carved out of translucent calcite. It is flanked with fretwork ornament symbolizing " Unity " and " Eternal Life." On each side is the name of Tut-ankh-Amen.

(*See* p. 30, Plate XLVI)

PLATE XLV

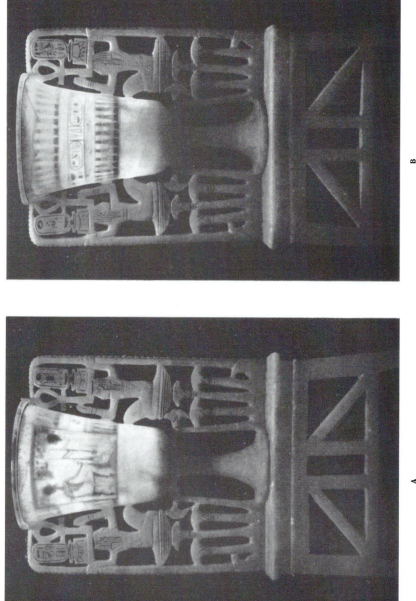

Plate XLVI

B

A

PLATE XLVI

THE ALABASTER (CALCITE) LAMP WHEN LIT

(A) Front, showing the king and queen in brilliant colours within the thickness of the translucent walls of the chalice-like cup.

(B) Back, in the same manner the prenomen and nomen of Tut-ankh-Amen are shown between garlands of floral ornament.

(*See* p. 30, Plate XLV)

Plate XLVII

A TRIPLE-LAMP

An exquisite triple-lamp of floral form, carved out of a single block of translucent calcite. In design it comprises three lotiform oil cups with stems and lotus leaves springing from a circular base. In all probability the lamp symbolizes the Theban Triad.

(*See* p. 31)

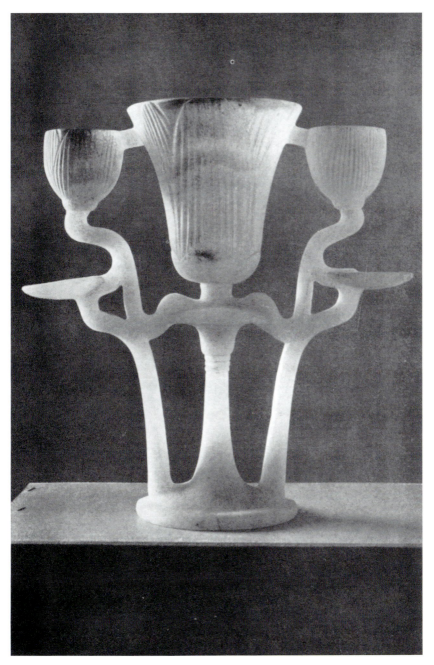

PLATE XLVII

PLATE XLVIII

PLATE XLVIII

THE PERFUME VASE OF THE KING AND QUEEN

This beautiful and intricate vase is carved out of four separate pieces of calcite cemented together, and is embellished with gold and painted ivory. The central vase has an open-work flanking ornament emblematical of " The Union of the Two Countries " (i.e. Upper and Lower Egypt) devised in the form of lotus (Up. Eg.) and papyrus (Low. Eg.) flowers, having their stalks knotted around the neck of the vase. On each side is an epicene figure of the Nile god Hapi. They support not only the flanking ornament, but also slender lotus and papyrus sceptres encircled by uræi, which bear upon their heads the white and red crowns (respectively) of the " Two Kingdoms." Upon the wide lip of the vase, and wearing the *Atef* crown of Osiris, is the goddess Mut in the form of a vulture with open wings. The device of the fretwork panels of the trellis-work pedestal comprises solar-hawks supporting with their wings the king's cartouche upon *Nub* (gold) symbols.

(*See* p. 34, Plate XLIX)

PLATE XLIX

PLATE L

PLATE L

A COSMETIC JAR

A cylindrical cosmetic jar carved out of semi-translucent and opaque calcite, with prisoners' heads of black and red hard stone. The tongue of the recumbent lion upon the revolving lid, the hinge and knobs, are of ivory stained red. The hunting scene and garland ornament upon the sides of the jar are engraved upon the stone and are filled in with different coloured pigments.

(See pp. 34, 35, 206, Plate LI)

PLATE LI

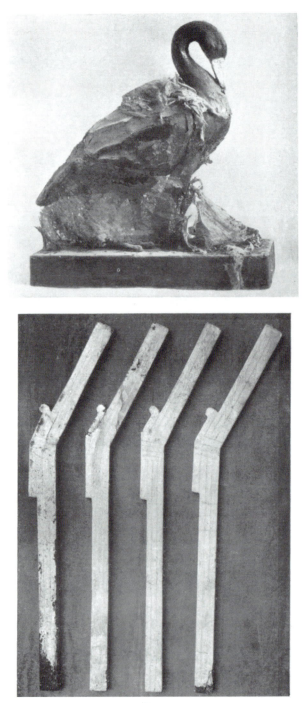

B

PLATE LII

Plate LII

(A) AMEN'S SACRED GOOSE

The Egyptian goose (*Chenalopex Ægyptiacus,* Linn.) carved out of wood, varnished with black resin, and swathed in fine cambric-like linen.

(*See* pp. 31, 32)

(B) FOUR CURIOUS GOLD WOOD SYMBOLS

These curious symbols of wood, covered with gesso-gilt, may possibly signify the swathing bandages of the mummy or, as they seem to give rise to the phonetic hieroglyph " to awake," they may have some connexion with the " awakening " of the dead.

(*See* p. 32)

PLATE LIII

(A) HES-VASE BETWEEN PROPYLÆ

This peculiar emblem, from the N.E. corner of the Burial Chamber, is carved out of wood and thickly varnished with a black resin.

(*See* p. 32)

(B) TWO WOODEN KIOSKS AND FEATHERS IN STONE

The wooden kiosks, varnished with black resin, contain blue faience cups filled respectively with natron and resin, from the N.W. corner of the Burial Chamber.

(*See* pp. 32, 214, Plate V, 193)

A

B

PLATE LIII

PLATE LIV

PLATE LIV

THE FIRST (OUTERMOST) SHRINE

17 feet by 11 feet, and 9 feet high, made of $2\frac{1}{4}$-inch oak-wood planking, overlaid with gold-work upon gesso, the side, end and door panels being inlaid with brilliant blue faience—their decoration mainly consists of alternate pairs of the protective symbols *Ded* and *Thet*.

(*See* p. 42, Plates IV, V and XI)

A

B

PLATE LV

PLATE LVI

PLATE LVI

THE WOODEN PERPENDICULAR PALL STRUTS
BETWEEN THE FIRST AND SECOND SHRINES

(*See* p. 44, Plates IV and LV)

PLATE LVII

THE SECOND SHRINE

A beautiful construction made, like the first (outermost) shrine, of oak-wood planking overlaid with gold upon gesso. Like the other shrines the whole of the exterior and interior surfaces are decorated with scenes and texts from the "Book of that which is in the Underworld" and the "Destruction of Mankind," etc.

(*See* p. 44, Plates LV and LVI)

PLATE LVII

PLATE LVIII

PLATE LVIII

THE FOURTH (INNERMOST) SHRINE

Made of oak-wood planking and overlaid with gold-work upon gesso. The decoration on this shrine is in bas-relief—in contradistinction to the incised work on the three preceding shrines. It exactly fits the great quartzite sarcophagus within.

(*See* p. 45, Plates XV and LIX)

s

PLATE LIX

A

B

C

PLATE LX

Plate LX

EXAMPLE OF SEALS UPON THE SEPULCHRAL SHRINES

The doors of the Second and Third Shrines were bolted with ebony bolts shot into metal staples, and (C), in the centre, fastened with cord ties to metal staples and sealed. The clay seal upon the cord bore impressions of two distinct seals: one (A) bearing Tut-ankh-Amen's cartouche, Kheperu-Neb-Re, and a recumbent Anubis jackal surmounting nine foes or captives, the other (B) the device of the Royal Necropolis " The Jackal over nine Foes," without other distinguishing mark or royal insignia.

(See p. 44)

PLATE LXI

FANS, BOWS AND ARROWS FOUND BETWEEN THE
THIRD AND FOURTH SHRINES

(A) THE GOLDEN FAN (Plate LXII) *in situ*,
west end of the Fourth (innermost) Shrine: note
the remains of the ostrich feathers.

(B) THE EBONY FAN (Plate LXIII), together
with bows and arrows *in situ*, south side of the
Fourth (innermost) Shrine. The stumps of the
ostrich feathers adhering to the palm of the fan
are still visible.

(C) A LONG BOW AND ARROWS *in situ* on the
north side of the Fourth (innermost) Shrine.

(*See* p. 46)

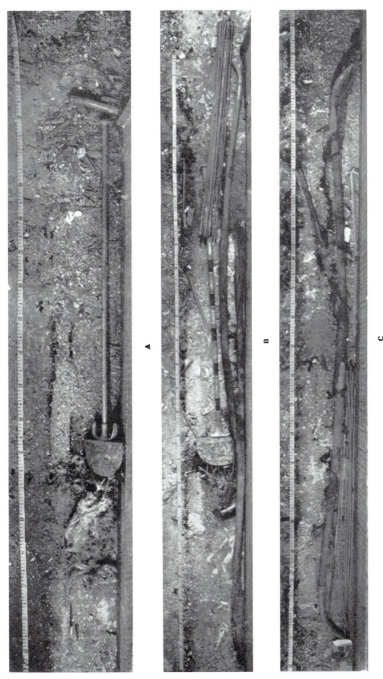

A

B

C

PLATE LXI

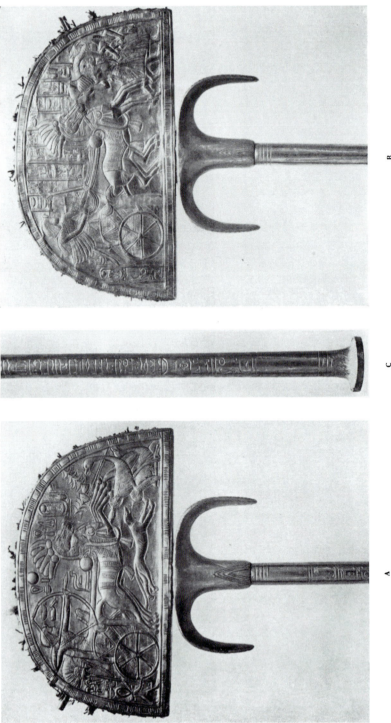

PLATE LXII

A

B

C

Plate LXII

THE GOLDEN FAN

(A) *Recto:* Embossed upon the gold surface is the young king in his chariot, accompanied by his slughi hound, hunting ostrich for plumes for the fan.

(B) *Verso:* The young " Lord of Valour " is here depicted returning from the chase with his quarry —two ostriches, borne by two attendants. The plumes are seen under his arms.

(c) THE HANDLE, incised upon which an inscription states that the episode took place in " The Eastern Desert of Heliopolis."

(*See* p. 46, Plate LXI, A)

PLATE LXIII

THE EBONY FAN

This fan, inscribed " Life to the Beautiful Ruler," is of ebony overlaid with sheet-gold and encrusted with glass of turquoise, lapis lazuli and carnelian colours, as well as translucent calcite. The palm (A) of the fan is emblazoned with the cartouches of Tut-ankh-Amen and the handle (B) at intervals with encrusted gold bands.

(*See* p. 46, Plate LXI, B)

A

B

PLATE LXIII

Plate LXIV

PLATE LXV

THE SARCOPHAGUS

THE GODDESS SELKIT—one of the four guardian goddesses carved in high relief on each of the four corners of the sarcophagus.

These goddesses, Isis (N.W.), Nephthys (S.W.), Neith (N.E.), and Selkit (S.E.), are so designed that their full spread wings and outstretched arms encircle the sarcophagus with a protective embrace.

On the south side, in the centre, stood a large painted wood *Ded* symbol.

(*See* pp. 47, 49, Plates XIV and LXIV)

PLATE LXV

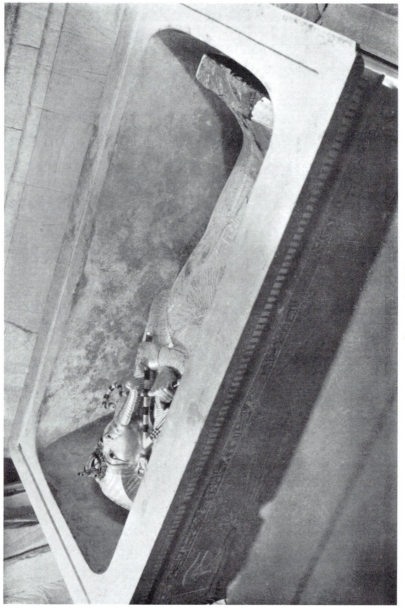

PLATE LXVI

PLATE LXVI

THE FIRST (OUTERMOST) COFFIN

The first coffin within the sarcophagus, after the covering linen shrouds had been removed. It measures 7 feet 4 inches in length and is carved out of a heavy wood, overlaid with thin gold upon gesso, the face and hands being of heavier gold. The insignia upon the forehead are inlaid with opaque coloured glass and faience. The eyebrows and eyelids are of lapis-coloured glass, the eyeballs of calcite and the pupils of obsidian. The Osiride emblems in the hands are encrusted with dark blue faience and coloured glass. Around the insignia upon the forehead of this effigy is a tiny floral wreath (*see* pp. 52, 190).

(*See* pp. 52, 70, Plates XVI and LXVII)

PLATE LXVII

THE HEAD OF THE EFFIGY UPON THE FIRST COFFIN

(*See* Plate LXVI)

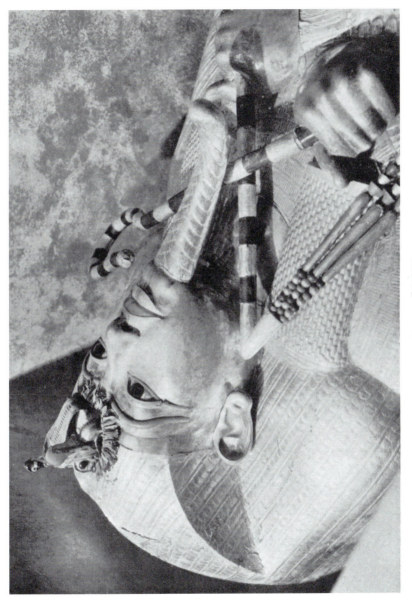

Plate LXVII

PLATE LXVIII

Plate LXVIII

THE SECOND COFFIN

This beautiful specimen of the New Empire Theban craftsmanship measures 6 feet 8 inches in length, it is carved out of a heavy (? oak) wood, overlaid with sheet-gold upon gesso, and is sumptuously inlaid with opaque polychrome glass, simulating red jasper, lapis lazuli and turquoise respectively. It has the *Nemes* head-dress, its ornamentation is of the feathered type, and over the arms and abdomen it has the additional decoration—the protective goddesses, Nekhebet and Buto, in the form of vultures.

(*See* pp. 74, 77, Plates XXII, XXIII and LXIX)

PLATE LXIX

THE LID OF THE SECOND COFFIN

This effigy, forming the lid of the second coffin, symbolizes the king as Osiris. For description, *see* p. 74.

(*See* Plates XXII, XXIII and LXVIII)

PLATE LXIX

PLATE LXX

Plate LXX

THE KING'S GOLD COFFIN

This unique third (innermost) coffin which contained the mummy is 6 feet 1¾ inches in length, and is wrought of gold, 2½ to 3½ millimetres in thickness, in the form of a recumbent figure of the young king, symbolizing Osiris.

The head-dress takes the *Nemes* form; the face, neck and hands are burnished; around the neck is a double necklace made up of red and yellow gold and blue faience disk-shaped beads; covering the chest is a conventional collarette of auxiliary cloisonné work. The whole of the surface of the coffin is engraved with *Rishi* (feathered) pattern, having over the legs additional winged figures of Isis and Nephthys; but the prominent feature of its ornamentation are two goddesses, Nekhebet and Buto, in the form of vultures, superimposed over the arms and abdomen, in sumptuous cloisonné work—the inlay on these goddesses, like that of the collarette, is of semi-precious stones and coloured glass.

(*See* p. 78, Plates XXIV, XXXVI, LXXI and LXXII)

PLATE LXXI

THE KING'S GOLD COFFIN

Details of the upper part of the third (inner-most) coffin wrought of gold and richly ornamented with cloisonné work.

(*See* p. 78, Plates LXX and LXXII)

PLATE LXXI

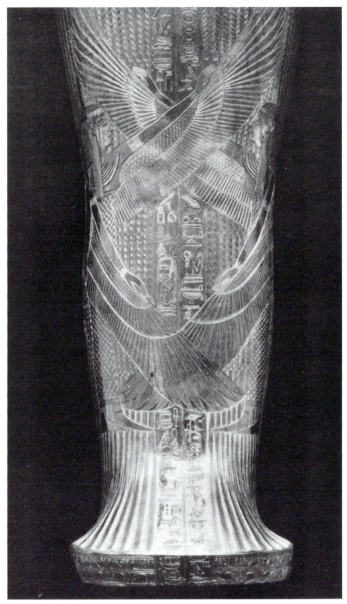

PLATE LXXII

PLATE LXXII

THE KING'S GOLD COFFIN

Details of the lower part of the third (inner-most) coffin wrought of gold and richly engraved with "feathered" pattern and the goddesses Isis and Nephthys.

(*See* p. 78, Plates LXX and LXXI)

PLATE LXXIII

THE GOLD MASK OF TUT·ANKH·AMEN

The profile view of the mask of Tut-ankh-Amen which covered the head and shoulders of his mummy. This beautiful portrait of the young king, from certain aspects recalls his father-in-law, Akh·en·Aten, in others, especially in this profile, an even stronger likeness of Queen Tyi (cf. Davis, *The Tomb of Queen Tiyi*, Plate XXXV), Akh·en·Aten's mother, in fact, there is visible a distinct affinity to both of these predecessors.

The mask, of natural size, is of beaten burnished gold, and is inlaid with opaque polychrome glass and lapis lazuli, green felspar, carnelian, calcite and obsidian. The triple necklace that was attached to the neck and the conventional beard (*see* Plate XXV) have been removed in order that the king's features may be better recognized.

(*See* pp. 83, 85, Frontispiece and Plate XXV)

PLATE LXXIII

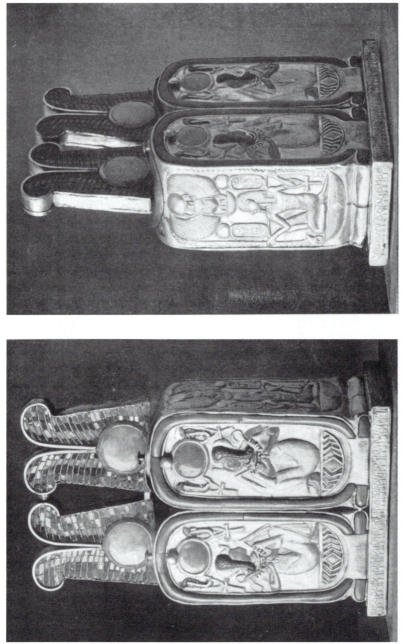

PLATE LXXIV

A

B

Plate LXXIV

THE KING'S PERFUME BOX

(A and B) This exquisite piece of jeweller's art, about 6 inches in height, is of gold with pedestal of silver. It is of double cartouche shape (each cartouche forming a separate receptacle for perfume) with highly embossed and chased ornamentation, the front and back being encrusted with opaque polychrome glass and translucent calcite. The figure within the cartouches upon the front represents the youthful king below the solar-disk wearing the Horus-lock seated upon *Heb* festival symbols. The device on the sides of the box incorporates the king's names and the figure *Heh*, " Eternity." The edges of the silver pedestal have chased *ankh uas* border, and, on the under surface, marsh and wild-fowl decoration recalling El Amarna art.

The double *Shu* feathers with solar-disk, that form the lid, are inlaid with polychrome glass.

(*See* p. 90)

T

Plate LXXV

THE KING'S DIADEM

(B) The diadem of fillet type discovered encircling the king's head. It is made of gold and is inlaid with contiguous circles of translucent carnelian, which have tiny gold bosses in their centres, and are bordered with a lapis lazuli and turquoise coloured glass pattern. The conventional floral and disk-shaped bow at the back of the fillet (c) is inlaid with malachite and sardonyx. The insignia (B)— i.e. the Nekhebet vulture and Buto serpent—are movable, and were found separate over the thighs of the mummy (cf. Plate XXX, R, s). The back pendant ribbons, and the side appendages (A and c) are hinged to the fillet, and were thus adaptable to the wig over which the diadem was worn.

(*See* p. 110)

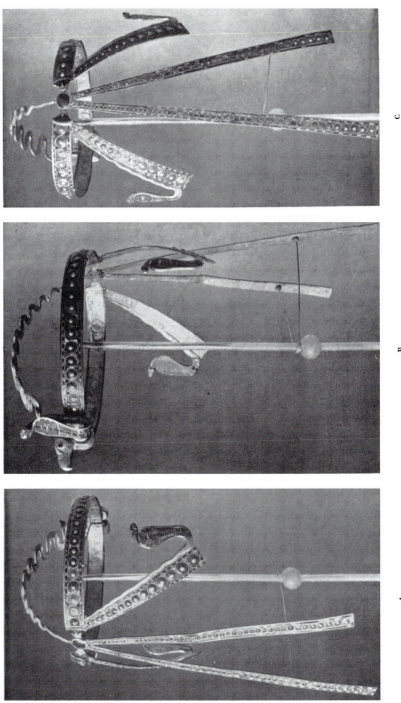

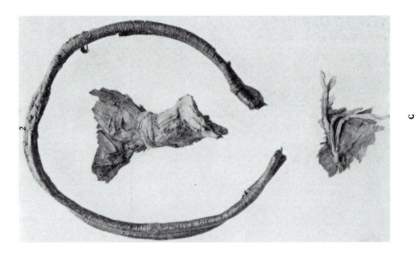

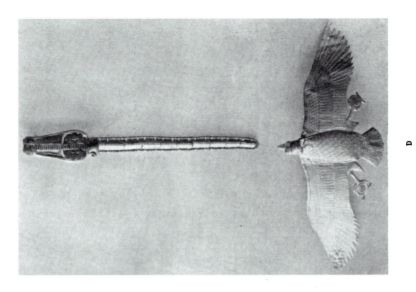

A

B

C

D

PLATE LXXVI

PLATE LXXVI

(A) THE NEKHEBET VULTURE OF GOLD WITH EYES OF OBSIDIAN

From the diadem (Plate LXXV, B).

(B) A MANKHET OF GOLD INLAID WITH POLYCHROME GLASS

From the collars (Plate LXXXI, A).

(C) 1. A DOUBLE CIRCLET DISCOVERED AROUND THE KING'S HEAD

It is made of fibre and bound with cord.

2. A PORTION OF THE PIG-TAIL OF THE LINEN *KHAT* HEAD-DRESS

3. BOW FROM THE RIBBON THAT HELD THE GOLD TEMPLE-BAND IN PLACE (Plate LXXVII, A)

(D) THE INSIGNIA OF THE *KHAT* HEAD-DRESS

The vulture is made of chased sheet-gold, and the inlaid serpent has a flexible tail made up of gold sections threaded together and bordered with minute faience beads.

(*See* pp. 110–112, 117, 124)

Plate LXXVII

OBJECTS FROM THE KING'S HEAD AND NECK

(A) Two gold temple-bands for holding the *Khat* head-dress and skull cap in place. Note the slots at the ends for ribbons for tying the bands at the back of the head, and eyelets on the edge for attaching the linen of the head-dress (cf. Plates XXXI and LXXVI, c. 3).

(B) A collar of four strings of gold and coloured glass beads, and an amuletic *urs* pillow or head-rest of iron (for other specimens in iron *see* Plates LXXXII, LXXXVII).

(*See* pp. 109, 112, 113, 118)

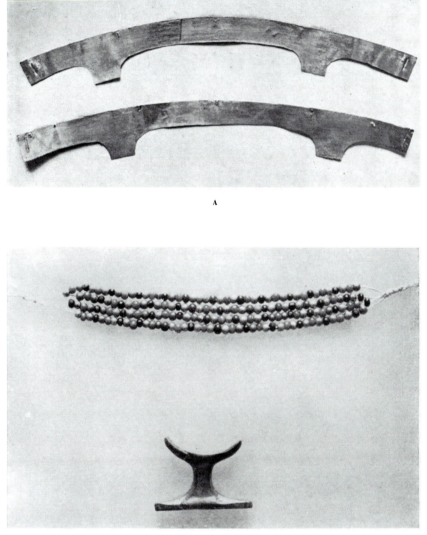

A

B

PLATE LXXVII

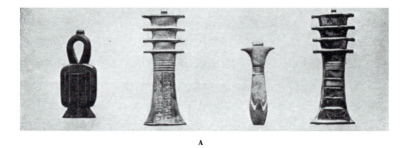

A

B

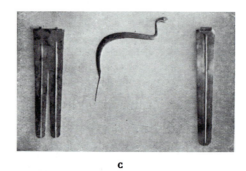

C

D

PLATE LXXVIII

Plate LXXVIII

AMULETS FROM THE KING'S NECK

(A) (From left to right) a jasper *Thet,* a gold *Ded,* a gold *Uaz* inlaid with green felspar, and a gold *Ded* inlaid with blue faience.

(B) (From left to right) a *Thoth* inlaid with green felspar, a serpent's head of carnelian mounted with gold and inlaid eyes, *Horus* in gold inlaid with lapis lazuli, *Anubis* in gold inlaid with green felspar, and an *Uaz* in gold inlaid with green felspar.

(C) Two curious pendant leaf-like amulets and a *Zt* serpent in sheet-gold.

(D) Eight amulets in chased sheet-gold, in the form of vultures, uræi and a human-headed winged uræus. They have eyelets at the back for suspension.

(*See* p. 117)

PLATE LXXIX

CHASED SHEET-GOLD AMULETIC COLLARS FROM THE
KING'S NECK AND CHEST

(A) "The Collar of Buto," and "The Collar of
Nebti" (i.e. Nekhebet and Buto).

(B) "The Collar of Nekhebet," "The Collar of
the Hawk" and "The Collar of Horus."

(*See* pp. 116, 120–122, Plates XXX, LXXX and
LXXXI)

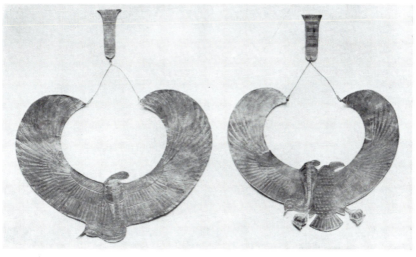

A

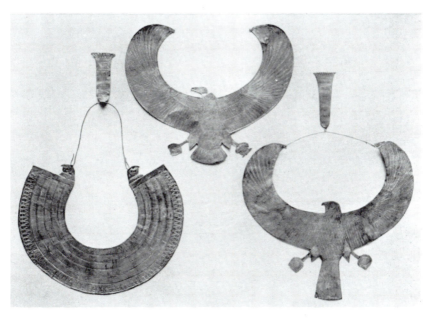

B

PLATE LXXIX

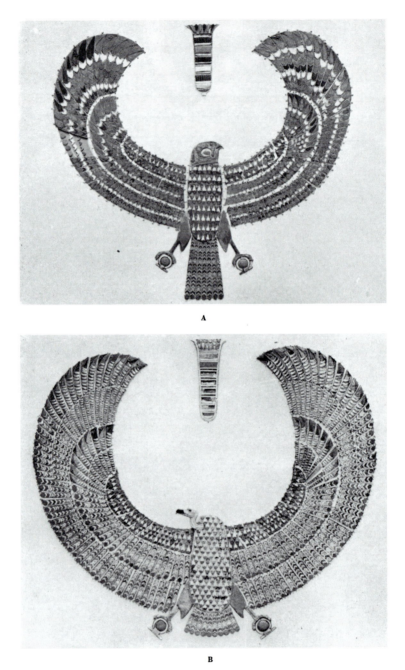

A

B

PLATE LXXX

PECTORAL COLLARS OF CLOISONNÉ WORK FROM
THE KING'S MUMMY

(A) Flexible " Collar of Horus," made up of 38
gold plaques elaborately inlaid with polychrome
glass, and threaded together with borders of minute
beads. From the thorax. (*See* pp. 122, 123)

(B) Flexible " Collar of Nekhebet," made up of
256 gold plaques elaborately inlaid with polychrome
glass, and threaded together with borders of minute
beads. From the thorax. (*See* pp. 122, 123)

(*See* Plates LXXIX and LXXXI)

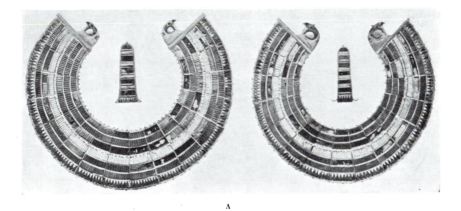

A

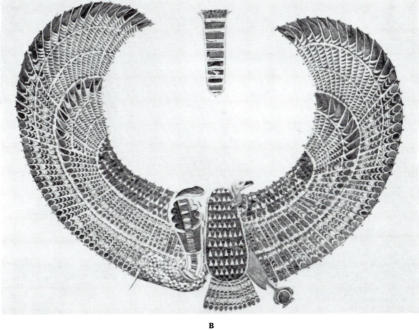

B

PLATE LXXXI

A

B

PLATE LXXXII

PLATE LXXXII

AMULETIC BRACELETS AND ANKLET FROM THE KING'S MUMMY

(A) From the thorax: 1, A gold bangle with lapis lazuli bead. 2, A gold bangle with inscribed carnelian bead, and 3, a gold bangle with *Uzat* eye of iron. From the arms: 4, A gold bangle with *Ment* bird in carnelian, and 5, a gold bangle with seven *Uzat* eyes and large head of various materials. (*See* pp. 122, 128, 131)

(B) Four pairs of gold circlets inlaid with coloured glass—from various parts of the body and legs; an anklet of gold and polychrome glass, from the abdomen; and a gold wire bangle from the right ankle. (*See* pp. 136, 137)

(*See* Plate XXX, N)

Plate LXXXIII

AMULETS AND AN AMULETIC APRON FROM THE
KING'S MUMMY

(A) Two knots from the thorax, a T-shaped
object from the abdomen, an oval plaque and an
Y-inverted shaped symbol from the left flank—
all of plain sheet-gold. (*See* pp. 122, 130)

(B) An apron made up of seven gold plaques,
inlaid with polychrome glass, and threaded together
by means of bead borders. It was found below the
abdomen and between the thighs. (*See* p. 134)

(*See* Plate XXX, J and M)

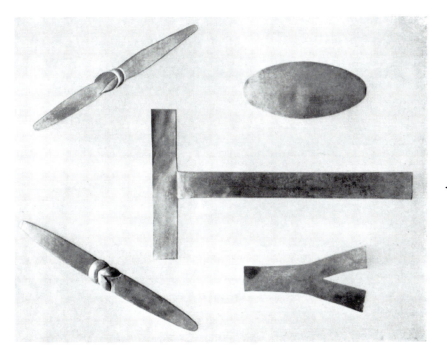

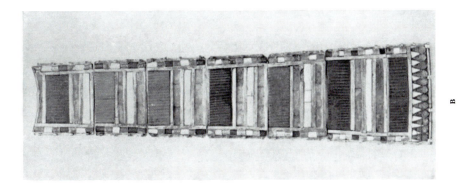

PLATE LXXXIII

A

B

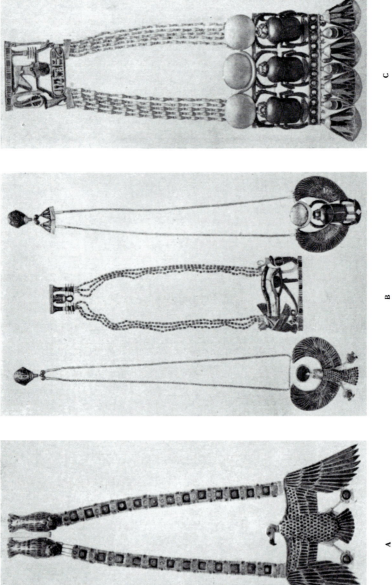

PLATE LXXXIV

A

B

C

PLATE LXXXIV

FIVE PECTORALS SUSPENDED FROM THE NECK OF
THE KING

(A) NEKHEBET VULTURE PECTORAL of gold inlaid
with green glass, lapis lazuli and carnelian.

It is suspended on flexible straps of gold and
lapis lazuli plaques, strung upon threads and bead
borders of gold and blue faience beads. The pair
of hawks forming the clasp are of gold cloisonné
work inlaid with coloured glass. (*See* p. 124)

(B) PECTORAL OF THE SOLAR-HAWK (Right Side)
of gold with body of open-work enclosing a green
stone.

PECTORAL OF THE LUNAR CRESCENT AND ORB
(Left Side) of gold inlaid with polychrome glass.

PECTORAL OF THE *Uzat* EYE (Centre) of gold
inlaid lapis lazuli, pale greenish stone, and polychrome glass.   (*See* p. 126)

(C) PECTORAL OF KHEPER BEETLES supporting
solar- and lunar-disks of gold (the crescent and lunar
orb of gold-silver alloy) and inlaid as follows:—

The beetles and marguerites are of lapis lazuli,
the small pendant buds of carnelian, the large
pendant lotus flowers and buds with polychrome
glass. It is suspended on five strings of plain and
granular gold beads; the clasp of gold open-work,
inlaid with polychrome glass, incorporates various
symbols and a cartouche reading "The Beautiful
God, Kheperu-neb-Re-Amen-Re, chosen of Re."

(*See* p. 124)

PLATE LXXXV

FINGER-RINGS FROM THE KING'S MUMMY

Finger-rings of gold, lapis lazuli, cloudy-white and green chalcedony, turquoise, and black resin. Note the private marks upon the sides of the rings suggesting an early form of hall-mark. The two rings (centre) were from the king's left hand, the group of five (left side) were found beside his right wrist, and the group of eight (right side) beside the left wrist. (See pp. 127, 130). The photographs show the rings from two points of view.

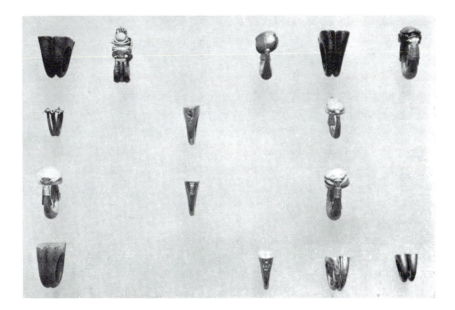

PLATE LXXXV

A   B

PLATE LXXXVI

Plate LXXXVI

BRACELETS FROM THE KING'S FOREARMS

(A) Seven bracelets from the right forearm, and (B) six bracelets from the left forearm. They are here arranged in the order in which they were placed upon the mummy : — (A) commencing from the elbow and ending at the wrist, (B) commencing at the wrist and ending at the elbow. They are made of gold and silver, and are inlaid with various kinds of semi-precious stones and polychrome glass.

(*See* pp. 128, 129, Plate XXXIII)

Plate LXXXVII

TWO DAGGERS FOUND UPON THE KING

(A) A GOLD DAGGER. The haft is ornamented with granulated gold-work and encircled by alternate bands of cloisonné work, terminating, at the hilt, with applied gold wire chain-scroll and rope decoration. The blade, of hardened gold, has two grooves down the centre surmounted by a " palmette " design and narrow frieze of geometric pattern. (*See* pp. 131–133, Plate LXXXVIII, A and B)

(B) AN IRON DAGGER. The gold haft with knob of rock crystal is ornamented with granulated gold-work and encircled by alternate bands of cloisonné work, the lower band terminating with applied gold wire-work. The blade of iron, when discovered, was quite bright and clean save for a few rust spots.

(*See* pp. 135, 136, Plates XXX, K, and LXXXVIII, C)

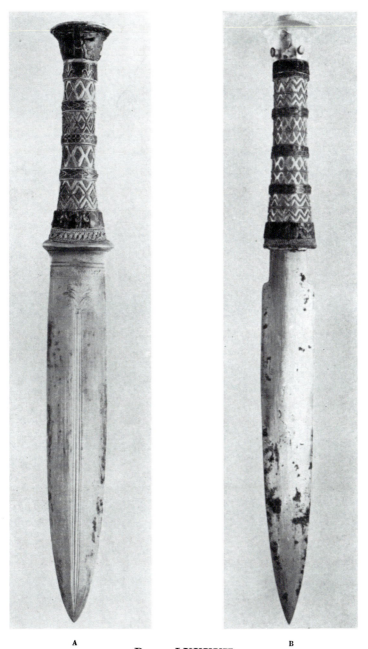

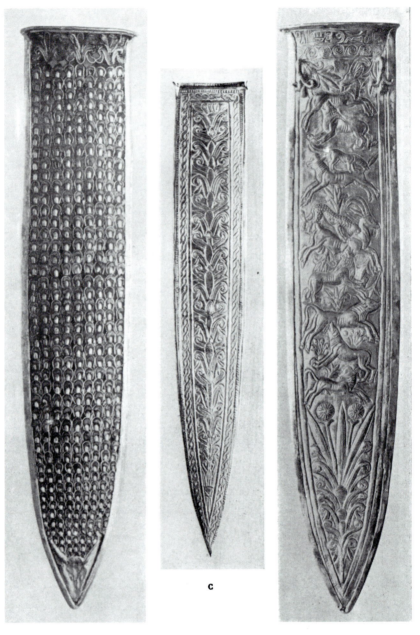

A

C

B

PLATE LXXXVIII

Plate LXXXVIII

THE SHEATHS OF THE DAGGERS

(A and B) Sheath of the Gold Dagger

With, on front (A) " palmette " frieze and feather-pattern in cloisonné work, terminating with a head of a jackal; embossed in high relief upon the back (B) below a frieze of coil-pattern and king's name and titles, is a scene of wild animals, terminating in an ornate floral device. (*See* pp. 132, 133, Plate LXXXVII, A)

(c) The Gold Sheath of the Iron Dagger

The back—shown in the photograph—is chased with an ornate floral device and rope border; the front with a simple pectinated feather-pattern, terminating with a head of a jackal similar to A. (*See* pp. 132, 133, 135, Plate LXXXVII, B)

INDEX

ABDEL HAMID PASHA BEDAWI, xiv, 67
Abdomen, objects on, 130
Adair, Mr. E. W., 166
Adhesives, 166
Ægean art, affinity to Egyptian, 132
After-life, Ancient Egyptian views of, 12
Ahmed Gerigar, xxiv
Akh·en·Aten, 38; measurements of, 160; remains of, 148; tomb of, 93; Tut·ankh·Amen's likeness to, xxiii, 19, 85, 113, 114; wives of, 115
Alabaster, 168 (*see* Calcite)
Alfieri, Mr. A., 166
Almina, Countess of Carnarvon, xii, xiv
Amen·hetep III, 102, 147, 148; mummy of, 150
Amethyst, 185
Amuletic bangles, 128
Amulets, *Ded*, 117, 118; duplicated, 119; Horus, 117; knot, 122; serpent's head, 119; T-shaped, 130; *Thet*, 117, 119; Thoth, 117; *Uas*, 119; *Uaz*, 117, 119; uraeus, 117; *Urs* pillow of iron, 109, 122; *uzat* eye, 126, 128; of blue faience, 134; of iron, 122; vulture, 117; winged serpent, 117; Y-shaped, 130; *Zt*, 117
Ankh·es·en·Amen, 14; accompanies King on fowling expedition, 14, 15; episodes of private life of, 14; offering sacred libations, flowers and collarettes to King, 14; supporting king's arm, 15
Anklet, 136
Anointing material, 177; mummy, 100
Antechamber, contents of, ix
Antelope, 18, 35
Antimony, compound of, 171
Anubis emblems, 32
Apron, ceremonial, 134
Aqal of Bedouin head dress, 110, 152
Aragonite in eyes of effigy, 52
Archery, practising, 15
Arms and forearms of mummy, 128

Army, Egyptian, 19; units of Re, Amen and Ptah, 31
Arrows, ceremonial, 15, 16, 46
Art, Eighteenth Dynasty ornamental, 125; of decoration in Burial Chamber, 29
Ass, wild, 18
Astor, Major the Hon. J. J., 51
Atef crown of Osiris, 109, 112
Aten cartouche, late form of, 113
Axles of the State Chariots, 62
Ay, King, 23, 24; officiates at funeral ceremony of Tut·ankh·Amen, 26, 28, 98

B

BA bird pectoral, 83
Bacteria, absence of, from the textiles, 199; from the tomb, 165
Bangle of gold wire, 137
Bangles of gold, 122
Barks, variegated, 35
Baskets, rush-work, 32
Batons, curved, 35
Battle scenes, 17
Beef fat, 177
Beeswax, 167
Beetles' wings, batons inlaid with, 35
Beetles with disks, significance of, 125
Beisan in Palestine, 31
Bennu bird, 121; ritual, 83
Bethell, The Hon. Richard, 51
Bier, lion-shaped, 52, 89
Bits for horses, 59
Bitumen, 177, 186
Blinkers, 60, 63
Body and limbs, Tut·ankh·Amen's mummy, 155 *et seq.*
Boodle, Mr. L. A., 39 (footnote)
Botanical specimens, 33; celery, wild, 191–193; cornflower, 190–193; lily, blue water-, 190–192, 195; mandrake, 192, 193; nightshade, woody, 191, 195; oak, 39; olive, leaves of, 190–192, 195; *Picris coronopifolia*, 192, 195; plants identified, 192; willow, 192, 195

Index

Index

Index

Herodotus, 8, 95
Hes vase, 32
Hill, Dr. A. W., 199, 212
Hor·em·heb, King, 23, 24, 104 ; tomb of, 93
Hounds, 16, 35 ; slughi, 17, 18
Humidity in tomb, 26 ; cause of, 164
Hunting denizens of the desert, 18 ; lion, 18 ; ostrich, 15 ; scenes, 17
Hussein Abou Owad, xxiv
Hussein Ahmed Saide, xxiv
Hyena, 18

Leyden Museum, diadem at, 112
Life, absence of, in tomb, 165
Limbs, wrapping of, 151
Linen, deterioration of, 185
Lion, 16, 18, 35 ; -cub of Tut·ankh·Amen, 14 ; hunt, 18
Lionesses, 18
Lucas, Mr. A., xx, 51, 65, 66, 67, 81, 106, 152, 197
Lunar disk of gold-silver alloy, 127
Lythgoe, Mr. A. M., 50

I

INLAY, deterioration of, 178
Insects, presence of, in tomb, 69, 166
Insignia of Northern and Southern sovereignty, 110, 112, 136
Inspector of Antiquities, the Chief, 50
Iron, objects of, xxiii, 109, 122, 135, 175
Isis, engraved figure of, 78 ; gold and gesso figure of, 52, 70

M

MACE, Mr. A. C., xix, 39, 51, 134
Maces, ceremonial, 35, 36
Magic oars, 32 ; spells, 119
Magical figures, 24, 37
Malachite, 180, 185
Mankhet, 117, 120, 123, 137
Marguerites, gilt bronze, 33
Marmour of Luxor, 67
Mask of gold, 9, 83, 154 ; extricating the, 87
Maspero, Sir Gaston, 24
Maxwell, Sir John, xiv
Mediterranean, characteristics of Eastern, 24
Mending, ancient, 215
Ment bird, 128
Merzbach Bey, Maître Georges, xiv, xv
Metal band round base of shrine, 205
Methods of work, 76
Mohamed Shaaban Effendi, 107
Mohamed Zaglûl Pasha, 50
Mond, Mr. Robert, 51
Mortar, 163
Mortuary chapel and sepulchre, 22
Mummies of the Eleventh Dynasty, 146 ; rewrapped, 144 ; royal, in Cairo Museum, 143 *et seq.*
Mummification, art of, 145 ; in Twenty-first Dynasty, 147 ; period for, 95, 97, 101
Mummy of Amen·hetep III, 147 ; anointing of, 105 ; condition of Tut·ankh·Amen's, xxi, 100, 148 *et seq.* ; description of Tut·ankh·Amen's, 148 ; discovery of Tut·ankh·Amen's, 82 ; drawn by courtiers to tomb, 98 ; examination of, 65, 87 ; fashioned to symbolize Osiris, 99 ; orientation of king's, 100 ; wrapping of king's, 107, 108
Mût vulture, 118

J

JAR, cosmetic, 34
Jasper, red, 185
Jewellery, personal, 124 ; of Middle Kingdom and of New Empire, 138

K

KHAT head-dress, 29, 70, 112, 113
Khensu, Karnak figure of, 6
Kheper-boat-of-Re, 28
King as *Sem* priest, 103

L

LACAU, Monsieur Pierre, 64–66, 106
Lamp, calcite, 30 ; triple, 31
Lapis lazuli, 185 ; beads of, 122 ; finger-rings of, 127 ; scarabs of, 124, 125
Lead, 175 ; compound of, 171
Leather, harness of, 59, 175
Leighton, Sir Frederic, quoted on Egyptian art, 8
Leonardo da Vinci, quoted, 5

Index

N

NAOS, golden, 14
Napkin, linen, 78
Natron, cup containing, 32
Nefertiti, children of, 115, 116
Neith, gold and gesso figure of, 52
Nekhebet, 74, 78, 83, 110, 111, 119, 120, 124, 126, 136
Nemes head-dress, 74, 78, 109
Nephthys, engraved figure of, 78
Newberry, Prof. P. E., xix, xxiv, 50

O

OAK, 39
Oars, magic, 32
Objects upon mummy, classification of, 137, 138
Obsidian in eyes of effigy, 52 ; in eyes of Nekhebet, 111
Ochre, red, 178 ; yellow, 178, 180
Oil, castor, 177
Oils, 176
Olive (*Olea Europa*), 33
Ornament, traditional, 19
Orpiment, 180
Osiris, 100, 104 ; *Atef* crown of, 109, 112
Ostrich, 18 ; feathers, 15, 46 ; hunt, 15

P

PAD upon head of king, 109
Padding within bandages, 134
Paint, mediums used in, 181
Painter, Court, 17
Painting, miniature, 18
Pall, linen, 33, 43 ; framework of, 43
Papyrus, 119, 122, 123 ; Turin, of tomb of Rameses IV, 94
Paraffin-wax treatment, 66, 80, 89
Partition wall, 25, 39 ; the erection of, 99
Pater, Walter, " The artist is the child of his time," 6
Pearson, Prof. Karl, formulæ devised by, 157
Pectoral, *Ba* bird, 83 ; of Nekhebet, 124 ; scarab, 124 ; solar-hawk, 126 ; *uzat* eye, 126, 134 ; winged scarab, 126
Perfume vase of king and queen, 34
Persea (*Mimasops Schimperi*), 33
Petrie, Sir William Flinders, 111

Pharaohs, wealth buried with, 79
Pickard, Dr. R. H., 176
Pigments, 178
Pink colour, 164
Plants, remarks on the identified, 192
Plaster, 162, 163
Plate, oval gold, 130
Plenderleith, Dr. H. J., 207
Pole of the State chariots, 62
Powder, brown, 199 ; greyish from kiosks, 215
Press, 66
Prisoners, African and Asiatic, 17, 19
Propylœ, 32

Q

QUIVERS, 60

R

RAMESES IV, tomb of, 94
Receptacle, gold and silver, for unguents, 90
Reed, cut by Tut·ankh·Amen, 13, 36
Refuse, workmen's, 48
Reins of chariot harness, 60
Resin, 167, 177, 183 ; black, finger-ring of, 127 ; scarab of, 83, 86, 121 ; cup containing, 32 ; red, 214
Resinous material on bronze tongues, 203
Rishi decoration, 70
Robbers, hole made by, 29
Royal insignia of Upper and Lower Egypt, 83
Ruskin upon Egyptian art, 4, 9 ; iron, 122

S

SADDLES of chariot harness, 63
Saleh Bey Hamdi, Dr., xx, 65, 66, 106, 113, 148
Saleh Enan Pasha, 106
Sandals, gold, 137, 151
Sarcophagus, the, 41, 45, 48 ; contents of, 51 ; lid of, 49–51 ; orientation of, 25
Sat·Hathor·iunut, diadem of Princess, 111
Sayed Fuad Bey El Khôli, 106
Scarab, black resin, 83, 86, 121 ; lapis-lazuli, 124, 125